Cathy and family!

This is just enough
to whet your interest.
all of these places are
"just over the hill!"

Merry Christmas - 1988

Tom

GHOST TOWNS OF THE PACIFIC FRONTIER

GHOST TOWNS OF THE PACIFIC FRONTIER

By Lambert Florin

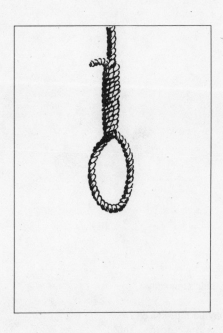

PROMONTORY PRESS

Published in 1987 by

Promontory Press
166 Fifth Avenue
New York, NY 10010

Abridged from Ghost Towns of the West
By arrangement with Darwin Publications

Library of Congress Catalog Card Number: 86-63845
ISBN: 0-88394-068-X

Printed in The United States of America

CONTENTS

WHAT IS A GHOST TOWN?

One of several dictionary definitions of "ghost" is "a shadowy semblance of its former self." We have elected to prefer this somewhat ambiguous phrase, because it accurately describes many towns on the borderline of being dead or alive. Most of the towns described and pictured in this book are "dead" ghosts, but some still have life, though nothing to compare with the lusty vigor they enjoyed in their heyday.

Some even have a future, and the shadowy remnants of a fascinating past are being sacrificed on the altar of a new strike, possibly of a newer metal such as Molybdenum. An example of this is Kokomo, Colorado. Here is a town full of interesting relics of Colorado's early mining days with a corner full of new buildings and developments.

Some have never really died but are much smaller than before, with a population sufficient to keep up a post office, a store or two and an eating place (and, of course, a tavern). Examples are Skamokawa, Washington; Shaniko, Oregon and Gem, Idaho. Many others still have a community spirit and hopes for a brighter future, perhaps more brilliant than the past.

Some are even crowded with people. The saloons are "revived," some buildings "restored" and in general are inflated with a sort of artificial respiration. Examples are Virginia City, Nevada and the town with the same name in Montana. These are well worth while, easily accessible and full of diversion, but they lack the charm of the deserted or nearly deserted places, for some, at least.

Our ideal is a town completely abandoned by all business and permanent residents, and many of the subjects included fall into this category.

GHOST TOWN ETIQUETTE

Such souvenirs as are found in the brush by the side of the road are legitimately carried home. Parts of buildings still standing, or furniture in them, we don't include in the souvenir category, however. The old towns are melting away too fast as it is.

One of the towns in our book, Shaniko, Oregon was written up in a local newspaper this year, and about the same time was a subject for a T. V. program. The results to the town were drastic. One of the tiny group of remaining inhabitants wrote to the newspaper as follows—"Today, your cameraman would find something new added to the panorama he viewed a few weeks ago," reads the letter. "The inhabitants have been forced to tack up 'No trespassing' signs, in order to preserve a bit of privacy and rights as property owners. Why? Because the public is carrying Shaniko away, piece by piece. . . . Among us are several who have had belongings of varied value, both sentimental and intrinsic, taken from their property, and the schoolhouse and surroundings have been devastated by souvenir-seekers. In short, our privacy has been invaded and we are irked to say the least . . ."

OREGON
GHOST TOWNS

HISTORIC OLD HOUSE was built, in part at least, in 1888 by William L. Brown in Apiary, now nearly vanished. It was named for beehives of early resident David M. Dorsey. William Brown had married Irene Lowman in Olive Hill, Kentucky, in 1885, and the couple came to nearby Rainier in 1887, taking homestead claim the next summer. When house was built, the Browns had one child, their first one having died earlier. In house shown thirteen more children were born to them, eight sons and five daughters. The father died here in 1932 and until 1964 the house was still occupied by a bachelor son.

ANTELOPE, OREGON

The gay 90's were not only gay in Antelope, but punctuated by shootings and brawls in the best western town tradition. And in common with so many tinder-dry and nearly waterless towns, it suffered trial by fire in 1898 and was nearly wiped out.

Antelope is situated in a small valley of the same name, so called first by someone in the party of Joseph H. Shearer, who was engaged in packing supplies to the John Day mines in 1862.

The road to Antelope consisted of two ruts through the sagebrush in the 60's and for a long time thereafter. Stagecoaches bumping along over rough terrain ran more smoothly when they entered the little valley where so many antelope fed and watered. Passengers were glad to stop and eat or stay overnight at the stage station, newly erected. This entailed a little hotel and a blacksmith shop. Also, inevitably, came a saloon. This was owned and operated by F. W. Silvertooth, who had driven a stage from The Dalles to Canyon City and decided to settle here.

By the year 1871, the place expanded to the point where a post office became possible, and on the seventh of August it was opened.

A prime figure in the history of Central Oregon was appointed first postmaster, intrepid Howard Maupin, who left his print on so many places in the state. It was he who, tiring of having stock stolen by Chief Paulina, tracked that wily Indian down and killed him near Paulina Basin, putting an end to depredations that had harassed the pioneers in the valley for years.

The town grew apace, being a natural center for cattlemen and later sheepmen. It was a convenient stopping place for supply wagons and enjoyed prosperity for a few years. More saloons went up. One of these was run by partners named Benjamin Pratt and Ed Gleason. All was not harmony between them, however, as rumors were rife that Mr. Pratt fancied the wife of his partner. One fine morning in '85, as Pratt was unlocking the door of their business establishment, Mr. Gleason, a believer in gossip, walked up and shot his partner dead with a rifle.

The trial was a cursory Kangaroo Court sort of affair. It was decided that the outraged husband was justified in eliminating Mr. Pratt from the scene.

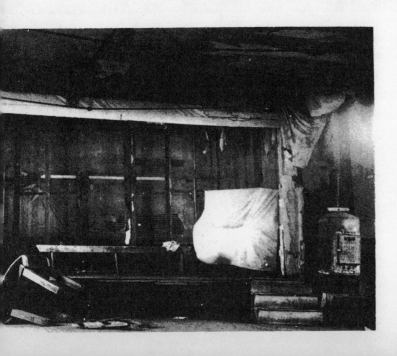

TINY STAGE AT END OF dance hall once looked on gay balls, Christmas parties, lodge gatherings and just plain dances.

SUPERIMPOSED SIGNS TELL varied occupancy over years. Starting out as carriage and blacksmith shop it served later as furniture store. At beginning of a u t o era, venerable building converted to garage for short time before dying completely.

R. J. Pilkington was Antelope's first doctor, serving the town all through the 90's. In addition to his practice, Dr. Pilkington operated a drugstore in the old saloon building.

The disastrous fire of '98 started in Tom Condon's Bowling Alley, above which were his family living quarters. After he had seen the women safely down, Condon's escape was cut off by flames. Outside the window was the pulley and rope by which water was raised to the apartment. Fortunately the bucket was at the top and ready. The resourceful Condon straddled the bucket and let himself down the rope. The town itself was not so lucky. After the holocaust, only one of the original buildings on the main street was left standing, as it still does today, at the far end of the street.

The town was rebuilt almost immediately, and things went pretty much as before. The little main street with its one surviving structure was solidly lined again, but this newer phase of the town's history was to end also. The town of Shaniko had been born only eight miles north as terminus of a railroad from the Columbia River. The new town drained off the population of Antelope and eventually left it an empty shell.

THE JAIL HOUSE, standing west of the dance hall was convenient place to hold rowdies.

LITTLE CHURCH SERVED Antelope for many years. Now idle, its doors stand open and town's few children romp up and down aisle. Tiny filigreed organ waits near pulpit, is in working order, birds nest in walls, their nesting holes can be seen in clapboards.

THE SILVERTOOTH ESTABLISHMENT also boasts a barbershop with business being conducted among relics of mining, cattle. Extensive rock collection completes resemblance of room to museum. Area is famous as source of agate of fancy quality, once abundant in huge chunks as "nuisances" in plowed fields. Gem stones are now much harder to find.

JAIL ITSELF WAS FRAIL, but "cell block" within was stout, and safely held most belligerent drunks, one of whom set fire to his thin straw mattress, hoping to escape in resultant confusion. However, fire hose was inserted through little window, drenching mattress *and* occupant, suddenly subduing the latter, completing the sobering-up process.

ASHWOOD, OREGON

"A volcanic butte and an early day family gave the ghost town of Ashwood, on Trout Creek in Jefferson County, its name," relates Phil F. Brogan, whose father owned a stock ranch seven miles east. "Near the site of the bustling village of the Oregon King mine days is Ash Butte. Settling close to it in the 1870s was Whitfield T. Wood and when the post office was established in 1898 the name of the butte was combined with that of the pioneer. The town grew on both sides of Trout Creek, spanned by a footbridge occasionally washed out by freshets, and into it for supplies and mail came ranchers from the range country.

"I remember all this as it was shortly after the turn of the century, with memories of riding into town from the east as a small boy to get the mail and pick up a few groceries. I can still hear the echoes of my horse's shod feet as we entered the big livery stable where the pony was rested and fed before starting home. When I walked past the open doors of saloons on warm summer days, I saw inside men standing at bars back of which were big mirrors. I have other memories of freight trains moving through town, headed for the end of the rails at Shaniko."

This part of central Oregon has a turbulent geological history. The area was covered at different times by lava flows and deposits of volcanic ash, layer by layer. As erosion progressed, many remains of long-extinct animals have been recovered which add to the store of valuable fossils in museums throughout the country. At the edge of one vast expanse of juniper trees, sagebrush and scanty grasses stands the prominent eroded cone which is Ash Butte, its sides covered by caked pumice and ash.

At the base of it, a promising region attracted pioneer Wood into settling there. The first spring

TYPICAL FALSE FRONTS of Ashwood's day. Saloon at left was one of several serving thirsty miners, ranch men and cattle drivers. Street once had small newspaper plant, printing weekly Ashwood *Prospector*, one of chain owned by Max Lueddeman. Editorials were embellished by florid prophecies of future wealth and productivity of Ashwood's mines and ranches. Town would grow to be "the metropolis of central Oregon . . . greatest producer of mercury ever known."

ASH BUTTE GRANGE for many years center of community affairs and even yet swept out for rare dances or celebrations. Was originally largest saloon in area, ground floor having bar on one side, small dance floor on other. Saturday nights saw wild times when cowboys, ranchers and miners "blew her in." Traces of windows upstairs can be seen. These opened into rooms for occupancy of short duration.

the little stream close by was a bountiful source of good water, the skies sunny and the soil soft and easily worked. But as spring became summer, hope became disillusionment. The stream shriveled and disappeared. The soil, composed largely of clay, turned as hard as concrete. Frosts persisted until late in the spring, freezing nights began in late summer. Discouraged at trying to farm in the face of these difficulties, Wood turned to raising cattle, a venture somewhat more successful, and soon the solitary rancher had neighbors, some as close as ten miles away.

"On a blustery March 27, 1897," recounts Phil Brogan, "Thomas J. Brown, herding sheep in a gulley leading into Trout Creek picked up a piece of quartz from a brushy, rocky slope. It proved rich in silver and free gold. Soon a mine boom town, with its frontier saloons, hotels, livery stables and stores, took shape on the floor of Trout Creek about three miles from the mine, and became Ashwood. It was not a wild pioneer town. On Trout Creek to the west, a lonely cove reminded the villagers that pioneer days were past. In that cove, the raider chief Paulina died under gunfire many years before to end the Indian unrest in the area."

The Oregon King mine gave Ashwood its start but there were other big producers in the Morning Star and Red Jacket as well as several lesser ones. With no smelters or milling facilities at hand, the ore was shipped out. There was talk of building a stamp mill and smelter, the weekly Ashwood *Prospector* pushing the project, but signs of the veins pinching out appeared and no backers were to be found. As ores became lower in assay values, and in quantity as well, the town settled into a period of doldrums, enlivened only slightly by occasional periods of mining.

Then came the discovery and working of a vein of cinnabar over Horseheaven way and since Ashwood was the supply center, it revived and sat up. But quicksilver in paying quantities did not pour forth for long. The company pulled out all its machinery, leaving the building to shrivel in the sun. The blight spread to Ashwood, which never recovered.

Brogan feels a bit wistful when he realizes Ashwood holds few of its buildings of pioneer days. "Gone are the livery stables, the hotels, stores and homes built close to the edge of Trout Creek. Most were lost in fires. Ashwood was a town of one main street with winding roads serving as side streets. One led past the Woods' orchard to the Axehandle highlands. One headed upstream to the T. H. Hamilton ranch and the big ranches near the head of the creek. Still another was routed down creek to the Columbus, Friend and Howard Maupin ranches, and up Little Trout Creek to Prineville."

Today the town has an open, sun-washed look. Magpies fly across the dirt road which is the main street and coyotes close in at night.

BLEAK, FORLORN ASHWOOD SCHOOL stands on knoll, surrounded by typical junipers, only trees of desert regions of Oregon. Cupola had bell which rang well in advance of schooltime, its peals reaching far across sagebrush hills, warning tardy pupils walking several miles. Schoolyard, surrounded by barbed wire fence, once held usual two outhouses.

"Alone? No!
... there was something else!"

AUBURN, OREGON

"Sweet Auburn! Lovliest village on the plain,
Where health and plenty cheered the laboring
swain."

These lines from the poem, "Deserted Village," inspired the naming of many towns and villages in the eastern states and at least one in California's Mother Lode country. Then when a group of restless prospectors from those diggings christened the first collection of shacks in the new Oregon gold fields Auburn was again a sentimental choice. And prophetic enough, this Auburn has long since been deserted and nearly vanished.

Early in 1861 a party headed by Henry Griffen and his partner David Littlefield, on the way to the Orofino diggings in what is now Idaho, paused in Portland for rest and supplies. In one of the bistros a man named Adams was loudly claiming full knowledge of the fabled Bluebucket Mine. He referred to the tale of the Meek Party which in 1845 was said to have camped by a creek in eastern Oregon while children of the emigrants amused themselves picking up yellow pebbles in a blue bucket. On the way again this dangled under the wagon for a while and then was lost. Later, on hearing tales of gold found in the mountains the pioneers had a sinking feeling they had likely overlooked a bonanza and now knowledge of the place was gone. They remembered only vaguely the stream, thought it probably a tributary of the John Day or Malheur Rivers.

Now here was a man claiming he knew the exact location! Gold conscious Griffen and Littlefield, imagination warmed by liquor, could not get to the man fast enough. They engaged him to lead them to the Bluebucket site in exchange for keep and a percentage of the gold found. Setting out in high spirits, the small party reached the arid central portion of Oregon in good time and after an extended rest, started for the location Adams claimed to have pin-pointed.

Now the guide changed directions erratically. Griffen and Littlefield thought little about it until Adams made an about-face twice and told them to camp in a dismal place without wood or good water. After more uncertain movements, the partners had a conference, called a halt near the head of Burnt River and demanded an explanation. Adams was forced to admit he had not the slightest notion where they were or where the Bluebucket might be. The man was summarily sent out of camp without food, arms or blankets and told he would be shot if found following the party. One soft-hearted member did get some food to him to save his life.

Unable to agree on a traveling plan, the party split, the majority deciding to retrace their steps as nearly as possible. Shortly after crossing Blue Canyon at noon, October 23, 1861, they reached a good camping spot in a gulch. While Littlefield shot some game and made supper Griffin sank the inevitable prospect hole at the creek. Next morning they worked the hole further, panning when

HEADFRAME is only standing remnant of town, surmounts shallow mine. Hard rock mining was secondary to panning and sluice operations, amounting to so little usual piles of waste dumps are almost absent.

down to bedrock. Suddenly Henry Griffen was swirling and sloshing the sands faster and faster as though glints of the yellow metal were showing before the dross was poured off. When the residue came clear it was of such value excitement broke like a rocket. Pan after pan was finished with about a dollar's worth of dust in each, with even small nuggets here and there. At a feverish pitch the partners and others staked out claims, twenty-two that fateful day. Even the forlorn Adams, trailing at a discreet distance, was called up and allowed to peg out a claim of his own.

Four of the men—Griffen, Littlefield, William Stafford and G. W. Schriver spent the winter at the diggings, just able to build a cabin before a terrific storm blew up. With three feet of snow

piled up, the weather suddenly turned warmer and rains melted the snow so fast flooding was general in the mountains and valleys. The men found they could not work without rubber boots and in the middle of December set out for Walla Walla for supplies.

They carried a poke full of Powder River gold dust which was not only accepted by merchants but sent by them to Portland and exhibited in a store window with a story that two men working on Powder River half a day had cleaned up two and a half pounds of gold dust! Almost by the time the four miners got back to the diggings a gold rush had set in. By spring thousands of gold-mad prospectors were panning every stream in the area. The ubiquitous William Packwood headed

RUINED STONE WALLS are sole remains of building in hell-for-leather gold camp of Auburn. Thickets of brush and weeds obscure site of town, once one of largest in Oregon. Living apple tree near ruins testifies miners sought respite from sowbelly and beans.

a group that laid out the town of Auburn on Blue Canyon Creek in April, 1862.

A population of 6,000 quickly made it the largest town in eastern Oregon and one of the largest in the state and it became the county seat in September of that year. It had all the trappings of boom town tradition—saloons, hook joints, dance halls. Murders and lynchings were part of it. In November of that action-packed first year miner Jack Desmond and gambler Henri Larabee became involved in an argument with an underworld character, Spanish Tom. The gambling debt quarrel simmered for several days and finally erupted in a shooting that ended with the deaths of Desmond and Larabee. The dead men were respected citizens where Spanish Tom was not and he was promptly snatched from custody to be strung up in a pine tree. All three victims were added to the growing population of Boot Hill. Next year Henry Griffen died at 59, was buried there. The stone now over his grave credits him as being "discoverer of gold in Eastern Oregon."

Auburn aged as rapidly as it grew, going into such a speedy decline its importance in 1864 was less than the upstart Baker, 14 miles northeast, and in June, 1868, a state election voted the county seat to that city. Sometime that spring the records were spirited away "very early one morning" and hauled to Baker in a wagon. Auburn citizens woke up to realize the town had reached the final step of ignominy, was fast headed toward oblivion and decay.

SITE OF OLD AUBURN

One quarter of a mile north of this spot on Blue Canyon Creek is the site of Old Auburn, early mining town and first county seat of Baker County founded in April 1862 after discovery by members of the "Adams Party" This was the goal of the first historic gold rush into Eastern Oregon.

The population at one time was over 5,000 one of the largest towns in the young State of Oregon

Sign Erected 1941 Whitman National Forest. By CO.644 CCC

SIGN ERECTED BY C.C.C. BOYS marks nearest approach of good road, rocky track leading steeply down into Blue Canyon to few remnants of Auburn's heyday.

AURORA, OREGON

If Cheyenne Chief Shot In The Hand saw the desert cavalcade he must have said to his medicine man in whatever way he said things to his medicine man — "Well, old herbs and skulls, I've seen everything now." Yet whatever the Indians did think of this "far out" procession on the Oregon Trail, they let it alone. Dr. Wilhelm Keil had a safety factor working for him.

The outfit would have startled any good honest settler. Leading the string of covered wagons were two mules pulling a hearse, inside it a lead-lined casket filled with alcohol in which was preserved the body of a nineteen-year-old boy. Beside the hearse rode several German band musicians playing doleful Teutonic hymns which were sung by others riding behind. Then followed the wagons with women and children and supplies of a large party head-

ing for the Willamette Valley. This was the wagon train of the fanatical religious leader, Dr. Wilhelm Keil and his followers.

Born in Bleicherod, District of Erfurt, Prussia on March 6, 1812, young Keil emigrated to the new world in 1836. Tailor by trade, he worked in a New York clothing factory and being diligent he would have done well but for his constant exhortations on religion among his fellow workers. They protested and Keil was discharged. German Methodism now took over his whole being and moving to Pittsburgh, he was ordained a Methodist preacher.

For a time dispensing gospel in the conventional manner satisfied his zeal but soon his radical tendencies set him in open revolt and he cut himself off from his church and moved to Shelby County, Missouri, where in 1845 he formed a colony of sym-

DR. WILHELM KEIL BUILT HUGE HOUSE in 1872 for favorite son and bride, architecture closely styled to "Das Grosse Haus" built for leader and family earlier. Mansion was stately but offered few comforts. Each of two floors has two large rooms, at end of each a large fireplace, only provision for heating and cooking. Resting on cedar stumps, practically indestructible as foundations, house is solid to this day.

FOUNDER OF COLONY is buried in family plot. Nearby is grave of daughter Aurora for whom village was named.

pathetic believers. Some six thousand acres were acquired, the center of it to be called Bethel, House of God. For a time the colony prospered but then came trouble — antagonism on the part of neighbors, several seasons of bad weather for crops and general discouragement.

By 1855 Keil had acquired the title "Doctor" and many ideas. The real New Jerusalem, he said, must be in the much talked about Oregon Territory and that was where the colony was going. The faithful gathered up their belongings, said farewell to loved ones and prepared to leave.

Also by this time the Doctor had five sons, the eldest named for his father and called Willie. He was nineteen and enthused about the trip west but was suddenly beset by malaria. Before he died he begged his father not to leave him in Missouri but take his body on the caravan and bury it in the new land. Following his promise, Keil placed the boy's body in the sealed casket with the alcohol and placed it on the lead wagon.

After four months of travel the party arrived at

ELIAS KEIL, born in father's house two years after it was built, two years before death of grandfather Keil, lived in structure all his life, never knew electricity or inside plumbing. Picture shows back porch covered by old grapevine.

Willapa, Washington Territory, the originally planned destination, and Willie was buried there. After a short stay, however, Dr. Kiel became dissatisfied with the place as a permanent site for his colony and again pulled up stakes.

Arriving in the Willamette Valley, the Doctor selected a location on the west bank of Mill Creek, just above its junction with the Pudding River and near the Willamette which received the waters of both.

It was share and share alike for everybody except Dr. Keil and many of the names of the colony founders might have come straight out of the Prussian army — Rapp, Steinbock, Wolff, Koch and Koenig. All members were to live by these tenets: "From every man according to his capacity to every man according to his needs, is the rule that runs through the law of love. Every man or woman must be a brother or sister to every man and woman in our family under the law of God."

The autocratic leader set standards of modesty for the homes of colony members yet his own, one of the first to be erected, was three stories tall. It had four very large rooms, two on each floor. There was no central heating system, large fireplaces at each end sufficed for heating and cooking. Two large balconies with railings of turned spindles graced the front of the imposing mansion.

Communal activities were varied and included working in the fine orchards and selling the fruit to neighboring settlers. A large furniture factory was set up, its products sold up and down the valley as were bakery goods. A fine band was organized, playing concerts from the balcony of one large building and for celebrations in neighboring towns. Dr. Keil was quite willing it should be so — for $50, of course. Proceeds of all projects were divided for the benefit of all — or so it was believed by devout members. Some detractors outside the colony claimed the funds went into a stout trunk which reposed under Dr. Keil's four-poster.

However no one in the colony seems to have suffered from want, especially of food. This item seems to have been all important in the progress of Aurora in true old country folk tradition. At all summer celebrations long tables were set up in the open and lavishly spread with German sausages, roasts, pies and pastries — all the rich indigestibles of peasant land. The band played loudly while everyone ate, the record says, and it is assumed the musicians had already eaten.

At Christmas huge baskets of cakes, fruits and candies were distributed to the colonists. Two large fir trees were trussed up in the forty by eighty church, where the altar was built in the shape of a star. Preaching and band concerts went on almost constantly, gifts accumulated under the trees until New Year's when they were passed out to the children.

Outsiders, even complete strangers, were welcome at all celebrations and came in droves. It was good business, spreading the good word of Aurora's products. When the railroad came through it stopped for meals at Aurora rather than at Portland which was much larger and only a few miles farther on. Schools operated the year around, allowing no such nonsense as summer vacations. Nor were any educational frivolities tolerated. Reading, writing and arithmetic were the only studies with the exception of music.

Dr. Keil's despotic rule prevailed for twenty-five years, then an undercurrent of change was felt. Many of the original colonists were aging, as was the leader himself. A younger generation was exposed to the outside world and this influence was working its way in. As long as the word of Dr. Keil was undisputed, the colony held together as a unit but he was failing, his word weakening, his grip loosening.

There was a reorganization, a deviation from the credo "Equal service, equal obligation, equal reward," yet still tempered to the older order while Dr. Keil lived. Upon his death in 1877, the colony was dissolved, all communally held property divided between members according to length of service. And as the years passed evidence of the original colony began to disappear, old buildings and houses falling victim to fire and slow decay.

Across the stream, on the highway, a town of Aurora grew up, somewhat as a development of the colony. It was a thriving community for years during the early twentieth century when it was on the main Pacific Highway and a center of the huge hop growing industry of the valley. It had at least one newspaper, the weekly AURORA BOREALIS, starting in 1900 and lasting eight years. Now the Portland-Salem freeway has bypassed the town which retains many reminders of more flourishing times. The community is beginning to realize the importance of its history and is making an effort to preserve its old buildings and visible reminders of its past.

SOUTH END of venerable house shows basement entrance at ground level. Elias Keil, grandson of colony leader, was born here August 17, 1875 and occupied it all his life. He played in famous Aurora Band most of these years, even participating in program at Aurora's Centennial in 1956 at over 80 years of age.

AUSTIN, OREGON

Austin was not itself a mining camp, but a supply depot for the many busy gold towns in the Blue Mountain area. The little narrow gauge railroad from Sumpter had its terminus here for many years in the earliest days, later being extended to Prairie City.

During this bustling period Austin was supposed by everyone to have a brilliant, permanent future. There were three large sawmills going full blast, turning out lumber for Greenhorn, Bonanza and other flourishing towns higher up in the densely forested mountains. A substantial jail was necessary for the many rowdies, drunks and more serious offenders. Several stores and office buildings for doctors, lawyers and real estate operators were built.

Already long established was the hotel and stagecoach way-station started by Mr. Newton. It was later bought by Mr. and Mrs. Minot Austin and called the "Austin House," giving the now growing community its name. The post office was incorporated in the building in 1888. The station was still being used as a hotel for hunters as late as W.P.A. days.

The decline of the gold camps spelled the death of Austin which had depended upon their existence. The population which had totaled about 500 at its height dwindled to 50 at the close of the second World War and is at the vanishing point now.

AUSTIN HOUSE LOOKS BETTER now than in photo of 1900. Wing extending south is long gone. Square structure on adjoining section shows at left. Original loghouse stands to right, out of range of camera.

LOAD AND PASSENGERS seem mostly to be on outside of stage in picture taken 60 years before our record. Picture was kindly loaned us by present tenants, the Alton E. Roods.

CENTER OF CITY GOVERNMENT in Austin heyday was this gaunt building. Inside on main floor are two stout cells with heavy doors with strong iron hinges and hasps. Upstairs were offices of city fathers.

ANCIENT LOG STRUCTURE dates back to earliest days of gold discoveries in Blue Mountains. Standing near Austin House, it antedates that building, is now regarded as "just the woodshed."

BONANZA, OREGON

Frank Roberts was an eager young man when he arrived in the rowdy mining town named after its main mine, the Bonanza. This was in 1900 and he planned to make teaching the mine roughnecks their three R's his work. And he did it, too, for a year or so. He had 25 to 30 scholars of all grades in the tiny Bonanza school.

At that time the big Bonanza mine had been operating since 1877 with a final depth of over 1,200 feet, and a thriving camp had grown up about it. Fifty men were employed in the mine alone and several were required to operate the aerial tram with its 20-to-30-foot towers suspending the cables well above deep winter snows. A constant stream of rich gold ore flowed down this web in buckets to be processed in the 20 stamp mills near the town, giving employment to another 40 or so.

Even this huge capacity could not process the increasing quantities of materials and the mill owners, about 1905, made the bold move of doubling the stamps. This was no simple job in such a remote mountain wilderness.

Pioneer Bonanza teacher, Frank Roberts, is now retired, living in Yamhill, Oregon, but he vividly remembers the various phases of that operation. "The snow was almost gone that spring when those 18 span of horses came up the hill from Whitney. They pulled two large pine logs laid parallel and on them was mounted the boiler necessary to steam power the 20 new stamps. They would come in a rush of 100 feet or so and then have to stop and blow."

During those days anyone could get a job and many did so, for the express purpose of "highgrading," pocketing "blossom rock," ore so heavily laced with gold that its theft paid more than wages. The practice was never wholly controlled and it was felt that many thousands of dollars were lost to the rightful owners this way. Even so, the estimates on total production ran from $1,500,000 to $5,000,000 and it is agreed that the Bonanza was one of the richest in the Baker sector. In addition, extensive placer, sluicing and dredging operations went on in the streams below the town, adding much to the total gained in "hard rock" methods.

Big operations closed down about 1910. Then Frank Dodson and his father took a lease on the property and worked it with more or less success for several years, after which the place died entirely.

MAIN STREET OF BON-ANZA is lined with ruins. Store on south side, near complete collapse, was center of commercial activity.

BOURNE, OREGON

Cracker was an honest, genuine gold mining and placering town in the 1870's and it had all the earmarks of the typical camp. A "Maiden Lane" section adjoined the several saloons and gambling houses; a large general store and hotel helped line the steeply inclined street. The main street was the only one, because the canyon sides all but squeezed out even that. At the upper end, however, there were several short, interesting "pieces" of streets perched here and there on the ledges. Each had its quota of businesses and residences in the days of Bourne's golden prosperity.

At the turn of the century Cracker began to deviate from honest mining and began to speculate. Somehow this more or less coincided with the change of name, although the new title honored a respected U.S. Senator, Jonathon Bourne. The Post Office of Bourne was established in March, 1895.

As Bourne, the place became a hotbed of inflationary get-rich-quick bubbles, all of which burst in short order.

Two newspapers emerged each week from the same printshop. One contained legitimate news. The other, meant for the outside world, promoted the myth that the town of Bourne was only a thin skin over a lode equal to the world's greatest bonanzas.

The closure of the post office in May, 1927, indicated the approaching end of this era and ten years later a cloudburst sent a wall of water down Cracker Creek and Main Street marking the finish of Bourne.

Enough remains to make a visit well worth while. Bourne is only about seven miles from Sumpter over a road typical of the more remote sections of the Blue Mountains, not good, not bad, not as steep as many, and lined with mementos of the boisterous days of gold placering along Cracker Creek.

UPPER END OF MAIN STREET of Bourne. Extensive foundations of large buildings are in background. Traces of all periods of former activity are scattered through town.

HYDRAULICKING GOES ON in small way along Cracker Creek below Bourne. Gold recovery still pays if not too much cost is involved. Here powerful head of water from small dam upstream is directed at gold-bearing mud and gravel; resulting thick liquid is channeled into sluice to settle out gold.

BUTTEVILLE, OREGON

The paddle-wheel steamer SHOALWATER was no more but her bones had been reshaped, her decks relaid, her defects covered with thick white paint. And there was her owner pointing proudly to her new name — FENIX. Funny name, people of the Willamette Valley said. What's it mean? "Why that," explained the owner, "that's the bird in the fable that rose up out of the ashes to fly again. See the point? I know how it should be spelled but this way I could make the letters bigger."

And what had happened to the SHOALWATER? One day in May, 1853, making her landing at the Butteville dock, above the falls where Oregon City is now, the Willamette River swollen by spring rains and flowing savagely, the skipper laid on all the steam she had and called for more. The SHOAL-WATER had the spirit but her flues were weak and a

great blast rent the boilers. On deck ready to dis-embark, the passengers suddenly found themselves in the cold currents. All were in luck to be saved from drowning but none of them ever wanted to hear the name SHOALWATER again.

Etienne Lucier planted the first crop in French Prairie, a flat, treeless area along the Willamette about 1830. The crop was wheat and from then on, until about the turn of the century wheat was al-most the only agricultural product of the area — this in a land where the soil was capable of produc-ing anything suitable to a temperate climate. Wheat found a ready market and that was enough. The only real difficulty at first was getting the crop to that market since there were no roads, only the river, and cargoes had to be portaged around large falls and rapids at Oregon City and transferred to

OLD BUTTEVILLE — picture taken from opposite bank of Willamette River about 1890, judging from fact concrete dock has replaced wooden one on pilings. Most buildings shown have vanished but white frame house upper right, ornate one center right and plainer frame with porch extreme left, still remain. Section of deeply rutted road leading to dock gives some idea of difficulties wagons encountered on most roads in western Oregon's rainy season.

ORIGINAL LANDINGS were built on pilings, some remarkably preserved after 100 years or more. Level of river shown here is average. Willamette has become much more tractable in recent years with flood control in main river and such tributaries as Santiam which originates in Cascade Mountains, although even now it goes on rampage when snows melt rapidly or during protracted rainfall.

other craft for the rest of the trip to Fort Vancouver.

All this effort caused a rash of little towns to spring up along the Willamette between the present Salem and Oregon City. Butteville, at the extreme northern end of the wheat belt called French Prairie, was one of these. It was primarily a river landing and never progressed much beyond that although it did boast a church, schools, stores and several saloons during the golden period of wheat shipping.

Joel Palmer, the man who had pioneered a route for the first wagons over the shoulder of Mt. Hood, mentioned the settlement in his journal in 1845; "Eight miles from Pudding River is a village called Butes. It was laid out by Messrs. Abernathy and Beers. There were but a few cabins there when I left. The proprietor had erected a warehouse to store wheat they might purchase of the settlers, who should find it convenient to sell their crops at this point. At this place are some conical hills called

Butes, which arise to considerable heights; the sides and tops of them are covered with tall fir trees which can be seen from the valley for sixty miles." All this was essentially true, the exceptions being one butte of noteworthy height and that only 427 feet, hardly noticeable except locally. His spelling of Bute was common enough in those days.

The village that grew up beside the first crude river landing about 1840 was first called by the preponderately French settlers La Butte but Americanized a few years later. When George Abernathy and Alanson Beers drove pilings at the edge of the river and laid out a simple town, they had big ideas of a metropolis that would outshine the rival Champoeg. For instance they planned to handle the buying and shipping of the settlers — almost to a man retired French Canadian trappers of the Hudson's Bay Co. — and later they would sell real estate, establish stores and saloons. Since there was little or no gold and business was done in trade, the rancher would get his pay in groceries and spend the rest of what he had coming for liquor or wine, Abernathy and Beers making a profit at every turn.

However this was not to come about. Abernathy became involved in the simple politics of the day and was so dedicated to seeing the provisional government get off on the right foot he was elected first governor of Oregon in 1845 and had no time to promote his interests in Butteville. The facts about Beers are obscure but it is known the first real store at the landing was started about 1850 by one Francis Xavier Mathieu, who talked the vacillating Etienne Lucier into casting his vote with the Americans at Champoeg (see Champoeg story).

Mathieu was one of the early French Canadian trappers who with the decline of the fur industry had settled on French Prairie in 1842. He lived with Lucier two years, making himself generally useful as a builder of wagons and houses, then married Rose Osant, daughter of another ex-trapper. Two years later he took a donation claim at La Butte. Mathieu had "a way with people" and after his successful persuasion of the deciding votes in Champoeg, he was elected constable, often settling disputes by inviting contestants to dinner and the difficulty was usually settled amicably over a bottle of French wine.

Mathieu decided against a comparative retirement to run the store. He cut trees on his claim and laid the logs for the lower half of the building and had some whipsawed for the upper section. Hand-adzed planks served for a floor and split cedar shakes for the roof. From then on for fifteen years Mathieu's Store was the most important place in Butteville. One good customer was Robert Newell of Champoeg, another the Hudson's Bay Co. emissary, Michael Framboise. For two years he had a partner, a George La Roque. A plat of Butteville in the Historical Atlas Map of Marion and Linn Counties, 1878, shows the La Roque claim as entirely surrounding the townsite of Butteville and seems to include it.

In 1860 an Episcopal Church was built, prudently quite high on the bank. Funds for construction came short of a bell but the congregation felt that God, in time, would provide. Next year the big flood that washed through so many river towns inundated Champoeg, wrecked the sister church there and carried its belfry, complete with bell, down to Butteville and depositing it in a thicket along the creek bank. Champoeg, utterly destroyed, had no more use for the bell, so it was joyfully reclaimed, cleaned of mud and hung in the Butteville steeple.

As long as there were few roads, and these almost impassable in wet weather, Butteville flourished. When rumors circulated that the Oregon and California Railroad would stop there, it was hoped farmers would continue to haul wheat in and that it would be shipped by train. But the rails bypassed Butteville and the town gradually faded. Today it is still alive, a tiny and picturesque hamlet with only one business, a modern little grocery store in one of the old, revamped buildings.

LITTLE OLD BUTTEVILLE SCHOOL shown here all prettied up and moved to grounds of Newell home at Champoeg, restored by D.A.R. While exterior of old structure has been renewed, interior is almost unchanged. Original flooring is of whipsawed planks, walls of lighter boards also showing whipsaw marks. School has two rooms, upper and lower grades in former days, is presumed same building as that of "Butteville Academy" incorporated at state legislature in 1869, Francois Xavier Mathieu being one of trustees. Howard McKinley Corning, in his definitive book, **Willamette Landings,** says the Academy "probably was a large name for a small public school." Dolores Purdue, now of Portland, remembers the time she attended graduation exercises at school; "There were three graduates from the 8th grade. After they received their diplomas there was a picnic followed by all kinds of games and races."

Oregon

GOLD — AND A GENIUS

Canyon City, Oregon

While its diggings yielded many millions in gold, Canyon City's history is colored more vividly by the character of one of its citizens. This was the bearded poet Cincinnatus Heine Miller, more familiarly known as Joaquin Miller who doubled as squaw man, prospector, printer's devil, supply packer and who as county judge claimed he "dispensed justice in Canyon City with a six-shooter in each hand."

In the early 1860s an unknown number of men combed the canyons and gulches of eastern Oregon, most of them on the trail of the mysterious Blue Bucket Mine. Although that location was never positively identified many other rich diggings were

located. No one can say how much gold may have been or still is in the Blue Bucket but certainly Canyon Creek gave up a whopping $8 million in dust and nuggets. Among many stories of the original discovery in 1862 is the one that has the unlikely elements so often founded on fact. One of these is that in the first party camping on Whiskey Flat, a scant half mile north of where the town would grow, was one Billy Aldred who strayed from the others to make his own explorations. Spotting a location he liked across a creek, he waded over and found the gravel promising. Being without a pan or container for samples he stripped off his long underwear and by knotting the ankles and wrists, made four long bags which he filled

HERE LIVED JOAQUIN MILLER, described as "a bit of a charlatan . . . a restless, spectacular character, capable of writing an occasional poem with a vigorous lilt." Arriving here with wife Minnie and baby in 1864, controversial poet brought first fruit trees, ornamental shrubs to raw mining camp on pack animals. Double white lilacs shown left and right could be survivors of original shrubs.

Chair, hand cut from single section of log is on porch of Joaquin Miller cabin at Canyon City. Long extended periods of sitting in it would seem to invite case of curvature of spine.

with gold laden sand. Three days later a saloon was erected on the spot and other structures followed it. Canyon City was on its way. At the peak of the rush some 10,000 people of every description thronged the narrow main street called Whiskey Gulch.

Breaking through the crowds were numerous trains of oxen, mules and horses bringing in supplies from The Dalles by way of the old Military Road, animals and wagons having crossed swollen rivers, stretches of desert sand and rocky mountain defiles. Indians lurked at several points, the danger increasing as they learned the value of gold coming back with the teams.

With the influx of packers, miners and traders came the inevitable gamblers and prostitutes. One of the former was a notorious card sharp known as Black Dan because of his swarthy complexion. The story told about him is the one credited to some gambler in almost every mountain camp, yet it could have happened to him. Caught by a bullet, Black Dan could see his end approaching but requested his saloon buddies to "lay him out" as already dead and bring in some of the girls. The going away party got rolling with a toast to the near-departed when it was discovered he had

been so inconsiderate as to spoil everything by not waiting for the glasses to be drained.

Independence Day celebrations in early mining camps were rated next to Christmas in importance and featured sack races, football games and volunteer fire department drills. In 1863 Canyon City staged a Fourth of July affair that got somewhat out of hand. With the Civil War raging there was some violence between miners, prospectors and hangers-on who had Confederate or Union sympathies and on this occasion with saloons filled quarrels sprang up quickly. Supporters of the South, largely from California, and Union men from Oregon, Washington and Idaho, let their feelings and tempers grow hotter as the day went on.

Shortly after noon rebels climbed the hill above town and raised a large Confederate flag, firing off a defiant volley. When the banner was seen from the street Union men quickly organized and armed themselves, stormed the hill and tore it down. Although some shots were fired in the melee, more were downed in the saloons. There were no fatalities but bitterness and resentment lasted for years. Lest anyone forget the incident the bluff, actually part of the rim rock above town, was named "Rebel Hill."

At the time of the party on the hill Col. Henry E. Dosch was on his way to Canyon City from St. Louis, Mo. Born in Germany June 17, 1841, and arriving in St. Louis in 1860, he lived there less than a year when he enlisted in the Union Army. By way of California young Dosch arrived at The Dalles on the Columbia River in 1864. There he set up an enterprise to pack supplies into roaring Canyon City. In later years, after he became a prominent citizen of Portland with a road named for him, he wrote an account of his adventure along the old Military Road in Eastern Oregon.

His partners John Snively and William Claffin furnished the money, Dosch wrote, and he the experience gained on his trip north. The packers carried about $25,000 worth of supplies to the camp, selling them at double the cost. "We didn't include flour in this, selling the staple which everyone must have, at cost—55 cents a pound. Nobody got rich but we made wages." The return load paid better. Canyon City gold was exceptionally pure without the infusion of copper that reduced value elsewhere. At $17 per ounce Dosch's pack animals were most attractive to road agents.

At this time Grant County had just been organized, the first election naming W. L. Laird as county judge and Tom Brents county clerk. After a short term the latter was replaced by saloon keeper Mike Goodwin and Dosch relates, "Mike didn't know the first thing about the duties required, so he named me as his deputy. I took over his job and served under C. H. Miller who had been elected county judge."

He refers to Cincinnatus Heine Miller who came across the plains in a covered wagon in his early teens. After a short stay with his parents he began a wandering career, fighting briefly in the Modoc War, traveling to the gold camps of northern California. As a youth of about eighteen he found life among the Digger Indians of the McCloud River country near Mt. Shasta very much to his liking because of the amiable Indian girls so easily available.

Going native, he shed his regular clothes for the fringed buckskins he was to affect during much of his life. Flitting from one acquiescent squaw to another he settled down with one whose "flowing hair," he wrote, "only partially screened the rounded young breasts of maidenhood." His white friend Jim Brock wrote later, "I should say a man would be crazy to live with one of them . . . the sight and smell of most would turn the stomach of any but a poet."

Of Miller's dalliance was born a daughter whom he named Cali-Shasta, then deserted both mother and child. Later he returned for the little girl and put her in the care of a friend in San Francisco. Moving to Eugene, Oregon, he worked on a newspaper which soon went out of business because of the editor's Confederate sympathies.

Some time later Miller and white wife Minnie and their small child joined a pack train for Canyon City, some of the animals carrying fruit trees, berry vines and ornamental shrubs. In the rough mining camp the family settled down in a cabin and Miller began writing the poetry that would bring him world fame. Dosch wrote of Miller, "He was an ardent admirer of Lord Byron, even affecting his idol's slight limp caused by a deformed foot. He wore his hair down to his shoulders and wore high boots, one of which was usually covered by a pant leg, the other leg being tucked inside. He loved to be conspicuous." Dosch, who often had to share the same office, complained that "Miller would often corner me so he could read me his stuff which I didn't much care for. I thought his wife Minnie wrote better, though her verses were never published."

But much of Miller's was, some of it in the Dalles *Times-Mountaineer*, sent out under a pen name—John Smith, Jr. Emboldened by success Miller submitted more material to his home town paper, the *Blue Mountain Eagle*, under his real name, Cincinnatus Heine Miller.

His marriage, ill-starred from the beginning, was dissolved and he moved to Portland where he continued his writings under a name that would be permanent—Joaquin Miller. Then came a European tour and in England his spectacular garb and flamboyant air "made a big hit," Dosch records. In 1907 Miller returned to his Canyon City home as a celebrity and there wrote "A Royal Highway of the World," actually a form of "letter to the editor." It was reproduced many times and sent to Grant and Harney County papers, commissioners and any other authorities he could think of. It protested the condition of the road from Canyon City to Burns. Miller claimed the "highway" was so clogged with brush that stage drivers had to carry axes and saws and cut their way through.

The road, now part of U.S. 395, is a modern paved highway, full of sharp curves as it skirts scenic Strawberry Mountain and many narrow canyons. It was formerly termed "Joaquin Miller Highway" but now the designation does not appear on maps.

MAIN STREET of Canyon City shows plunder taken by market hunters. Birds beaten out of swarming marshes bordering some sections of John Day River were ruthlessly slaughtered, even rare swans. Hunters pose with guns, butcher in apron. (Courtesy Oregon Historical Society).

CHAMPOEG, OREGON

"A ball was given on the floor of Dr. John Mc-Loughlin's mill in Oregon City. Lt. Peel bet the wine with the late Dr. Robert Newell that most of those present would take the British side in case of a contest. Lt. Peel lost the bet and showing some chagrin in his manner, offered to bet another bottle of wine that a man he indicated sitting right opposite to him across the floor would fight under the British flag. Dr. Newell took the bet. The man was asked to cross the floor when the question was put to him. 'Sir, which flag would you support in case of a war for this country?' The answer was quick and clear. 'I fight underneath the Stars and Stripes, myself'. The man was Willard H. Reese."

This incident was related by S. F. Chadwick a number of years later. It gives a vivid glimpse into the way events were building up to trouble with Great Britain over the Oregon country, as to whose flag was to fly over it. "Oregon" at that time was a vast territory extending from Pacific Ocean to Rocky Mountains, between parallels 42 and 54-40. The controversy centered in a rolling, grassy "prairie" area extending from the Indian village of Chemeketa, near where the State Capitol at Salem now stands, northward to a point just south of the Willamette falls at Oregon City. Possibly this land had once been covered by the same dense forests that mantled the surrounding country but native

OLD PICTURE, said to have been taken at Champoeg is undated but scene is typical of early days in busy river town. River is low, exposing bare banks where normal highway would bring it near grass. Phenomenal flood which destroyed Champoeg sent waters high above any point shown here.

"DOCTOR" ROBERT NEWELL, whose title was given for courtesy and affection, was one of earliest and most picturesque of Oregon pioneers. All his buildings and property in Champoeg, except home on higher ground, were washed away in disastrous flood of 1861. Newell persisted in trying to rebuild town for time but became disheartened and moved to Lapwai, Idaho, in middle '60s. Indian friends donated land to him in what became the heart of Lewiston. Portrait here was made on visit to Washington with Indian group to agitate for betterment of their situation.

Indian tribes, loosely grouped as Calapooias, had long been in a habit of setting fire to the grass and brush each fall, to corral game for easy killing and discourage forest growth.

To the earliest settlers in the 1820s the land seemed waiting to be planted to wheat. Etienne Lucier, born in the District of St. Edouard near Montreal, came to this part of the Willamette Valley in those years. He had been a recruited member of the Wilson Price Hunt Expedition overland to Astoria, arriving there in 1812. The arduous trip was part of Astor's great venture to establish a branch of the Pacific Fur Co. at the mouth of the Columbia River. Lucier became a trapper and guide, saw the fertile fields of the Willamette Valley and decided to settle there, planting wheat he brought from the post at Fort Vancouver, Lucier was Oregon's first farmer.

During the '30s more French Canadians gave up trapping, "married" Indian girls, termed "infidel women" by the priests who established missions at nearby St. Louis and St. Paul. Inept at farming to begin with, these "Mountain Men" were soon producing wheat in a golden flood, using it to pay for all manner of food and supplies in place of money.

A system was established to get the grain to market. Many of the farms centered on the banks of the Willamette River at a point called "Encampment du Sable". A landing and warehouse were built there, "batteaux" loaded with grain and floated to the falls at Oregon City where larger boats reloaded the cargo below the falls. Dr. John McLoughlin at Fort Vancouver found a good sale for the crop in Russian settlements along the coast.

Encampment du Sable took on the more convenient name of the Indian village nearby—Champoeg. The origin of the name, according to one version is that it is a combination of two Indian words for "weed" — "champoo" and "coich", pronunciation similar to "shampooik".

By 1840 there were fifty families on the "French Prairie", most of them near Champoeg. At first all were French Canadians with Calapooia or Nez Perce wives and numerous progeny, but later Americans joined the community so that Protestants, particularly Methodists, mingled with the Catholics. There was little friction since in this remote country every man had to rely closely on his neighbor.

Yet there was a storm of vaster implications brewing in high levels — the dispute between the United States and Great Britain as to who would control these fertile lands of the entire Oregon area. On October 28, 1818 a treaty of joint occupancy had been signed in London. In 1827 this was renewed but now more and more American settlers began to chafe at the idea of a possible English government. When the discontent finally reached an explosive stage, it was less a quarrel than the need to settle a private estate amicably.

Ewing Young, who became one of the wealthiest settlers, died in 1841 without an heir, his lands, buildings and stocks unclaimed. Now in place of the social and religious meetings the settlers were accustomed to have, they gathered to appoint an executor. At the same time another kind of meeting was called to cope with losses of livestock from wolves and other predatory animals, specifically losses of cattle and horses running wild on the Young place after his death.

On February 2, 1843 the farmers met again and levied an assessment of five dollars on each to pay bounty for carcasses of marauding wolves, mountain lions, lynx or bear. It was aptly termed a "Wolf Meeting" and the phrase applied to others following. A second Wolf Meeting was held on March 2 but this time wolves were not discussed.

The Americans, now about equal in number to those of foreign origin, were in some ferment over fear of British control and it was agreed by all that a local government of some kind must be established. A committee of twelve was appointed to "take into consideration the propriety for taking measures for civil and military protection of this colony." The committee met at Willamette Falls within a few days and arranged for a general gathering at Champoeg on May 2 to vote on the situation.

That meeting was the most momentous and dramatic in the history of the Oregon country, resulting in a bloodless decision that the vast territory should be under the control of the United States rather than Great Britain.

It was called to order in a corner of the wheat warehouse, used as an office by the Hudson's Bay Co. The first resolutions, calling for organization into a self-governing body, generated such excitement and confusion in the confined quarters that many voters went unheard and many of those who did hear voted improperly, even for the opposing side. The whole gathering then moved outdoors to the middle of a field and while the situation was

NEWELL HOME about turn of century, prudently built on high ground above Champoeg. House fell rapidly into disrepair after abandonment and when it collapsed, D.A.R. made project of restoring it. Present house on site is relic-filled museum, containing some original boards and fireplace bricks, is maintained as historical shrine.

OLD CHAMPOEG CEMETERY was on ground too high for flood-waters. Section shown here was planted with lilacs, now gnarled, lichen-encrusted, but still blooming in spring. Contrary to fate of some old cemeteries, this one is maintained for historical significance.

improved, a voice vote was hopeless. Trapper Joe Meek, tall, dark-eyed and black-bearded, raised his penetrating voice against the uproar, urging the men to "side up" in the field and declaring he would start things by taking the American side. French Canadian G. W. LeBriton made the formal motion that this be done and it was seconded by American William Gray, a Methodist mission worker. Joe Meek stepped out and called on all those of the one hundred and two present who wanted an American government established to gather around him.

With a loud hallooing forty-nine men went to the American side to make fifty in all. And fifty remained where they were. The other two? They were Etienne Lucier and F. X. Mathieu, standing in the middle, hesitating. Everyone waited impatiently for them to make up their minds. Lucier said he had

heard that under American rule, the very windows of his house would be taxed. Mathieu, who owned much land and property in nearby Butteville where he was surrounded by American sympathizers, suddenly decided to go with them and persuaded Lucier to do the same. They joined Meek and swayed the vote. The immense area sandwiched between Mexican California and Canada, so tenuously held by England, was now safely under the flag of the United States — at least as far as the inhabitants were concerned. Succeeding events soon made it official.

A group of nine was named to set up the beginnings of the infant government and a short time later Champoeg was declared "The Capital." A crude State House was erected of split cedar slabs and poles, roofed with cedar bark.

England was not willing to go along with all this quite so easily and in 1844 was still contending with Washington although it had ceased any activities in the Oregon country, the issue seeming dangerous to everybody but the Oregonians. There was even talk of war but the increasing influx of American immigrants to the Willamette Valley over the Oregon Trail made it obvious to the British that their cause was lost.

Champoeg began to take on the appearance of a permanent town, largely through the efforts of Robert Newell. Two places in Ohio, Putnam and Zanesville, are mentioned as his birthplace, in 1807. At eighteen he became a Rocky Mountain trapper, then as the fur trade declined, he teamed up with Joe Meek on a trip to the Oregon country, spending some time in Idaho and acquiring Nez Perce wives. They were sisters, daughters of sub-chief Kow-e-so-te. With a third man they brought the first wagons from Fort Hill into Oregon, although half dismantled. When they stopped at the mission in Walla Walla, Marcus Whitman congratulated the young men, saying: "You will never regret your efforts. Now that you have brought the first wagons, others will follow."

Newell, often referred to as "Doctor" or more familiarly as "Doc", took up residence in Champoeg and began to raise a family. He bought and fitted up two batteaux, starting a regular run between the town and the falls above Oregon City. They were called MOGUL and BEN FRANKLIN, power provided by Indian paddlers.

By 1851, when steamboats reached the town, Newell abandoned his primitive vessels and turned to real estate. Having taken up the 360-acre claim of Walter Pomeroy at the southern edges of Champoeg, he laid out a sub-division and sold lots. When need for land access became acute, he persuaded the provisional legislature to survey and construct a stage road from Salem to his property which he called Oxford. The Salem-St. Paul-Champoeg road is essentially the same route today.

By the 1850s there were about a hundred and fifty buildings in Champoeg including adjoining Oxford where Newell had built a fine home on a higher level above the Willamette. Peter Skene Ogden and James Douglas reported in 1847 that the Hudson's Bay Co. property in Champoeg was worth about $8,500 and the concern sold out in 1852 for some $17,000. Values and building continued to increase until the catastrophe of 1861 which all but wiped out the progressing city.

The Willamette had risen in 1853-54 to the point where water flowed through the edges of Champoeg and nibbled at the foundations of buildings. The stream subsided with little damage but Champoeg citizens were not alert to the warning.

In 1861, September and October passed with almost no precipitation. Then it began to rain in earnest and November brought an unending deluge which turned to snow. Temperatures rose, rain continued and the snowbanks melted.

Every tributary of the main stream, particularly the raging Santiam, swelled the Willamette almost a foot an hour until by December 2 the river was fifty-five feet higher than summer stage and twelve feet above the level of the '53-'54 flood. This time the murky, roaring waters swept over the town seven feet deep with terrific force, large logs acting as battering rams, and one by one Champoeg's buildings were carried away. The river stayed up for several days then slowly subsided to reveal a townsite "bare as a sandy beach". Three hundred and fifty houses were washed downstream yet the destruction was not quite total. Two solidly constructed structures remained standing — the two saloons.

The higher bench where Robert Newell had his house remained dry, the house intact. Newell, however, was financially ruined, his holdings in town entirely swept away. His Indian wife had died long before and now he took his new white wife and many offsprings to Lewiston, Idaho, the scene of his youthful dalliance.

Attempts were made to lay out a new town on the old site but with its moving spirit gone, once so strong many people thought of the place as Newellsville, nothing much happened. The green

meadow where the fateful vote was taken is now marked by a granite shaft, its exact location determined in 1900 by the last surviving voter, Francois Xavier Mathieu. It is emblazoned with the names believed on best authority to be of those siding with Meek and the United States. Surrounding all is Champoeg State Park where thousands hold summer picnics. The author visits there often, one such occasion in November when heavy rain was making a lake of the picnic grounds, tables and benches floating. The Willamette will continue periodic rampages; present and future dams along the tributaries such as the Detroit and Santiam appreciably restraining flood levels.

UNIQUE MONUMENT in Champoeg burial ground shows full maiden name of wife in accordance with Catholic custom. Object is partly to maintain evidence of accuracy of birth, baptismal records. English ivy, established and growing wild in much of Willamette Valley, clambers around base of marker. At least one marker in cemetery dates back to 1853. It is thought long-vanished wooden ones were first placed by settlers in '30s.

CHITWOOD, OREGON

Grace Davis left her telephone switchboard only once. It taught her a stern lesson. Now Mrs. Collins of Portland she thinks back to 1906, to her life in the rugged, timbered mountains of the Oregon coast.

There were only about twenty telephone subscribers but their calls kept Grace Davis busy almost the whole twenty-four hours she was on duty. Although she loved the job there were jangling interruptions while she was busy with other necessary duties that "got on her nerves" some days. This one day she made up her mind she would finish her lunch, buzzing or no buzzing. She tried to shut her ears until she finished eating and then sweetly answered the signal.

The voice was that of Chauncey Trapp, conductor of the eastbound train, telling her it had been wrecked below Chitwood and he had been trying to get her for fifteen minutes and he was about crazy, that she must get out there and stop the westbound train when it passed through Chitwood to avoid a terrible collision. Grace jumped and barely had time to warn the engineer as the train was pulling out. "That was the only time I ever ignored the switchboard," Grace says now. "And I haven't really felt safe in telling the story until now, almost sixty years later."

The area was a primeval wilderness in the 1860s when M. L. Trapp and his wife settled on a land claim a short distance below where the town would be. Life was lonely for the solitary woman until the Barney Morrisons took the next location. In a few more years more hardy pioneers came to cut the trees and till the soil. Some had families, more children were born and the need for a school arose. A house with one large room a half mile west of Chitwood was pressed into service, a fireplace at one end being the only source of heat. No one seemed to have time to cut firewood of proper length so the teacher, Thomas J. Brannan, poked the ends of large branches in the blaze and moved them farther in as they burned. There were no desks or tables so the pupils sat on benches and did their sums on slates in their laps.

After a few years of hardships some of the settlers gave up and moved away, taking their children with them, so education languished for a while. Then Mr. Trapp, one of the persistent ones, offered the use of a room in his home and hired a teacher who "lived in."

It was not until 1887 that a real school was built, its location near Chitwood and built by donated labor. It became the center for all community affairs — box socials, committee meetings, farm group get-togethers, Christmas parties and even weddings. Sometimes itinerant evangelists would hold revival meetings in the little "hall". A collection of books donated by residents, became the nucleus of a growing library shortly after the turn of the century and the "hello girl," Grace Davis, served as librarian.

During the early years many adherents of the Seventh Day Adventist faith wanted a church which could double as a school, but lumber was scarce and the dream had to be postponed. Then a little farm building in nearby Elk City which was already fading was dismantled and the material hauled to Chitwood by a sturdy pair of oxen—Lep and Lion. Lep was conspicuously spotted and was first called Leopard until it proved cumbersome. Oxen were best for hauling on the deeply rutted, muddy roads, but their doom was spelled when at last the railroad came—and with it P. A. Miller.

He had been Per Anderson in Sweden but that country's army complained there were already too many Andersons and would Per please change his name? The young Swede borrowed one of his cousin's and became Per Moeller. After the army service he took his new bride, Marie, to Chitwood and they lived in a section house while the Corvallis and Eastern Railroad was being built. And his name got "in the road" again. His daughter Lillie tells about it. "My father was quick to embrace new ideas, new things. As soon as he realized his name was awkward to American tongues he abbreviated Per to P, then inserted an A for the original Anderson and simplified Moeller to Miller. For the rest of his life he was P. A. Miller."

He was soon transferred to Mill City in the Willamette Valley at the very edge of the Cascade Mountains and helped build some of the bridges for frequent crossings of the Santiam River which

TRACKS OF CORVALLIS AND EASTERN, later branch line of Southern Pacific, run close by old George Smith store at right. Line ran from Corvallis in Willamette Valley over Coast Range to Yaquina on bay of same name, connecting agricultural area to coast, was started in 1880. Trains were first composed of flat car or two, a few box cars and about three coaches, hauled by puffing, wood-burning engine. Number of farmers added to income by cutting fuel on private wood lots, stacking it beside track. When train crew saw a pile ready, they would stop train and load it on tender. Passenger service was finally discontinued, tracks taken up between Yaquina and Toledo. Covered bridge is 96 feet long, was built in early 1920s, replacing hand-hewn span.

SNOW IS RARE in coastal area of Oregon, helps to delineate buildings shown in picture made about 1900. At extreme left is store built by Lafayette Pepin, rented to Rogers two years, then run by Pepin. Next right is old bridge of hand-hewn beams, above it Seventh Day Adventist Church. Large house with surrounding porch was originally owned by Mr. Durkee, later housing telephone office and switchboard, and still stands but long unoccupied. Next right is post office, shown in modern photo without porch. Next is railway depot, back of that old Whitney store, later operated by George Smith. Above is old Chitwood family home. Forest fire nearly denuded hills now covered with luxurious growth.

twisted down its narrow canyon. But he was dissatisfied because the job kept him away from home where his young wife was expecting her first child. He applied for the job of track maintenance on the Chitwood line where he could have permanent residence with his family. His request was granted six months after the baby girl was born, so the little family moved to a train stop called Morrison Station just below Chitwood, close enough for Lillie to go to school when ready.

Young Miller did well at his job and managed to improve his small home too but with the birth of two sons he started building a much larger one. Lillie's memories really begin with this house. "It had lots of bedrooms and a huge kitchen with a big wood range. Just above it, on the side of the steep hill was a woodshed which seemed as large as the house and appeared attached to it. One of the many people who stopped with my folks remarked: 'This

is the first time I ever saw a two-story woodshed'. There was always company at our house, salesman or drummer, itinerant preacher and, of course the school teacher. Everyone seemed to think it was expected he stay with the Millers, and mother, on whom the largest share of the extra work fell, never protested although it must have seemed she was running a boarding house."

The wagon road was a sea of mud in winter, with dust a foot deep in summer. Much later when the first automobiles began to filter in, it was said: "One car would raise so much dust that another couldn't follow it for a long time." In the muddy season the road was completely impassable but this did not handicap the section foreman. He had access to a hand car — a tiny, four-wheeled platform that ran on rails, powered by a handle bar worked up and down. It was a back-breaking job for one man but was easier when two used the rig, one facing forward and one backward, each man alternately lowering and raising the handles like the operation of a see-saw.

Just as the patient Mrs. Miller was relied upon to "put up" all stray visitors, so was P. A. trusted to take care of any emergency such as fetching the doctor when someone was desperately ill or an imminent childbirth. When called upon he would jump on the hand car and pump madly to Elk City where the doctor lived and with that worthy's help on the other end of the handle, speed to wherever needed. Since most of these calls came at night when the trains did not run, there was little danger on the rails. When Elk City declined and could no longer maintain a doctor, Miller was forced to pump his rig all the way to Toledo.

The right of way ignored most of the twistings of the Yaquina River along which it was built with spidery trestles and tunnels through projecting points of rock. When Lillie started going to school in Chitwood, she and other children walked the ties to avoid the muddy road. "We got very expert at hurrying over the trestles," she says, "so as not to be on one when a train came." In a year or two she was joined on the walk by her little brother whose twin had died in infancy.

Coming home from school one day the children came to a pile of glowing embers where the section crew had been burning old ties. The children put more wood on the dying fire and fanned it to a blaze. As Lillie stooped low over the flames her dress caught fire. In a panic she ran back to the school house and fortunately the teacher was still there. She tore most of the clothes from the little girl's body and rolled her in a coat. Lillie was a long time recovering from her burns, the scars still showing faintly.

It was about this period that a "prospector" from San Francisco discovered a fine vein of sandstone nearby, the material deemed most suitable for construction of the mint and post office in his home city. The Corvallis and Eastern ran a spur line into the quarry, the sandstone cut and loaded by hand on flat cars hauled to Yaquina, the lower terminus on Yaquina Bay, and trans-shipped on vessels to San Francisco. The industry caused quite an influx of workers for a time, "inflating" the tiny community to some extent.

In 1905 a movement was started for a telephone line to serve Chitwood, P. A. Miller in particular feeling the telegraph was not adequate. It was his responsibility to see that the long stretch of track was kept in good repair and he needed better communi-

cations with those who lived along the route. So on December 14, 1905, the Rural Telephone Co. was organized with A. L. McDonald as chairman, George T. Smith as secretary-treasurer. The list of signed members starts with P. A. Miller, includes most of the responsible residents including the Pepins, Wilsons, the younger Trapp and W. N. Cook. The office and switchboard was set up in the Durky house, owned by Miss Jean Robertson. It was here Grace Davis took over as switchboard operator. At first the line went only to Morrison Station but was soon expanded and eventually connected to the outside world for long distance calls, at first a big thrill for Grace Davis.

The coming of the Corvallis and Eastern changed things for Chitwood more than any other factor. When travel was confined to the wagon road, the stages sometimes got through and sometimes did not. The first fall rains turned the heavy dust into a quagmire in which wagons and stages were bogged down to the hubs.

CHITWOOD POST OFFICE was for years in George Smith store with Smith as postmaster. Later it was transferred to this little building. After it was closed out, door was enlarged and building served as garage. This business also has gone but pigeon-hole racks still hang on walls where they held letters. Huge chestnut tree once shaded front, was cut down some years ago, new growth springing up, as shown here in bloom.

When stages did get through they were useful. A man with a freshly killed deer carcass who lacked flour could wrap up a hind quarter in a sack, take the stage to Corvallis, make a trade in the store and return by stage with his flour.

When the puffing, wood-burners started pulling trains from Corvallis to Yaquina, Chitwood became an important stop. The little depot was close by George Smith's store and post office and train time always stirred the town into a frenzy. Grace Davis, in addition to her switchboard and library, saw that the mail sack was thrown on board, the incoming one taken off.

Since George Smith was the butcher as well as grocer there was always a smelly bale of cowhides ready for shipping. There would be sacks of dried and crushed cascara bark gathered in the woods where the trees abounded and carried out in bundles strapped to the pickers' backs. Cord upon cord of wood would be stacked beside the tracks for train crews to load as fuel for the boiler. Cutters got 90 cents a cord delivered on right-of-way. And trains brought large shipments of goods for George Smith's store.

The store had its beginnings in a small building put up by Joshua Chitwood who served as first postmaster as well, selling out later to a Mr. Whitney. George Smith worked in the store and later married the owner's daughter, taking over ownership after Whitney's retirement.

You could buy anything you needed at George's store. If it was not on hand it would be "sent for" from Corvallis and come in on the train. Bee keeping was an important part of the economy, Smith himself having an apiary and selling his neighbors a complete line of supplies, hives, supers and even queens on occasion. He sold meat but allowed customers to use his facilities for their own slaughtering.

Growing up and going to school here was Smith's son Morris. When he was old enough to work he did many jobs and then at 24 was elated to get steady work at another, later stone quarry. The stone was regularly blasted out of the solid vein by chipping out a "coyote" hole, placing the charge, then plugging up the hole with tapered rock with the wide ends out so they would jam tightly with the explosion, causing the full force of the blast to go upward instead of out the hole. Morris had gone to the cook shack for lunch one day which had been delayed for the scheduled twelve o'clock blast. This time a shower of badly placed rocks arched high overhead and came hurtling down through the roof of the shack, pinning Morris to the floor by his leg, crushing it from the ankle to above the knee. After a year of hospitalization, the knee was left rigid and ankle almost so.

GAY TIMES WERE HAD in olden days at Chitwood's dance hall.

PHOTO TAKEN FROM CHITWOOD'S covered bridge looks toward U.S. 20, shows old Pepin store. At other end of bridge was George Smith's, both stores necessary to service Chitwood in heyday, were friendly rivals. Lafayette Pepin came to Chitwood about 1878, married Flora Akey who bore him four sons. He built store in 1908, first rented it, took it over two years later. He died in 1917, Flora continuing to operate store. One son Archie, who had worked as logger 22 years, returned to care for ailing mother. When she died in 1948, Archie ran store in same old-fashioned way until about 1959 when he retired to Salem Nursing Home.

When Morris left the hospital he found the depression in full swing. With few jobs available he was happy when his father offered to take him into the store and as he kept busy, the leg improved. He cultivated berries and orchard fruit near the store, sold the produce there or with honey to the coast resorts at Newport.

When Lillie Miller graduated from the Chitwood grade school she went to high school in Toledo, thirteen miles away. It was hard to get there and lonely staying there so after the first year she took courses at home. When ready she taught in several of the small area schools and saving her money, took a summer course at Oregon Agricultural College at Corvallis, western terminus of Corvallis and Eastern. She had a stint of teaching at West Linn across the Willamette from Oregon City, graduating from the University of Oregon at Eugene. After a few years she married Charles A. Nutt and moved to Portland where she now lives, a widow.

When the old wagon road was rerouted and paved the improvement was hailed in Chitwood as a great thing. Automobiles, coming rapidly into popularity, used the new, short route to the coast. Soon no one was riding the train and with increasingly large tonnage of freight shipped by truck, the railroad reduced service to a minimum, discontinuing passenger service. The depot was torn down and many people moved away. Business was so slow at the Pepin and Smith stores, now that larger stores and markets were so readily reached by automobile, both owners quit trying. Chitwood, although retaining a few residents who love the place, is now a virtual ghost.

35

RIDERS IN THE SKY

CORNUCOPIA, OREGON

Cornucopia was once a rip-roaring gold mining camp with over a thousand people. It boomed not once but several times, as each new lode of fabulously rich gold ore was followed up. Some of the ore was so full of free gold that nuggets could be shaken out of it. Eight saloons provided refreshment and entertainment to hundreds of rough miners, many of them from Cornwall, England and called, for some obscure reason, "Cousin Jacks."

The first big boom years were from 1884 to 1886. The Union Companion Mine was the big one then, but several others ranged on up the rugged slopes, the Last Chance being at 7,000 feet. As for the name of the town, Cornucopia, with its connotation of wealth and abundance, has always been a popular name for mining towns. Some of the early miners here had come from Cornucopia, Nevada, and named the new camp for the old.

Erma Cole was a child of eight when she arrived with her father and mother in Cornucopia. Her father had been mining in the Yellow Jacket near what is now Sun Valley, Idaho, but had been told to quit the mines as he suffered "miner's consumption." The little family traveled on horseback to Weiser, then to Red Bluff, California. Here Mr. Cole heard that a Mr. Shipman, who had been the bookkeeper of the Yellow Jacket, was now in charge at the mines at Cornucopia. Not having found work elsewhere, he decided to cast his lot in the mines again. The family set out in horse and buggy for Cornucopia, a long and arduous trip in those days.

When they arrived there in October, 1898, Cornucopia had already shed its first site and moved farther up the slope to be nearer the mines, although the school, several saloons and office of the only physician, Dr. O'Conner, remained on the old townsite.

The little girl and her mother sat in their buggy on Main Street for half an hour. "When father returned," Erma remembers, "he told us that he had a job at top wages; $3.50 a day. He had already rented a tiny house and bought a stove so we would be warm." Mother Cole was not happy; Joseph ought not work in the mines again, but there was no choice. The family was destitute. And sure enough, "Father lasted just 15 days and came down terribly ill with pneumonia." The Irish physician, Dr. O'Conner, was summoned from the lower town and reassured the frightened family by telling them he had never yet lost a pneumonia patient. Joseph Cole did get well, but could not return to the mine.

At this time the one street was lined on both sides for several blocks by the typical false fronts and many cabins. There was a livery stable across from the post office. The meat market boasted two floors, the residence of the proprietor being over the shop. Mr. Estes was the butcher, a huge man with very short legs. He went everywhere on his mule named Becky, pulling himself up into the saddle by sheer strength. A good-sized general store was on the west side of the street, owned by Tom Turner in those early days. Later he took in a partner named Brown.

One of the buildings was a hotel and, at that critical period in the fortunes of the Coles, it needed a cook and manager. "Mother was a wonderful cook and Father was able by now to take over the duties of clerk and manager. Together they made a go of it and for a time it seemed as though this would be permanent. The hotel was always full, as living quarters were scarce and Mother's cooking attracted business."

Winter snows were and are of a prodigious depth in that section of the Wallowa Mountains. Total depth in winter often reached 30 feet, or a settled depth of 10 feet. The two stages which came daily, one from Baker and the other from Union, used sled runners instead of wheels. All winter the little street lay buried deeply and the trail rose higher and higher, much above the level of the doorways.

"Father cut a tunnel from the door up to the trail, and carefully made beautiful steps in the hard-packed snow. As soon as he turned his back we kids used them for a delightfully bumpy ride on our sleds and it soon took the sharp edges off the steps and Father would have to make them all over again. Little brother, Robert, who was five, would never come down stairs the conventional way, but jumped out of his upstairs window onto the snow, often with all too few clothes on his small body. This particular winter he became ill with rheumatic fever and mother had to devote her full time to nursing the boy.

BARBERSHOP AND "CANDY STORE" are among buildings on Main Street of Cornucopia. Barbershop was post office before tonsorial conversion. Space between buildings was boarded up during winters and soon filled up with snow. It packed and was handy during summer for making ice cream treats.

EARLY-DAY BARN of logs still stands. Shake roof was steeply pitched to shed enormous winter snows. Even so, snow piled up and had to be removed by hand.

The cooking had to be turned over to hired help, an unsatisfactory arrangement which resulted in the sale of the hotel to George Herbert, who later was sheriff of Baker County."

At this time the mines were using huge amounts of timber for shoring up the tunnels and shafts, for sluice trestles and many other purposes. Although the town was surrounded by an immense stand of virgin timber, wood and timbers were in short supply for lack of cutters. So Mr. Cole turned to this occupation and it proved to be successful.

Things became easier for the Coles and another strike helped produce a new boom for the town. Had the rich streaks of gold been mined systematically the situation would have been more stable, but some companies gutted them, and miners had to be searched on leaving to go home at night. Their pockets and lunch boxes would sometimes be found to have golden linings.

Mine accidents were frequent. Men were blown to bits by premature blasts, tunnel walls caved in or were flooded. Fire took its toll and avalanches were frequent. Huge slides of snow sometimes buried buildings entirely, entombing luckless inhabitants.

An explosion made fatherless one of the playmates of the Cole children. He was Christopher Schneider, and at 12, he had to get a job to support his mother and sisters. He was industrious and well liked and soon was doing the important work of sharpening drills.

Erma and other camp children usually played near where Chris was working. They ranged the mine tunnels and, since there was little room left when the ore-filled cars came rolling along, they flattened themselves against the walls whenever this happened. Shafts hundreds of feet deep connected to the tunnels, but strangely, no child ever fell down one of them.

EARLY-DAY CONSTRUCTION shows interesting wood textures. This is corner of huge barn which sheltered large part of important population of mules and horses, used mostly in hauling of firewood, shoring and stope timbers for mines.

FORGOTTEN WAG nailed shoes to weathered pump house.

Cornucopia lacked the wild shooting frays and killings so characteristic of other mining towns in early days, but in common with them, had the usual quota of women who lived in a couple of buildings by themselves. Miss Cole delicately refers to these as "Sporting Ladies."

The madam of one of these was familiarly known as Fanny, and she took her meals at the hotel where the Coles stayed. Around the corner from the dining room was a closet in which was a barrel. The hotel's official mouser, a big white cat named "Snowball," had selected this as a nursery for her new litter of kittens. Came dinner time and Fanny swept in with one of her girls named Nelly. They were followed by her several dogs whose custom it was to wait attentively on the chance of a bone. But now the dogs were irresistibly attracted to the barrel. When Snowball exploded in their faces, the resulting confusion in the dining room was such that both Fanny and Nelly jumped up on the table and held their voluminous skirts well up out of the way. To quote Erma Cole again, "I was somewhat bold in those days and I couldn't help laughing at them, but they were very upset."

As Erma grew up she also worked, usually helping wait table for the single men, in the company mess hall. "It was all I could do to carry those enormous platters heaped high with steaks, and the tureens of soup, each with a big ladle. The men helped themselves and ate like beasts. They piled up outside the door, and at the signal, fell over each other in their haste to get into the dining hall. And, while they looked at us girls, it would have been as much as his life was worth for one of them to so much as touch us. The company saw to that."

Now Cornucopia is slowly reverting to wilderness, sagging and empty buildings sparsely line the main street. Trees grow up through collapsing porches and cedar shakes rattle in the winds, playing a wild tattoo on steeply pitched roofs. Pack rats frolic where miners and gay ladies danced on rough plank floors, and where games of "21" lasted all winter.

TRESTLE LED DOWN FROM mill and carried pipe line to pump house. Tailings in soupy sludge dropped by gravity and then were lifted to top of huge pile by pumps. House was near to being engulfed by its own dumpings when town died.

ORE CAR STANDS WHERE it was left at mouth of Coulter Tunnel. Mines, whose upper workings were many hundreds of feet higher on mountain, dropped their shafts to level of tunnel which was well lighted in later years and had a restaurant for miners carved out of solid granite and gold ore a mile and a quarter back in the mountain. Blast of icy air emerges from mouth.

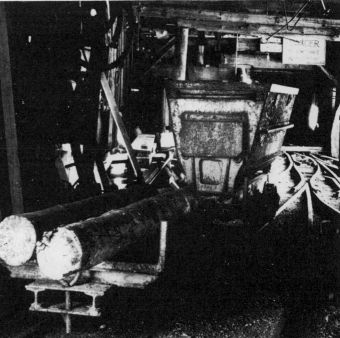

GRANITE, OREGON

When the original prospectors and settlers arrived at Granite in 1862, they realized the date was July 4th and accordingly named the future town Independence. But the postal authorities said no, there already was an "Independence" in Oregon. Further consultation produced "Granite," for the prevailing rock of the region.

Until about twenty years ago the general store had a good supply of derby hats, black corsets with beaded tops, heavy "snuggy" underwear and brilliantly spangled women's garters.

Now the faded buildings stand empty and deserted, their ranks thinning by fire and collapse under winter snows.

IN FRONT OF OLD CEMETERY stands tiny school-house. Later it served as polling place, a sort of "city hall." Pine-covered hill in background is typical of Blue Mountains. Seen from a distance through haze, heavy stands of ponderosa pines take on bluish look. Ancient headboards totter over forgotten graves behind plank fence at right.

NICKELODEON FACES drugstore across street. Until rather recent years structure also served as store and filling station. Grass-grown streets attest to lack of traffic now. Road carries cars to going mine in mountains and small private claims.

GREENHORN, OREGON

The two young men fresh from the East were as ignorant as they could possibly be on mining lore. They were determined, however, to strike it rich with a gold mine. They had heard that almost anywhere "Out West" they could simply strike a pick in the ground and there would be gold in unlimited quantities. Why they picked on this tiny camp high in the Blue Mountains of Oregon no one knows. But they did, one day, about 1890, walk brashly up to the bar of the little saloon and ask the barkeep, "Where can we dig for gold in this place?"

After the man with the towel recovered his composure, he turned to some of the more seasoned customers and in turn inquired, "Well, where would *you* say these boys might hit a vein of gold?" One of the "regulars" seeing an opportunity for a joke, took them outside and at random pointed to the side of the hill above town, saying, "There's a likely looking spot to dig!"

And dig they dutifully did. In a moment they came back down to the now uproariously merry group lugging a chunk of rock, with the naive question, "How does this look?" Laughter died among the gathering. The piece of rock was "blossom" stuff, richer than anything yet discovered in the camp.

Ridicule vanished, the old-timers in all honesty directed the innocents to stake their claims immediately, but the mine's discoverers didn't get the chance to name their find. The wiseacres had already christened it, "The Greenhorn Mine." The camp changed *its* name to Greenhorn and as such burgeoned and grew into a real, full-scale town, complete with several hotels besides the big one called the "Red Lion." Inevitably, several saloons were established and a newspaper, *The Greenhorn News,* was published every Friday.

TROUBLE OF ALL SORTS, involving shooting scrapes, thefts and holdups plagued Greenhorn in early days. Stout, though tiny jail was built as a consequence, had chastening effect, contained only half dozen tenants during following years. Structure is used now as shelter by deer hunters who cook meals in rock fireplace in front.

A water system was built, possibly unique among mining camps in that every house had its water piped directly to the kitchen. The source was on Vinegar Hill and the water company laid wooden pipes bound with wire to conduct the supply. Everything worked fine, except that elk wallowed in the spring and frequently broke the pipes.

By 1895, some 3,200 people were living their lives in this green wilderness and the nearby forest slopes boasted several large mines besides the Greenhorn, among them the Phoenix, I.X.L., Humbolt and Virginia.

The place had no regular post office until May, 1902, with Burton Miller as first postmaster. The town is divided by the line between Grant and Baker Counties, with the post office in the latter. Why postal facilities were not established for so many years after the original gold rush in the 1860's is a mystery.

The Greenhorn Mine was purchased by Richard Baird in 1914 and was operated by him until 1925. Some years after that, with increasing cost of mining and non-advancing price of gold, this and other mines became unprofitable to work and Greenhorn died a slow death.

Its people moved away and many of its buildings fell into decay, to be replaced by the magnificent White Firs, *(Abies Conocolor)*, of the area.

ORIGINAL CLAIM CABIN stands in small clearing. Section marker is visible in front of house. Here in infant mining camp lived Mr. Carpenter, the first miner to build a permanent home. Staking out homestead claim he did his necessary "improvement work," mined his discovery and built his cabin long before Greenhorn attained its status as town.

WHERE SPIRITS ROOST

HARDMAN, OREGON

In the days of stagecoaches two small Oregon towns were bitter rivals for the stage depot in their area. They were Raw Dog and Yellow Dog, about a mile apart in Morrow County, Oregon.

In the 1870's many stagecoaches and wagon trains traveling north and south through eastern Oregon and Washington, found one or the other of the two towns a convenient overnight resting place. This business was much more lucrative and easy than the regular ranching and cattle operation. Passengers found themselves shunted from one place to the other as drivers were favored or even bribed to stay the night.

Then, late in the decade, the rivalry became even more intense because it became known that a post office would be established in the area.

The whole thing was settled when Raw Dog was found to have several more people than Yellow Dog and was declared to be the metropolis and a fitting location for a United States Post Office. This move also decided the location of a more permanent stagecoach station and the demise of Yellow Dog was complete. Its remaining inhabitants moved over to the town that "had everything"' and their abandoned stores and buildings, such as they were, completely disappeared.

Now, as a veritable kennel of "dog towns," Raw Dog became just that . . . Dog Town and was so known for many years. When the post office was officially established in 1881, however, the dignitaries frowned on the name Dog Town and instead called the newborn

GENERAL VIEW OF TOWN from cemetery on hill above town. Clouds sweep in from south, but promise of rain is false in summer, usually dry. Two painted buildings are permanently occupied, others temporarily or not at all.

post office Hardman, after the man who had homesteaded the site. So Hardman it was officially known, but the dog tag hung on it for many years.

The town flourished and grew. A large hotel was built just south of the Odd Fellows Hall, and smaller hostelries sprang up along the main street.

There was even a jail, built of 2 x 6 inch lumber laid flat, and considered impregnable. One morning after a particularly boisterous Halloween, however, it was found tipped over on its side. It stayed that way until the following Halloween, when it was set afire, and "made a very hot blaze" according to an old resident.

Parker's Sawmill was located about 15 miles southeast near the pine woods, and contributed much to the economy. More important to the more lively element was the big all-day celebration and dance held every Fourth of July. These annual events were not always conducted with as much decorum as they might have been.

A large flour mill did a good business grinding the local wheat. It stood at the extreme south end of town. A drugstore with the typical false front of its day was built just north of the present grocery store. In front, in the middle of a wooden platform extended from the board sidewalk, was a handpump for water. Since there was no central water system and many people had no well, the pump was a community affair, and news of the townspeople spread rapidly from there.

With the decline of the stagecoaches and wagon trains, and as travel speeded up, the main usefulness of Hardman began to fade away and the town pump served fewer and fewer people. The community slid into a decline from which it will never recover.

HARDMAN MARKS southern edge of wheatfields. Drugstore in background once stood on Main Street.

HOSKINS, OREGON

The remains of Hoskins nestle in a hollow at the edge of the Coast Range, just where the mountains merge with the level flood plain of the Willamette River.

Due to a concentration of Indians at Siletz Agency in 1856, Fort Hoskins was established on the Luckiamute River near the mouth of what is now Bonner Creek, on July 26th of that year. The Fort was named for Lt. Charles Hoskins who had been killed in the battle of Monterrey, Mexico, ten years before.

Lumber was king in those days and the timber to be sawed grew densely there. Virgin forests were so dense as to shut out the light of day except at noon. Sawmills sprang up all along the coast range.

As the woods were depleted close by, short logging railways were extended to the diminishing forests. About 1918 the Valley and Siletz Railroad laid tracks through Hoskins displacing the old store, a relic of the 1880's. The venerable building was moved to a new location a few hundred feet down the slope and beside the tracks.

Mr. Earl Lonie, who now owns the store, says, "But I guess they had some wild times upstairs in the old days." It is easy to imagine the ladies and gentlemen, perspiring from the performance of a lively two-step, walking out on the little balcony for a cooling breath of air.

A number of abandoned houses and cabins are scattered about, no pattern of streets exists any more for Hoskins, and as Mr. Lonie sadly remarked, "The place seems to be a thing of the past."

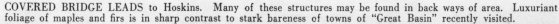

COVERED BRIDGE LEADS to Hoskins. Many of these structures may be found in back ways of area. Luxuriant foliage of maples and firs is in sharp contrast to stark bareness of towns of "Great Basin" recently visited.

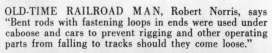

OLD GROCERY PRE-
SENTS architectural study
from rear. Front has bal-
cony extending from upper
story.

ANTIQUE CABOOSE dates from 1870's. Crossed bars
on sides were for reinforcement. Probably even they
would not hold venerable car together now. Repair
shops with walls full of parts is in background.

OLD-TIME RAILROAD MAN, Robert Norris, says
"Bent rods with fastening loops in ends were used under
caboose and cars to prevent rigging and other operating
parts from falling to tracks should they come loose."

PHANTOMS OF THE FAR WEST

JACKSONVILLE, OREGON

Original discoveries of gold were on Jackson Creek, in December, 1851. By the middle of the summer the place was already swarming with prospectors and miners of claims already staked out and the city of Jacksonville was on its way.

This frenzied activity was interrupted for a time when the Rogue River Indian wars of 1855 broke out, but resumed at the cessation of hostilities.

A smallpox epidemic in 1868, a flood in 1869 and fire upon fire ravaged the village, but never seriously discouraged the populace.

Advent of the Civil War split the people into factions, however, and did more to cause of dissension and strife than all the natural disasters put together. But that too, passed away and left the town in the peace it still enjoys today in a somnolent but living atmosphere.

Jacksonville is not a dead ghost, but neither is it a lively one, except for the tourists who visit this fascinating monument to Oregon's mining history.

CROWDED GRAVES ARE SUBMERGED in dense grove of cypress and madrona. These last are indigenous to area and are striking with peeling red trunks and evergreen leaves, clusters of orange-yellow berries.

FIRST PROTESTANT CHURCH west of the Rockies. Covered wagon is "prop" of Oregon's centennial year.

WELL-FORTIFIED AGAINST bandits and Indians was this building, dating from 1856.

PETER BRITT STANDS OUT among early-day photographers. His studio is set up in the museum located in the old courthouse. Beautiful structure was built in 1883. Courtroom upstairs is preserved intact.

KERBY, OREGON

James Kerby (or Kerbey) spelled his name first one way, then the other, and confusion still hovers over the spelling, not only of his name, but that of the town named for him. The town seems to have first been called Kirbey's Ranch, then Kerbyville. Then for a time it was named Napoleon! In 1857, D. S. Holton got control of most of the town and decided, since it was in Josephine County, Napoleon would be an elegant and appropriate title. The name was popular only with him and the town soon reverted to plain Kerby.

Kerby was well established by 1850, and in 1858 took over the position of county seat. As usual, gold was the main attraction, but many other minerals have been mined in the area, including iron, quicksilver, cobalt and ilmenite. Infusoria earth and quartz have had their day, too.

At its best, Kerby had a population of 500 or more miners and the usual proportion of hangers-on.

About this time, a neighboring mining town contracted for an elegant pool table, to be packed in in sections on the backs of mules. The expedition started from Crescent City, California. On camping one night near Kerby, one mule with the most important part of the table turned up missing. When found in the morning, he was dead. The packer decided he had gone far enough, buried his mule and established his pool hall in Kerby.

The town populace has dwindled to a mere handful, but a typical group of buildings remains, including the Masonic Temple, a tiny store, and several false fronts.

Across the street is a huge oak which is supposed to have been the inevitable "Hanging Tree," for the only ghost town without a "Hanging Tree" is a town with no trees at all. In this case, since the old Courthouse stood in its shade, and convicted prisoners were dragged out and hanged immediately, the tree certainly would have been convenient for this grisly use.

"HANGING TREE" broods over remnant of Kerby.

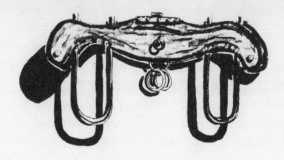

KINGS VALLEY, OREGON

The words had a deep and tragic significance. Samuel Parker, the wagon master, wrote them as they sounded. "We tuck what is called the Meek cut of", and later in view of what happened, he added: "A bad cut of fore all that tuck it." It was indeed a bad cutoff for all who took it.

Destiny interfered with the crunchingly slow progress of the wagon trains at Fort Boise. A number of them bound for Oregon's Willamette Valley met there, the emigrants exhausted and dispirited, yet trying feebly to answer the question — "Shall we keep on and if we do, do we go by the established Oregon Trail or follow this Steven Meek and pay him $5 a wagon? Maybe he's right and maybe he's wrong. All we know about him is he's a brother of Joe Meek who is a trusted mountain guide."

One party did follow Meek, the train of Nahum King, his young daughter Sarah and her husband Rowland Chambers. And then deep trouble began. The ox-drawn wagons were in the country named by French trappers "Malheur", meaning "evil hour", and so it proved. Sarah died, near the place the hamlet Beulah appeared forty years later, and a crudely lettered stone was set to mark the grave — "Mrs. S. Chambers   Sept. 3, 1845."

The procession toiled on at a maddeningly slow pace. In two days it stopped at a stream, a much disputed spot where, legend says, the children picked up gold nuggets and played with them in a little blue bucket which they hung under the wagon when it began moving. When the long journey ended its contents were discovered and the wild excitement caused many searches for the spot on the stream and many tales about the mythical Blue Bucket Mine, which was never found. The weary emigrants did not join in the hunt or lift their spirits in wondering. They were just thankful to be

YOUNG LT. GARBER just couldn't win, even at the end. Tombstone, paid for by collection among soldiers stationed at Fort Hoskins came from stone-cutters with "r" in name transposed to "s," was erected anyway.

GRIST MILL, built in summer of 1854, is among oldest in Oregon country. Located on banks of Luckiamute River, it utilized water power generated by overflow from rock dam built by partners Rowland Chambers and A. H. Reynolds. Upper story was storage space for grain to be ground.

able to settle down in the peaceful valley with no wish to return to the place of tribulation even if they found it.

The fertile little valley the Nahum King family and widowed Rowland Chambers selected was separated from the Willamette Valley by a low line of hills. It came to be called Kings Valley and the apostrophe, if any, has long since disappeared.

The lonely Chambers wooed and won another of King's daughters. He built a little house and planted a large acreage in wheat as did most early settlers there. But instead of shipping out his grain, he built a grist mill on the creek called Luckiamute. By means of a stone dam he was able to get enough fall in the slow moving creek to turn an old-fashioned water wheel which transferred power to the

mill higher on the bank by means of huge, handmade leather belts. Chambers had an able partner in the project, A. H. Reynolds, whose lately discovered diary records the time of construction "We started work on the grist mill in June, 1854."

On April 13 of the next year the Kings Valley post office was established with Rowland Chambers as first postmaster. From then on the town grew rapidly, supporting a sawmill, store and several saloons. Although a log school house dated as early as 1849, a church had to wait for popular subscription to get a frame building, 36 by 58 feet.

Indian troubles ended with the surrender of Old John, one of the main trouble makers, the last chief to come to the treaty grounds on the Rogue River. He set his gun against a rock during negotiations

51

UPPER FLOOR of grist mill had V-shaped floor, divided by partition, bottom on each side having opening for chute through which either of two kinds of grain could be fed to grinding stones. These photos were made in spring of 1963 when historic mill was due to be burned. Dam in river remains, impounded pool still providing neighboring children with swimming hole.

and at one point grabbed it to shoot down the officer reading the terms. When fifty soldiers aimed their rifles at him he gave up, temporarily, and surrendered his weapon. He was first sent with other Indians to the reservation at Grande Ronde, northeast of Kings Valley. When the neighboring farmers complained "the ground here is too good to waste on redskins. They ought to be thrown out so we can farm it", the Indians were transferred to the Siletz agency, farther south and near the Coast. A fort was ordered built at the western gate of the reservation, not so much to protect the settlers from the Indians as to guard the natives from being debauched by the whites. In this lofty aim the authorities were not entirely successful.

The site selected for Fort Hoskins was on a bench of a gently rising hill overlooking the lower part of the Luckiamute Valley, beautifully serene but considered the most likely spot for Indian up-

risings. The land was at the southern end of the town of Kings Valley and belonged to Rowland Chambers who sold it willingly enough.

At the rear of the bench and set against the hill was the largest building, the barracks. Immediately to the left was the latrine, then the commissary, water tower and bakery. The guard house was placed at the right of the barracks and farther down, near the foot of the bench, a hospital with Dr. D. G. Campbell of Corvallis in charge. The building still stands. At the left of it were the several buildings serving as officers' quarters which completed the square. In the center was a spacious parade ground.

Lt. Philip Sheridan, active in the Oregon wars in 1859, was the first in charge of Fort Hoskins but he was soon promoted to higher rank in the Civil War which followed. Taking his place was Capt. Augur, the unfortunate who had to take the brunt of complaints from neighboring farmers as to the behavior of his soldiers. One such protest was strongly worded. "The garrison at Fort Hoskins has a strong predilection for wine, women and song. Details are so indelicate they will not bear repeating." The report obviously lacked the savory details some wanted but ended with the definite statement: "The soldiers are a menace to the peace and prosperity of the community."

The captain is reported to have been "upset". He wrote letters to the farmers and neighbors ranging from Kings Valley itself to the little town on the other side of the fort called Fort Hoskins requesting

ROWLAND CHAMBERS with some of brood. Picture is thin, positive film on cracked glass, provided some problems in copying by this photographer. It is about 100 years old.

FAMILY GATHERING photo was taken after Rowland Chambers passed away but not before he had started population explosion. First wife died on journey to Oregon, second probably woman at right of infant in center, eldest daughter at left. Relationship of others vague. Many now rest in old Kings Valley cemetery not far away.

them to state their feelings on the matter. As reports came in Augur held a plebiscite with Rowland Chambers, L. Norton, O. King — son of the late Nahum — and other parties concerned. The somewhat surprising consensus was stated: "Either the farmers have had a change of heart or else the chief complainant, Mr. Ross Browne, was a liar." True, one farmer did say that although he had made good money selling the soldiers milk and eggs, the profit was nullified by their thefts of his hogs which they butchered and added to the commissary as a change of diet.

There was also continual trouble from Indians who insisted on coming over from the Siletz reservation and getting into trouble with the white settlers. One was caught peeking into the bedroom window of a farm house. The owner swore he would kill the next Indian Peeping Tom and he promptly did. This caused an uproar but the bereaved family was quickly placated with a payment of $200 by the army.

Then there was the incident concerning the beautiful Indian girl and young Lieutenant Garber. On duty at Fort Hoskins, he became acquainted with the girl in the early spring of 1850. She was soon visiting the reputedly "very handsome" officer in his quarters and then moving in, apparently tolerated by fellow officers until her parents complained, not so much on moral grounds as they needed her at home. Hoping to put an end to the affair, Augur sent Garber to Fort Vancouver to cool off, but reckoned without the persistence of the young squaw who walked all the way to the fort on the Columbia River to rejoin her lover. Garber was returned to Fort Hoskins and brought before Captain Augur for a dressing down and a warning to stop seeing the girl. This was supposed to end the matter but the Indian maiden was again discovered in the lieutenant's rooms. Again sent for by Augur, tempers flared on both sides and Garber made some insubordinate remarks. He was sentenced to six months in the guard house but died of unstated causes in a few months. He was buried in the Kings Valley cemetery, his grave identified only by the regular army marker for a time. Then his fellow soldiers contributed funds for a marble marker which stands today. Ironically, as though pointing up his ill luck, his name is misspelled.

OCCASIONAL BEAR was killed by soldiers and civilians at Fort Hoskins. Comment of one soldier: "It was a treat to get something we could eat once in a while." This and other very old pictures were loaned by descendant of Rowland Chambers.

LONEROCK, OREGON

Scotland's greatest export is Scots and the newly married Spaldings were two of them, making the incongruous jump from the fishing village of Banff, Aberdeenshire, to the raw and bleak wilderness of Lonerock in 1898.

At 17, David Spalding went to the arid eastern section of Oregon to establish a ranch home for his intended bride, Sophia Essom, choosing the locality near Trailfork in an almost barren area of sagebrush and juniper trees. The nearest large settlement was Condon, some 20 miles away but a smaller one, Lonerock, was only five miles distant and David felt Sophia would not be too lonely with such near neighbors. After five years of improving the ranch he returned to Scotland and claimed his bride. She had been taking nurses' training, a skill of inestimable value in a land so far from doctors and hospitals.

On arrival at the lonely farm the young couple set to work in earnest to establish a few of the comforts, and these were few indeed. One deprivation was being almost completely cut off from the outside world. Both were eager for news from Scotland but getting mail was a chore. Their small home was some distance from the mail route and a temporary system was set up that gave the ranch its name. When the mail carrier came by the road intersection he would put the Spaldings' mail in a heavy paper bag and stuff it in the crotch of a large juniper. Before long the Spalding place was the "Paper Sack Ranch."

Sophia and David worked their place for a number of years, then moved to the comparative comfort of Lonerock. This town had been settled as a crossroads gathering place for ranchers and sheepherders and being on the main emigrant route a supply center was needed. Two ranch partners, R. G. Robinson and Albert Henshaw, laid out the town in 1881, seeing to proper platting the next year. Prior to this, in '72, a post office

TINY JAIL held last prisoner, drunken Indian, 25 years ago, once was crowded when sheep were moved to higher pastures by sheepherders who celebrated at crossroads settlement. After last tenant was freed, fire hose cart was moved in. Little shed at right held wood supply for stove. Just past corner of jail is seen edge of early hotel, the Williams.

was established, with Robinson carrying the mail from The Dalles in a buckboard or on horseback.

The arrival of the Spaldings was an occasion for rejoicing, both young people being popular in this new country as they were back home, and social life enjoyed a lift. Since David was an accomplished musician with accordion and piano, and Sophia with a pleasing voice, an entertainment group was started at their ten-room home with neighbors gathering in the evenings for songs and dances.

The couple had two children, Lovena and Cecil. Their mother would make a batch of cookies and leave the lid off for all nearby children to help themselves. She and David became close friends of the Robinsons, Hardies, Maddens and Campbells. Sophia's nursing ability stood her in good stead as she aided in many an emergency as unofficial midwife. She often helped a birth before the only doctor, overworked George Gaunt who might be miles out in the country, could get to the scene.

Busy as she was, Sophia planted a row of little trees along the side of the house and in dry spells carried water from the creek to keep them alive and pumped water from the well when the creek dried up.

People began to move away from Lonerock about the end of the first World War. Water was getting scarce to the point of crop failures every few years, the climate always rigorous, reaching 16 degrees below zero and 100 above. The Spaldings stayed on and even after David's death in 1935, Sophia kept the big house tidy and the front yard full of flowers, still administering to the needs of her dwindling neighbors.

In 1956 she fell, fracturing her hip, was taken to a Portland hospital. Upon recovering she stayed with her married daughter Lovena in Condon. Another fall two years later resulted in breaking her other hip requiring more hospitalization. From her wheelchair she cheered other patients as she ignored her own pain. In July of 1961 she died and was returned to the little Lonerock church for the funeral.

By this time the town was almost completely deserted but on that Sunday, July 29, the church was filled beyond capacity, more than three hundred people coming from far and wide to say goodbye to the woman who had held such an important place in their lives.

IMPOSING SCHOOL was once alive with children, even housed higher grades in one room 2 to 5 years ago, high school later moved to Condon. Sophia Spalding's daughter, Lovena Palmer, taught here between 1934 and 1942, another teacher, Ruth Potter. Only seven pupils remained in '60-'61 taught by Geraldine Overhulse. Old school is now entirely deserted, cupola still holding silent bell.

LONEROCK M. E. CHURCH dates from before turn of century, saw regular services for many years. Now worshipers gather only on rare occasions when minister of Assembly of God Church of Condon makes visit. Huge rock behind church gave town its name. Funeral services for pioneer, Mrs. David Spalding were held here.

MALHEUR CITY, OREGON

There is a story that Malheur City received its name in the early days of mining there when a tunnel caved in trapping a French miner who died of his injuries. "Tam" McArthur, in his book "Oregon Place Names" thinks this is highly improbable, that the name came from the same source as did Malheur River. His version concerns Peter Skene Ogden, a Hudson Bay trapper, who made an expedition into the Snake River country and noted in his journal: "Tuesday, Feb. 14, 1826. We encamped on *River Au Malheur* (unfortunate river) so called on account of property and furs having been hid here formerly, discovered and stolen by natives."

As for Malheur City itself, it is not on the Malheur River but the much smaller Willow Creek close by and it was in this stream that gold was discovered in 1863. A group of miners who had left the exhausted El Dorado nearby, were prospecting for other diggings and made their find about the time they were ready to give up and go back to California.

The gravels of Willow Creek had plenty of gold and at first, when miners were easily satisfied, they panned and sluiced the stream when there was water in it and quit when there wasn't —which was often. Getting impatient at these enforced delays they made efforts to get water to the diggings and this resulted in the El Dorado Ditch, in that day an immense undertaking. The largest of its kind on the West Coast, it was planned and carried out by W. H. Packwood who engineered the Auburn and Sparta ditches.

The project was started in 1863 and was at first

FIRE LEVELLED ALL WOODEN HEADBOARDS in Malheur cemetery. Identification of these graves was lost, partially restored by memory, a few new markers erected. Some are pathetic in their brevity, such as: "A Mother and Her Three Children."

MANY YEARS HAVE PASSED over Malheur City since any mail was placed in box. Malheur is hot in summer, cold in winter and dugout style of home building had advantages besides making use of available materials. Rock and dirt walls had excellent insulating qualities, were only type to survive fire.

called the Burnt River Ditch since it was to carry water from that stream. The digging got off to a slow start but by '67 eleven miles had been built; forty-six more in the next two years. In 1870 the project was bought by an Illinois firm which speeded things up by putting 1,000 Chinese laborers on it. By some default the ditch was back in Packwood's hands in '74 and he kept at it four more years.

When the channel was carrying water it was 134 miles long and cut through many a big hill on its way to El Dorado and Malheur City, costing between a quarter and a half million dollars. An issue of the *Portland Oregonian* of that day report-

ed: "El Dorado Ditch in Baker County is now carrying . . . about 800 inches of water, from which is realized about $600 every 24 hours, over and above running expenses." This was below its capacity, as historian Isaac Hiatt wrote. "The main ditch was five feet wide at the bottom, seven at the top, with a carrying capacity of 2,400 miner's inches." But it was large enough to float logs for building purposes and proved to be a boon to Malheur City for five years, even if it did not pay for itself.

In 1887 Malheur County was formed and the town found itself out of Baker County and in the

FIRE IN 1957 started in tinder-dry grass, swept unhindered through Malheur, destroyed all wooden buildings remaining from mining heyday.

extreme northern end of the new one. El Dorado was dead, placer mining unproductive there and going out in Malheur. The ditch was no longer used by miners and its owners tried to find new uses for it. In 1911 the Eastern Oregon Agricultural Co. was formed to convert it to irrigation purposes but Baker County farmers were not willing to share the water with those in Malheur County and the costly project was dropped. And as the ditch dried up, so did Malheur City. On August 16, 1957 a disastrous grass fire devastated the few lingering remains of the town.

MARYSVILLE, OREGON

Nostalgia must have soon taken over the little group of prospectors from California. They had discovered traces of gold in Dog Creek near John Day, traced them to a good ledge on the hill and there founded a little town. This was in April of 1862, and they christened the infant camp Marysville after their home town.

In two years the place already had a population of several hundred and the juvenile element needed, though likely did not desire, a school. With contributions and a poll-tax one was built, this being the second school district in Grant County. It started off with twenty-one pupils and one teacher. This brave soul was a girl named Elizabeth Chope. The community spent $97.34 that first year.

The town was started so early, the buildings were so impermanent and have been abandoned so long that tracing its plan is difficult. Almost all of Marysville has melted away, leaving only the collapsed shell of the schoolhouse. Before long this, too, will have vanished.

PATHETIC REMAINS of little school crown bluff above canyon of John Day River. Rimrock scene is typical of eastern Oregon where low elevation and rainfall do not permit stand of timber.

STAGE LINE BLUES

Mitchell, Oregon

It did not take long for Canyon City to boil over after the news of the gold discovery spread east and west. There were no facilities for the people who thronged the place, no way for mail to get there. A mail route was a prime necessity and one was hurriedly established from The Dalles on the Columbia River, mainly over ancient Indian trails, twisting over flats and hills.

Mail was put in tightly strapped saddle bags. Daring riders carried letters at 50 cents each, newspapers, even though outdated, at $1. Some riders were waylaid and killed by Indians but dangers were accepted as part of the job.

Dust and nuggets in the veritable flood of gold from Canyon City were shipped to Portland by way of Sherar's Bridge and over the Barlow Road, or to The Dalles by the mail route. As Indian attacks along the way became more acute, the Federal Government improved the latter route to expedite the movement of soldiers to base camps and it was thenceforth called The Dalles-Canyon City Military Road.

Pony express and pack train were soon followed by regular stage lines, the first one operated by the man for whom Wheeler County would be named, Henry H. Wheeler. On May 1, 1864, he placed stock, wagons and coaches on the 180-mile run between the Columbia River town and the gold camp in the John Day Valley. Later he often related the next four years were the most exciting ones of his life.

Wheeler's first trip conveyed 11 passengers to Canyon City, about as many on the return, each paying a fare of $40. Then regular trips three times a week were established, Wheeler driving his rig with four horses. In 1865 he was awarded the mail contract. Encounters with Indians were varied and frequent, enough of them, Wheeler said, to fill a book, one in particular being a bloody hair-raiser.

On Sept. 7, 1866 he was driving the route between Dayville and Mitchell, accompanied by H. C. Page, Wells Fargo agent. Among the valuables were the usual mail, $10,000 in greenbacks, $300 in coin and several diamond rings. Near Mitchell a band of about twenty Indians appeared on horseback, opening fire almost at the same instant, the first bullet going through both of Wheeler's cheeks and taking out several teeth with a section of jawbone. Unable to speak he signaled Page to hold the Indians at bay as long as possible and jumping to the ground he managed to unhitch the horses. Then the two mounted a pair of animals never before ridden and got away to the road house at the Meyers ranch.

After Wheeler's wounds were dressed, he and Page returned to the scene of the attack to find the mail bags ripped open and contents scattered about. Valueless to the Indians they had strewn the greenbacks to the winds. Except for a small part of the currency all valuables including rings were recovered.

One of the several stopping places along the Military Road was named for J. H. Mitchell, former U.S. Senator from Oregon. By the time the place became large enough to be platted it already had two stores, blacksmith and hotel. Its location was not chosen but happened to be a good camping place. A stream called Bridge Creek afforded year around water and cottonwood trees shaded the small level area. The fact that the spot was at the bottom of a narrow canyon coming out of

BRONZE PLAQUE marks site of stage driver Wheeler's most notable encounter with Indians.

DOORWAY to old homestead cabin near Mitchell.

barren mountains was overlooked while the town grew.

In the summer of 1884 Mitchell was flourishing, its many buildings crowded into the narrow confines of the canyon mouth. The season produced numerous heavy thunderstorms in the nearby mountains and one of them dumped a deluge concentrating in a tributary to Bridge Creek canyon. Ignoring the small watercourse at the junction, a nine-foot wall of water burst over a cliff and inundated the town. Damage was tremendous in proportion to the size and isolated situation. Entire buildings were carried away, the street covered with several feet of mud, boulders and debris. This flood, the first in a disastrous series, failed to take any lives. Having made such an ominous roar in going over the cliff all residents were warned and able to escape.

In 1904 another and even worse flood hit the community, sending down a thirty-foot wall of water that took out a total of twenty-eight buildings and killed two citizens. Phil Brogan, well-beloved historian of his area, writes in *East of the Cascades,* "Those who escaped to the hills watched the heavens blaze with lightning and heard the crash of thunder echoing from cliffs that were once ocean ooze." Most recent was a disastrous flood about 1960.

Calamitous fires were added to the unusual drama of Mitchell's existence. One blaze on March 25, 1896, destroyed nine buildings and ten more were lost in August of 1899.

Although the days of gold and pony express are long since finished, Mitchell did some rebuilding from destruction time and again, and still lives. Strategically located on U.S. 26 it provides supplies for far-flung ranches and gas for the traveler between Willamette Valley points and Eastern Oregon and Idaho.

61

BUILDINGS dating from Mitchell's early days of gold and stage coaches are few. This one of stone survives a few feet back of the row of main street stores. Solid metal door attests its use as a vault in early days Canyon walls rising directly behind gives hint of narrowness.

FAST DECAYING REMNANTS of barn in Ochoco Mountains above Mitchell shakily survive elements. Gate post, well rubbed by stock, is near collapse.

62

THE RABBITS ALMOST HAD IT

Narrows, Oregon

In the sparsely populated area south of Burns the now defunct village of Narrows was built on an unusual site, unusual in that the two lakes between which it lies are twins except that one contains fresh, potable water, the other being brackish and undrinkable.

One of the lakes, its French name "Malheur" meaning "evil hour" since early day trappers discovered there a valuable cache of furs stolen by natives or other trappers, is fed by fresh water from Donner und Blitzen River. It appears this stream was crossed by a troop of cavalrymen en-gaged in the Snake Indian War in 1864, a furious electrical storm raging at the time and leader Col. George B. Curry gave it an apt German name.

Harney Lake is by nature isolated from any supply of fresh water, receiving only scanty rainwater and in times of flood a supply from its twin Malheur which overflows into a channel connecting the two. Harney's water, its salts gradually concentrated by evaporation, has become unusable for any purpose.

In 1892 on the narrow strip of land Charles A. Haines built a home centering a cattle ranch he hoped to establish. The single house turned out to be the nucleus for a good sized town because of its isolated position, the only stopping place in a vast lonely land south of Burns and north of Frenchglen where famed Peter French had his domain.

Haines put up several buildings to serve travelers in the otherwise uninhabited 80 miles of desert. In five years the settlement required a post office, in a few more a hotel, several saloons, livery stable and gambling house. A large store did a good business in merchandise brought by freight wagons from Burns. One oldtimer in the area, a rancher from Happy Valley recalls, "I was born at Narrows. It wasn't that my parents were living here, there was a midwife in the place and where else could a woman go to have a baby in this country?"

The only boom or rush Narrows had was on the side of the rabbits. The story is well remembered by Ray Novotny, county extension agent. There were always plenty of rabbits around but during the '20s not particularly troublesome to ranchers.

SCHOOLHOUSE from rear with corner of stone jail visible, about all left of Narrows' town center. No forest exists in this arid section except sparsest growth of junipers, few seen in right distance.

63

DESERTED SCHOOLHOUSE stands alone on treeless plain. Only family now living at Narrows is that of property owner, Henry Church, whose father came here in 1916. "I was a student in that schoolhouse until 1941," he says. "I was only in the fifth grade then but they had to close the school for lack of pupils."

Then unexplainably there was a population explosion among the long-eared, long-geared jacks. They made such inroads of forage and crops that the county placed a five cent bounty on each pair of rabbit ears brought in. Not in the habit of bothering much about such small game, ranchers now found some profit in shooting the pests and on the next trip to Burns collecting the bounty. Some, with only a few dozen pairs to turn in, were glad to do business with the Narrows storekeeper who paid three cents a pair in trade and who collected a nickel in Burns. When the depression came its effects seemed to extend even to the Narrows rabbits, keeping population down to a minimum.

Other fauna fared better. Both Malheur and Harney Lakes are bordered by lush growths of aquatic plants. From pre-historic times immense flocks of water birds have bred in thickets of reedy growths. Migratory fowl including herons, pelicans, egrets and geese gathered in such flocks as to temporarily obscure the sun. In 1908 the area just south of Narrows was set aside and dedicated by President Roosevelt as the Malheur Migratory Bird Refuge, the original area later expanded to 159,872 acres.

In the 1930s the road to Burns was paved and nearly all the ranchers around Narrows owned cars. They drove handily to the larger town to find more variety in the stores and Narrows was as good as doomed, its demise conceded when the hotel burned down.

Henry Church and his family are now the only residents. He owns the property adjoining the bird refuge, raising cattle on the vast acreage. The Churches live in a picturesque old house in the middle of the deserted town. They are interested in antiquities and during the last 20 years have uncovered over 100 arrowheads and other Indian artifacts around the farm. An obsidian knife they found was checked out at the University of Oregon which established its age as about 1000 years. Almost certainly the material came from Glass Buttes deposits of obsidian not far west of Burns.

The Churches find that owning a ghost town has its drawbacks. Some visitors have displayed a regrettable lack of respect for private property. When interviewed in 1966 by Robert Olmos, Portland *Oregonian* writer, Church said, "People have damaged and almost carried off the old buildings. I put up no trespassing signs in self-defense, but they are ignored, so I have had to tear down some of the old houses and expect to raze the rest."

PONDEROSA PINE is familiar tree in Ochocos, intricate textural pattern of plated bark shown here.

SOLIDLY BUILT JAIL, only stone building in Narrows. Not far from jail Mrs. Church found nearly buried Colt pistol. Although stock was rotted away serial number 107335 is still clearly visible.

ORTLEY, OREGON

The Cascade Mountain range, extending in a north and south direction through Washington and Oregon, exerts a very strong climatic effect on the western and eastern sections of both states. The barrier causes most marine storms common to the area to deposit most of their moisture on the westerly slope and holds back much of the colder air prevailing in winter on the eastern side. But there is a rift in this wall, the gorge cut through the Cascades by the Columbia River. Terrific winds whistle through the gorge much of the time at some seasons, their direction depending upon the location of high and low pressure areas. Strangely enough, this geographical peculiarity had a direct effect in making a ghost of a thriving, growing town.

On an exposed plateau on the eastern side of the summit of the Cascades high above the Columbia huddle the few remnants of Ortley, once bustling with 300 people dedicated to the dream of making a fortune growing Ortley apples.

About 1908, a group of business men in Hood River, Oregon, began to work on the idea of establishing a European type of community for the purpose of establishing a large orchard of apples and of creating a world-wide market for them. They selected comparatively level fields on a bluff surmounting high cliffs facing the Columbia — a spectacular setting offering a view of many miles up and down the river and of several snow-clad mountain peaks.

In 1911 the plat was filed in Wasco County for the Town of Ortley by the Hood River Orchard and Land Co. Business buildings were to be centralized near the only source of water, a small stream. Close to these stores were to be the residences of the settlers, who would have to radiate out some little distance to their orchards, which would surround the whole. Lots for homes were an acre in size, orchard space was laid out in 5 and 10 acre plots.

As soon as building was begun the need for expert carpenters and other artisans became apparent and ads were inserted in the Portland newspapers.

A Mr. Hallyburton was one carpenter who responded, his skill so evident he was put in charge of the whole building operation. A school was erected, several stores, a fancy two-story hotel elegantly fitted with bath both upstairs and down, and a saloon. In the rear was a huge barn capable of sheltering 200 horses for working the land.

People moved in eager to set out their little apple trees. Early arrivals had to go down the steep mountainside to Mosier, 7 miles away, for mail but on April 9, 1912, the post office was opened with L. D. Firebaugh as first postmaster. As soon as the new Ortley Hotel was completed the post office was moved into the lobby. The hotel also housed a fine dance hall and Saturday nights people came from Mosier, The Dalles and surrounding farms to relax in a big way.

Kerosene lamps provided the only illumination at first but the developers invited the power company in The Dalles to come up and see what was going on. Duly impressed the purveyors of power invested $10,000 in the up and coming community which soon had electric lights.

A garage was built near the hotel to house two elegant new automobiles, a Franklin and a Cadillac. Prospective settlers were met at the train in style and carried up the twisting mountain road to the town on the heights. Here they were put up at the hotel, wined, dined and importuned to buy an apple orchard. And buy they did until young trees

NATIVE TREES on high windswept plateau are hardy pines, firs and oaks, well adapted to fend for selves. Oaks were left around barns and buildings for shade, removed in areas where apple trees were to be grown.

LITTLE SCHOOL HOUSE stands almost intact but long ago converted to shelter for farm machinery. Water stands in road in foreground. Snowy Cascades show in distance.

flanked the whole countryside. By this time the land company had sunk $200,000 in the project, and had the settlers paid cash for their property, it would at least have broken even. But they had not paid even a fraction of what they owed.

Then some painful truths began to appear. Many apple trees died from lack of water in summer, drowning in an excess of it in winter, there being little or no drainage. And the trees that lived were having their troubles. There were many large

fir trees along the bluffs with branches on only one side due to the strong prevailing winds blowing up the river in the growing season. So eager were the settlers to cultivate their ground and get their trees started, they did not question the reason for the lopsided firs until the apple trees began to be distorted the same way.

This discouraging state of affairs caused the orchardists who had bought on contract to quit and move away. Before long the population had dwin-

68

HOUSES AND BUILDINGS not razed or salvaged for lumber soon disintegrated among native trees which formed grove around nucleus of town. Soil is almost impermeable, rains of winter stand as surface ground water. In summer ground dries into something resembling adobe bricks, cracking and killing roots of susceptible apple trees.

dled to a low point and the post office was closed in November, 1922. Ortley was getting to be a very lonely place for Mr. Hallyburton, the builder, who had decided to hang on, no matter what. And remain he did until he was the sole resident.

The power company was anxious to take its poles and lines down, salvaging what it could from the fiasco but old Hallyburton paid his electric service bill of $1.10 per month regularly and promptly and all the company could do was sit on its hands, hoping for a slip up in the payments. The Community Hall, hotel and other buildings were torn down and the old man held on tenaciously until 1946. Then even he abandoned the place, the light poles and most of the apple trees still living pulled up and desolation in Ortley was complete.

PAISLEY, OREGON

All is quiet on the Paisley front. With the sawmill shut down, the general lethargy of the little town was sharpened to the edge of frustration. Credit at the general store became a problem although people did seem to have enough money to drink at the tavern. But idleness was only incidental the day big trouble came. It started at the post office, shattering the quiet with gunfire and murder.

Postmistress Mrs. Anita Bannister, a grandmother at forty-one, saw the two men come in the door. "They were dressed like cowboys," she said, " and seemed drunk, asking silly questions. They both carried guns and I was worried."

The men staggered through the knot of loungers, then suddenly one of them stiffened, shifted his gun and demanded the "payroll." The second man, Jesse Thurman Hibdon, who had formerly worked in the Paisley sawmill and was unaware that it had closed and there was no payroll, moved back toward the door. One of the trapped onlookers was too quick, breaking outside.

"The first bandit was still threatening me," recalled Mrs. Bannister, "and kept shouting, 'I'm goin' to blow yer brains out.' I told him there was no payroll and I guess he finally believed it, poking me and saying— 'You want to see yer family again? Give us all the the money you got.'

"He jabbed the gun barrel into my head and told me not to look at his face. I gave him everything, our V.F.W. money and even the postal orders. He handed it all to Hibdon who ran to the door and

yelled—'Let's get out of here! One of them's escaped already.' But the man holding the gun at my head didn't go. He said, 'I'm goin' to think about this a few minutes' and I was sure I was going to be killed."

Now there was a shotgun blast outside and Donald Lee Ferguson who was still holding his gun at Mrs. Bannister's head, dropped it and ran outside. A man lay bleeding in the doorway and from the car with motor running Hibdon screamed—"Come on, hurry up!" Ferguson piled in and the car took off.

The man who had escaped from the post office earlier saw 65-year-old Troy Lawson with a rifle. It was the deer season and the plumber, like every other man in Paisley, was never far from a gun. Lawson ran toward the post office and, about to go in, turned to warn a woman—Mrs. Norman Carlon with baby Lana in her arms—"Get away or you'll get hurt!" The hesitation was fatal. As Lawson turned, he exposed himself to Hibdon in the car and received a shower of lead pellets in his abdomen. As he dropped, a second blast from Hibdon's gun ripped a big hole in the side of the building. Mrs. Bannister had followed Ferguson outside and later recounted: "Although the women inside were crying all the time of the holdup, I didn't—until I went outside and found Troy dead."

All available townsmen quickly gathered into a posse, every member armed with a deer rifle. One remained in town to telephone Summer Lake Lodge, thirty miles up the road the car had taken, to arrange for a roadblock.

When the bandits came to the makeshift barricade

70

they swung the car off the road in a desperate effort to clear it, but crashed into the boulders below the rimrock about a hundred yards from the highway. Then the posse arrived, swarming up the hillside. Logging truck driver Doug Houston, 25, sent a shot that nailed Ferguson behind a boulder. "I told him to come out but he fired and almost got me. Then he stepped out and I let him have it in the arm. He was thirty yards away and I could have killed him but didn't have the nerve."

Houston then ran up to the wounded man who had dropped in a pool of his own blood and was trying to reach his gun. Houston kicked it away as his grandfather came up. "Ferguson made a pass for grandpa's rifle and I hit him over the head with the butt of mine. He didn't go down so I hit him again. That's all there was to it."

Hibdon had escaped into the sagebrush and disappeared into the juniper-covered, boulder-strewn hills. Next day at dawn an armed group made a systematic search of Paisley on the chance Hibdon had circled back to get some shelter and food. The hunt widened into the surrounding area, every farm combed, every haystack stabbed with pitchforks. Famed bloodhound man, Norman Wilson, brought his dogs from Dallas to help and once one of them seemed to have picked up a trail but no lead developed.

All this time Hibdon was slogging over the hills to the northeast, keeping out of sight of the highway. Nearing exhaustion and starvation, he reached the Jack Pine Motel about ten miles south of La Pine. He asked the proprietor, William Schabener, if he could rent a cabin, saying his car had broken down. Suspicious of his appearance and actions, Schabener refused and alerted the State Police. Officer William Aveline tried to follow Hibdon's trail through the brush but lost it.

The robbery and murder had taken place on Thursday. The next Tuesday, Harold J. Broderick, 50, fire chief of Hammond, was hunting deer in the area with his two sons, Harold, Jr., and Pat. They had worked north from Paisley where they learned of the trouble. Broderick was about three-quarters of a mile from the Jack Pine Motel when he saw a man walking furtively among the pine trees. "He must have heard me," Broderick said of his experience, "and started going faster, almost breaking into a run. I had my rifle aimed at him and shouted to him to halt." Hibdon did and, surrendering, allowed himself to be walked back to camp where he was given the drink of water he asked for.

"He must have gulped down a quart," said Broderick, "like a horse in the desert." The fire chief had a siren on his pickup and wound it up. The boys came running. Tying Hibdon to the tailgate, they drove to the motel and called the State Police. Hibdon

MAIN STREET OF PAISLEY conforms to State Highway 31, only road through town. Peaceful setting was scene of violence when post office (center) was held up and citizen shot to death. Jagged hole in wall made by second blast can be seen in lower boards at left of deposit box. Post office saw lighter incident later. For more than 20 years after-hours patrons had dropped mail in slot in building front. Some letters, instead of sliding completely through, fell to floor between walls, accumulating until October, 1961. Then R. G. Greene was hired to modernize mail deposit and on opening wall, discovered old cards and letters. When Anita Bannister, postmistress, was told of it "she darned near fainted" said Greene. Her comment: "I thought everyone in town would be mad at me but they took it right good." Postal authorities made effort to deliver lost mail even though postage had become insufficient. At least one letter would be late, regardless. It was from a mother who wrote her daughter 20 years earlier just before Thanksgiving Day: "Please bring the cream for the pie."

offered no resistance, obviously at the end of his endurance. He had walked over 150 miles in common oxford shoes over a rugged terrain. When asked what he had eaten, he said: "I had a quart of milk" but that was the only question he would answer. That evening he was back in Paisley where he was identified by burns on his legs received in a gasoline fire some years before.

He joined Ferguson in the jail at nearby Lakeview and later confessed it was he who had fired the shot that killed Lawson. Both men were sentenced to life imprisonment. After its brief excursion into violence, Paisley dropped back into its rut of peace. The townspeople still patronize its general store, post office and tavern and do not expect to see another holdup.

WALL OF PAISLEY POST OFFICE is still scarred by effects of shot gun blast, one of two fired by would-be bandit. First was lethal, second hit wall.

TOWER CARRIES BELL rung in all emergencies, particularly fire. Paisley Mercantile is only store and, like old Chewaucan Hotel, shows signs of decay. Town was plagued by spring floods when rising temperatures released ice-blocked Chewaucan River. Ice would jam against bridges, divert rising waters into farms and town. *Morning Oregonian*, Portland newspaper of Feb. 4, 1951, said: "The ice-jammed waters of the Chewaucan River have been channeled back into the river bed and this Lake County community is totaling the flood damage. The Forest Service blasted a channel from near the Adams Mill bridge to the Z.B. ranch, . . . Icy waters that covered pasture lands and flooded homes did considerable damage, Bob Parker of Paisley Mercantile said."

MILL STREET runs at right angles to Main, between post office and Chewaucan Hotel. Hostelry, long unused, was named for marsh and the river emptying into it. Word "chewaucan" derived from two Klamath Indian words — *tchua*, a swamp root variously known in Oregon and Washington as *wapato*, sagitaria and arrowhead, and *keni*, a general suffix meaning locality or place. At right is post office with fraternal hall above serving several lodges. Ubiquitous poplar trees stand bare in early March, lit by near-setting sun.

RICHMOND, OREGON

In 1889 a number of ranches were settled in the rolling sage-covered hills of Wheeler County, Oregon. Ranchers had to go all the way to Mitchell, about 19 miles to the south, or to Spray, about the same distance north, for their supplies. Their children were growing up without education except a little home instruction and many of the settlers felt the need of public worship. A meeting was held in one of the farmer's homes to see what could be done about a population center.

Among the earliest settlers here were the Gil-

liams, Donnellys, Keyes and Walters. These families attended the meeting as did several interested men from nearby communities, representatives of the cattle firm of Smith and Waterman from Waterman Flat and Caleb N. Thornburg who ran stock at Spanish Flat in the John Day area, was receiver of the land office at The Dalles and for whom the little community and post office at Caleb were named.

The meeting was successful in establishing plans for a town and all agreed the first building would

OLD COMMUNITY CENTER almost swamped by sagebrush and poplars. Starting as a residence, building expanded into general store, post office with T. B. Elrod as first postmaster, and general cracker barrel meeting place.

LITTLE M. E. CHURCH was among earliest structures in Richmond, steeple an architectural gem. Weathered walls are riddled with woodpecker's holes. Hill behind is sparsely dotted with junipers and sagebrush, typical of the eastern Oregon terrain.

be a school. The name for the new city was not so easily settled, the effort almost breaking into hostilities. R. N. Donnelly and William Walters disagreed over the school site, Walters objecting to everything Donnelly proposed. Even the Civil War got into the controversy and Donnelly called Walters "Jeff Davis" because of his rebellious tendencies, vowing that if things ever did get ironed out the town would be called Richmond after the capitol of the Confederacy. When tempers cooled, Donnelly donated three acres of land for the school. And the name of the town agreed upon? Richmond.

Construction of the small schoolhouse was started as soon as lumber could be hauled to the site. This had to come from the sawmill at Six Shooter owned by E. M. Howell. A store was built and immediately prospered, people coming from many small outlying communities such as Waterman to trade at the new Emporium. Next was the Meth-

odist Church and a large I.O.O.F. Lodge Hall. Other buildings followed and Richmond was a real town.

The biggest gathering ever held here was the get-together of the Wheeler County Pioneers. 450 attended and the festivities lasted a week. This was in 1901 and is still remembered by a few old timers.

Many factors contributed to the slow decay of Richmond. The "Tin Lizzy" and better roads made it possible for the farmers and cattle men to get to larger cities to buy their goods. The younger generation was not enthusiastic about ranching or the isolation involved and the older land owners died or moved away. Gradually the buildings were deserted and fell into disrepair, many collapsing or were burned. The few remaining ones, gray and shabby, present a picturesque and bona fide ghost town.

SANGER, OREGON

The little Wallowa Mountain community of Sanger, built on the flat just below the Sanger mine, and the mine itself, were originally named Hogum as a commentary on the nature of some of the earliest placer mines in the area. After the joke grew stale and the town sought a more dignified title, in 1871, the name of Augusta was selected, honoring Miss Augusta Parkwood, the first unmarried resident. After a year another change was made—to Sanger, the name of an early mine owner. The Sanger post office was established August 17, 1887, with William Aldersley the first postmaster. What the miners did for mail distribution for fifteen years, remains a mystery.

The Sanger mine on the road between Medical Springs and Lilly White was the largest producer in the district. The old placer camp operated for many years before the mine was started, yielding some half a million in easily obtained nugget and dust gold, separated from the granite gravels by panning, sluicing and Long Toms—when there was water. This was before ditches were so frequently constructed to bring water from Eagle Creek.

In 1870 the vein from which most of this loose gold came was discovered and named the Summit Lode. In 1874 this mine produced $60,000 from ore assaying $16 to the ton. A mint report shows it turned out $813,000 from '89 to '92. It closed in '97, opened for a short interval in 1900 then shut down for good with a total production of a million and a half.

The Sanger is on the west side of Eagle Creek and close to an older placer camp which had been a good producer. The Sanger had a long period of activity, closed for a time, opened again at the turn of the century, was then defunct. In 1915, the Oregon Almanac reported there were thirty people in the community. There was a little prospecting at Lilly White in 1930 with no result.

In the summer of 1936 there was a short reopen-

OLD SANGER HOTEL later occupied for many years by Charley Marks and his eighteen dogs. Cabin is placed in meadow among pines and deciduous trees of Wallowas. In summer wagons could be driven under upper floor for cool shade. In time of heavy snows sleighs were pulled directly to front door. In rear clear stream of cool water flows year around and spring house over it kept milk and perishables fresh.

ing of the Sanger. Baker druggist E. B. Cochrane with partner Harry Belden worked here all season but when the snow came to the Wallowas, they decided the results were not worth the effort and the mine died. The Wendts of Baker, its present owners, have placed a new roof on the old mill and hope to revive the workings when and if the price of gold goes up.

A large and impressive log cabin still standing on the flat below the mine has a varied and obscure history though it seems to have been a hotel at one time, the spring house just above the building being much too large to have served a private house. The first tangible story of it is, it was occupied for years by Charley Marks.

Old Charley graduated from Stanford, it is said, and went to Alaska with the gold rush using a dog team of Alaskan huskies. When he came to the Sanger cabin after the mines were down, he brought some of the sled dogs and bought others until he had eighteen. They all lived and ate with him in the house. On one of his rare visits to the biggest town in the area, Baker, he heard of a police dog which had bitten a child and might be destroyed. Charley brought the dog, Rex, home, made the huskies accept him, which they did after some fights.

The Wallowas see a heavy fall of snow every winter and Charley built up a complete dog team to haul a modified toboggan Alaska-style. In the winter trapping season he carried supplies to several line cabins and on one occasion he was following his marten traps when he came to an open spot in a frozen stream. There were several large fish

stranded here and Charley hankered to get one and change his diet.

As he walked out his snowshoes broke through the thin ice and he took a bad fall, his gun flying out of his hand and a bullet going through his knee. He crawled back to the line cabin, made a makeshift splint from a snowshoe and crawled on the sled. His lead dog was a veteran husky but the German shepherd Rex held the most important position, that of turning the sled. The dogs had been to the large Basin Mine workings many times and understood the word "Basin." Charley told them to head there and weak from loss of blood, blacked out. The timber was heavy and the snow deep but the dogs struck out and Rex carefully maneuvered the sled away from low-hanging branches. They reached the mine after several hours and the men there rushed Charley to a doctor.

He recovered from the ordeal with only a slight limp. He is 82 years old and lives in the same area at Keating. He has only four dogs now but they live with him in his little two-room shack and eat their bones there too.

VIEW THROUGH BROKEN WINDOW shows living room and fireplace of old log hotel.

ABOUT 100 FEET FROM LOG HOUSE is pile of beef bones where Charley Marks did butchering for dogs. Mr. Wendt of Baker, present owner of Sanger mine says: "I was out there once when I was a boy. It was in the summer and the smell from the pile of bones was pretty strong."

SHANIKO, OREGON

"Shaniko is the wool center of the world" proudly boasted its citizens of an earlier day. Cornered, they might admit, "Well, if not of the world, at least of the Pacific Northwest." And this came very near the truth.

Shaniko owed its birth to wool, and to wheat. No accidental gold strike or gradual accretion of farmers produced the town. Shaniko's was a planned birth.

Central Oregon, in the 1890's was, in effect, one huge sheep ranch. Wool was produced in enormous quantities and the only outlet for these thousands of bales of fleece was The Dalles, Oregon. Then in 1898, in order to expedite the shipment of wool from the countless bands of sheep which extended to Lakeview and the California line, a railroad was constructed from Biggs Junction, on the Columbia River.

Since a railroad couldn't be useful without some kind of terminal, Shaniko was built for that express purpose. It was the brainchild of a group of bankers and businessmen in The Dalles and Moro and was first laid out as a tent town, but by 1900 many permanent buildings were put up, including the hotel, a combination City Hall, Fire Hall and jail, and a general store, all of which still stand. In rapid succession followed many other structures. Many of these have succumbed to time, fire and vandals. A school was built with funds raised by popular subscription.

Actually, Shaniko was preceded by another settlement, or rather a small community, gathered around a stagecoach station called Cross Hollows, because of the two gullies

OLD SCHOOL WAS BUILT in 1902 with funds raised by "passing the hat" according to Frank Wagner who lived there 43 years. Any school children now must make trip to Maupin schools.

HOTEL WAS BUILT AT turn of century, still serves excellent home-cooked meals at long table, "family style." Tall "City Hall" across street had council chambers upstairs. Fire hose-cart and jail cells occupy ground floor. Structure is surrounded by empty spaces once filled by business buildings.

PRESENT POST OFFICE was established in this building about 1906. Structure in background was drugstore, smaller one leaning against it was pool hall. Rotting wooden sidewalks extend many empty blocks beyond in sagebrush.

having their intersection there. The spot was a natural stopping place for stagecoaches on their way from The Dalles and other points. The station was owned and operated by John and Elizabeth Ward. In 1874, a German immigrant named August Scherneckau arrived and bought out the Wards. Being industrious and possessed of many other good qualities, he prospered. A post office was established for the expanding village on May 23, 1879 with the benevolent and bearded head man as first postmaster.

By 1887, Mr. Scherneckau was well off financially and decided to retire, and spend the rest of his days in California. All the Indians in that part of central Oregon were fond of him and regretted his going, although none of them could correctly pronounce his Germanic name. And so they called the place Shaniko. Having sold out to one Gustav Schmidt, Scherneckau departed to Astoria to catch a ship south. But the city of Astoria so appealed to him that he stayed there until 1923, when he decided to take a long deferred trip to California. This he did, but his stay was short. He died in 1925 and was returned to Astoria, where he is buried.

The site for Shaniko had been chosen for the same reason the original station was built there. A good reliable water supply existed on the spot.

The Cross Hollows post office ceased to exist in 1887 with the departure of its Postmaster. With the establishment of Shaniko Post Office on March 31, 1900, with John D. Wilcox as postmaster, the era of the original Cross Hollows settlement was officially ended.

Shaniko now is only a faint shadow of its former self. Wooden sidewalks run out to nothing and are bordered only by grass and weeds.

SHELBURN, OREGON

In the old graveyard on the hill there are stones dating back to the 1850s, more from the '60s, the decade in which a cholera epidemic carried away so many of the early settlers in this section of the fertile Willamette Valley.

By the time the '90s arrived, the need for some sort of centralization of stores, school and a post office became obvious and several buildings were erected around the old blacksmith shop. This authentic gem of the false-front period of western architecture is still standing though the roof leaks and windows lack glass. With the establishing of a post office in June, 1890, a name for the town had to be selected.

Two of the leading citizens, Shelton and Washburn, were honored by having parts of their names spliced together to form the title, Shelburn.

Sawmills sprang up in this land of virgin fir and spruce and the railroad came to haul out their products as well as potatoes and farm produce. A large hotel was built and operated by Stanley Strylewicz who, for some reason, was simply called Stan. J. R. Moses was the lone barber for several years and if there was anything going on he didn't know about, "it hadn't happened yet," as one oldtimer puts it. A large dancehall was erected and on Saturday nights the sawmill hands and farmers performed the two-

ED ZINK, now gnarled and grizzled, was born on farm in 1879 before Shelburn was a town. With his older brother Eph, he lives in small shack built from lumber salvaged from old home which had begun to disintegrate and was hard to heat. "Eph and I worked in the sawmills as long as they were running," he says, "then did some farming on the old place. We used to think we could get jobs in Shelburn but the old place is sort of going downhill now."

79

step and Black Hawk waltz with their ladies. The perfect serenity of this was altered by the weekly thirst build-up. Because of a rash of accidents in the sawmill, hard liquor was forbidden there and the men slaked their thirsts at the Saturday night hoe down. Dances were often interrupted by drunken brawls and several bullet holes in the wall of the hall remain as evidence of broken romances.

When the surrounding timber was cut out, the mills began to close down. The once healthy potatoes developed a scabby disease and train stops were made only for passengers to buy bread and cheese for lunch. With the coming of the automobile, Shelburn residents went to Salem or Stayton for many of their needs and the local stores dropped away.

Today the place is almost deserted. The dance-hall, having suffered ignominy as a chickenhouse, now stands empty. And yet not silent. Metal feeders, hanging on their wires, creak and groan with the vagrant winds sweeping through the glassless windows.

BLACKSMITH SHOP, oldest building in Shelburn, dates from early 1890s. Many horses in logging and farming made it one of busiest in new community. Concern also sold and repaired harness gear, saddles and bridles, later became supply center for farm equipment, growing into general store when mechanized equipment and "tin lizzie" caused blacksmithing to fall off. Little "wing" served as millinery shop, early phone office and residence. Roof is deteriorating in heavy rain of Willamette Valley, building having small chance for long survival.

THE RIVER WAS A CHALLENGE

Sherar's Bridge, Ore.

In 1826-7 Peter Skene Ogden took an exploring party down the long miles of arid territory east of the Cascade Mountains, a major portion of "Oregon." One large river he encountered, tumbling in falls and rapids most of its length, was termed by the French Riviere aux Chutes and Riviere des Chutes, and by Lewis and Clark, the Clark. Ogden wrote of his crossing, "On Thursday September 26 we reached the River of the Falls and found an Indian camp of about 20 families. Finding a canoe and a bridge made of slender wood, which we began crossing, 5 horses were lost through the bridge."

Years later, John Y. Todd, whose father, John Y., built the first substantial bridge over the cataract, wrote, "It is difficult to believe that there could have been much of a bridge there when Peter Skene Ogden crossed it. It seems as if Ogden must have been blinded by the snow, because it is hard to think the Indians could possibly have built a structure that would support a horse."

The first John Y. Todd was born in Missouri, Nov. 30, 1830. Determined to join the forces going overland to fight the war with Mexico in 1846 and refused enlistment as being too young, he went along as driver of an ox team. Once in Mexico, however, young Todd was "drafted" as a regular soldier and returned to his home in Missouri in 1848, a veteran at 18.

When he heard the news of gold in California he went to the West Coast to try his luck at finding a bonanza. Denied this and depressed by summer's dry heat in the gold country, he went to San Francisco and boarded a steamer for Portland. At Astoria he was transferred to the steamboat *Lot Whitcomb* (see *Tales the Western Tombstones Tell*).

He sold wheat harvesting machinery up and down the Willamette Valley for several years and then turned Indian fighter, joining the Yamhill Company which attempted to subdue the Yakimas. After that the young Missourian went into the cattle business and eventually settled in Oregon's Tygh Valley on the eastern flank of Mount Hood.

Some pioneer wagon trains bound for the Wil-

OLD PHOTO gives hint of town-like settlement at crossing, no trace of Indian fishing village which developed more recently. After Todd built first bridge in 1860 most weary immigrants abandoned dusty Oregon Trail, taking short cut by way of Grass Valley and the Wamic approach to Barlow Road over Cascade Mountains. Location is narrowest defile in entire course of Deschutes River, deeply cut channel crowding river into black, swirling torrent rather than white rapids and cascades generally characteristic of river. Tolls of $3.75 for each yoke of oxen or team of horses plus $1 for driver were charged. Users beside immigrants were miners or freighters passing to and from Canyon City and John Day gold mines.

lamette Valley and nearing the goal, chose the Columbia River route for the last push. Others pressed on by land and encountered several difficult river crossings, the tumultous Deschutes by far the worst. Todd saw he could help his fellow pioneers and make money at it so in 1860 he built a bridge over the stream at a point where it deepened and narrowed between waterfalls.

For two years the bridge served well, then came a winter of heavy snows in the nearby mountains and hard spring rains which caused severe flooding, a surge in the Deschutes carrying away the span. Since Todd had put all his money into his buildings and logs necessary for rebuilding would have to come from mountain forests as before, he was forced to take in two partners, Ezra Hemingway and Robert Mays, before he could build a new bridge. When the new firm was organized and second span built, Hemingway bought out the other two and shortly, in 1871, sold out to a man named O'Brien who in turn sold to Joseph Sherar, the bridge bearing his name since.

Born in Vermont in 1833, Sherar also arrived in the West via the California mines, his digging done in the northern section and later the John Day mines of eastern Oregon. He saw in the bridge far greater opportunity for investment than had Todd and the other owners. Paying only $7,040 for the structure itself, he invested $75,000 in building approaching roads. Then he put up a stage station which soon developed into a 33-room hotel, large and elaborate for those primitive parts.

In 1868 a post office was established at the site with Hemingway as postmaster and now Sherar improved the building to succeed him. In addition to hotel and postal facilities the location had a store, livery stables and many other buildings.

MODERN "SHERAR'S BRIDGE" is part of State Highway 216. No trace exists of village once established here for early immigrants to Oregon Country. Instead large but transitory Indian village stands along both banks. Existing only during salmon runs, settlement consists of habitations ranging from stinking, garbage-surrounded tent shacks to luxurious campers. Indian fishermen erect temporary and seemingly precarious platforms suspended above water from which they wield long-handled nets. Salmon are particularly vulnerable here while resting after leaping falls just below and before ascending equally difficult one immediately above.

SPARTA, OREGON

At the southwestern edge of the snowy peaks in Oregon's Wallowa Mountains which nearly fill the northeastern corner of the state, is the Eagle Creek area of old mining camps. Here on a small "island" of granite in the center of a rather recent lava flow is Sparta, where in 1863, Squire Morris and his partner Neales Donnelly, made their Shanghai Gulch strike of small gold nuggets and dust in the stream gravels. A short time later Tom Koster made his find at the head of Maiden Gulch.

There was great excitement. These new finds were just what was needed to take up where the depleted mines of the area left off, and the town of Koster sprang up on the slope. Friends of the first discoverers renamed it Eagle City but authorities found the new name a duplication and the post office was established as Gem, after one of the larger mines. This was on August 7, 1871 and the name lasted over a year.

William H. Packwood, pioneer prospector, farmer, engineer and civic leader in Gem, proposed the town to be renamed in honor of his home town—Sparta, Illinois. Three other pillars of the community had home towns and weren't willing to go along without a struggle. The four inscribed their choices on the sides of a square top and needless to say the side showing up was Sparta. Even if the others had heard of loaded dice, they accepted fate peaceably.

Sparta flourished. Gold dust up to $15,000 a week was sent through the mails, other large amounts by express and individuals. E. E. Clough and his father took $25,000 in dust and nuggets to Baker by horse and wagon.

But the water supply was inadequate for the placering equipment and Packwood backed a daring venture called the Sparta Ditch. Raising capital, he had the survey made and the 32-mile ditch built in two years. The placers had plenty of water but now the gold supply was thinning out.

With the richest mines abandoned, the Chinese workers from the completed transcontinental railroad moved in, content with placer gleanings. The luckless Orientals were harassed by wrathful whites, robbed, murdered and finally ejected. In 1915 all hard rock mining ceased and most of the shafts caved in. About two years later even the placering came to a stop.

SPARTA STORE only remaining business structure was solidly built to resist robbers. Erected in 1873 by W. H. Heilmer, 24x50'. Opening was celebrated with ball, attracting everyone in whole area, many from "metropolis" of 'Baker, 30 miles away. Store was operated for many years by Joseph Wright.

SUMPTER, OREGON

The railroad came to Sumpter in 1896 because of the new veins of ore being opened and developed . . . or maybe it was the other way around. In any event, the population zoomed to 3,000 in no time. This was a big increase from the few hundred pioneer-type individuals who had patiently panned in the Powder River, and pecked away at the hard rock streaks of gold in the previous 20 years.

In 1862 three men from North Carolina built a log cabin on the site. They intended to farm the land, an ambition later swamped by the tide of gold mining.

They found a spherical rock almost like a cannonball nearby and were inspired by this discovery, along with severe nostalgia, to call their new home "Fort Sumter," a name prominent in those Civil War days.

The "Fort" was lost, but the "Sumter" remained, picking up a "P" somewhere along the way. Spelling in those days was regarded lightly.

For a good many years Sumpter flourished, feeding on new lodes opened by improved methods and the substantial returns from the huge dredges in the river. As these sources died out, so did Sumpter. Several disastrous fires took heavy toll as evidenced by parts of brick walls and exposed bank vaults.

Dredging operations have continued until the whole valley is in ruins, tailings occupying the creek bed and both banks. But since 1916 the town has declined. A few newer buildings are scattered among the ruins, and Sumpter would have had a chance to become a farming community, but for the preponderance of granite tailings over good soil.

VAULT IS ALL THAT remains of old b a n k, burned years ago in Sumpter. White Masonic Hall is on hill in background, was one of few wooden structures spared in holocaust.

WHITNEY, OREGON

Whitney was never a mining camp, though it lived in company with many gold towns. It was strictly a center for logging operations, the surrounding Blue Mountains having heavy stands of Ponderosa Pine and, at higher elevations, Alpine White Fir. The place is wild and wooly, though murders were not as frequent as in some. There *was* a lynching in the spring of 1915 some eight miles south of Whitney. The case involved the rape of a girl and murder of a boy, and the aroused populace had taken justice into its own hands. Law officers, later trying to track down those responsible, met a tight-lipped silence, and soon gave up.

Our same Miss Erma Cole, who figures in our Cornucopia story, taught school in Whitney in the winter of 1919-1920. She had all the children of the first five grades in the tiny schoolhouse on a small knoll near town. Although she started with 28 pupils in the fall and finished with 28 in the spring, only two were continuous, so transient was the logging population.

"I boarded in one of the small hotels near the saloon on the east side of one street," she relates. "The walls were just boards with battens more or less covering the cracks. I had a little sheet iron stove, a bed and a little table for furniture in my 9 x 10 foot room. That winter was extra cold; the thermometer stayed at 55 degrees below zero for a spell, and although the little stove was bright red all the time, I was still cold. When the temperature rose to only 50 degrees below, it seemed almost balmy."

MAIN STREET OF WHITNEY, once thronged with roistering loggers, is now almost silent. Cattle graze in meadow beyond.

HUGE SAWMILL STANDS ROTTING on shore of log pond. Logs were snaked up chute to upper floor to emerge on ground floor at other end as sawn lumber. Spur of narrow gauge ran close by, busily hauled product to all northeastern Oregon.

Each Saturday saw a big dance, and the hotel man made a trip to Prairie City on the narrow gauge earlier each week to replenish his supply of bootleg booze so the festivities would be a success.

That old narrow gauge, the Sumpter Valley Railroad, figures prominently in all the history of our Blue Mountain group of towns. Ahead went the tiny engine, then the little box cars and, trailing behind, a passenger car or two. The trestle crossing a deep canyon between Sumpter and Whitney had a short life, but it is said by the editor of the Sumpter newspaper to have been the second highest in the world, surpassed only by one in the Bavarian Alps. Due to its impressive height it was too shaky and dangerous and was removed in 1915; the grade run around the mountain instead. The little station in Whitney was a neat, well-kept building.

A nearly level meadow is centered by the weathered buildings that are Whitney now. There is no school, depot, hotel or saloon, but a dozen or so residences remain scattered along the main street. Here and there are the ties of the little railroad. At the south end of town is a really imposing sawmill, or the shell of one, the height of a three-story building. A large log pond adjoins it.

EXCEPT FOR HAY, crops did poorly in Whitney. Summers were too short, frosts came late in spring, early in fall, sometimes in August. Machinery stands long idle, rusting away in barnyard.

WASHINGTON GHOST TOWNS

ALTOONA, WASHINGTON

If you were a salmon fisherman living in Altoona, mused a newspaper reporter, on the north shore of the Columbia River near it mouth, you would be one of a hardy breed. You rode out into that turbulent, treacherous river, usually out over the bar where she spreads murkily into the heaving Pacific and where a storm can blow up like the temper of a shrew. You tossed out your small gill net and staked your life on the catch. It was a hard life but a glad one and you didn't complain. But the going got really tough when that old devil river choked herself on ice and your isolated village was cut off from the outside world for two weeks and you got so hungry you could eat your oilskins.

The Portland OREGONIAN of January 23, 1930 carried a dramatic story of relief for the near-starving residents of Altoona. The whole Pacific Northwest shivered in below zero temperatures for thirteen days, the worst weather in forty years. Even the lower Columbia region, usually subject to no more cold than occasional frosts, was in deep freeze with temperatures as low as 10 above, and the river was covered with an unbroken crust of ice.

Altoona, like several other communities on the river with no roads, depending entirely on water traffic, began to get hungry when boats did not dock. Then on the 21st a freezing rain started to fall, soon coating wires with ice, the weight of it threatening to ground the single telephone line to the outside. Before it came down the people sent out a distress call which got to Astoria, Oregon, across the river.

Next day the Arrow Tug and Barge Co. of Astoria dispatched a sturdy tug loaded with food. It broke ice successfully in the faster running channel but was unable to get nearer than 350 feet from the North Shore. So the hungry Altoonans walked out on the ice to where the supplies were dumped from the tug, five of them fighting the numbing cold river water to get aboard the vessel, wanting to see Altoona never again. The others worked their way back and the emergency was relieved.

Pillar Rock in the Columbia River just east of Altoona, is an historic landmark around which much of the lower river activity has centered. A rugged column rising some twenty feet above deep channel water level, it was noted by British explorer Lt. William Robert Broughton in 1792 when he sailed up to it in the armed tender *Chatham* and commented it was "a remarkable pillar of rock." Later Lewis and Clark made notes about the rock in their journal.

Around 1840 the Hudson's Bay Co. established a salmon barreling operation near Pillar Rock and the local Chinook Indians caught salmon in their

WAHKIAKUM COUNTY COMMUNITY of Altoona was largely built on docks. Pilings supported huge cannery operations, space for drying and repairing nets, segregated housing for Chinese workers and general store, Altoona Mercantile. Closed for many years, store was last operated by W. L. Smith who turned to fishing. Cavernous cannery buildings sit on more solid section of same wharf.

COVERED BRIDGE over Gray's River close to mouth at Gray's Bay, is unique in having no windows. Gravels of stream yield agates and rock specimens especially after spring freshets.

willow weirs and nets, packing them down with salt, sailing vessels loading the barrels as cargo for London. Ships heading upriver to Vancouver would tie up at the rock to wait for favorable winds and tides. The respite from a long voyage was so welcome to the sailors they usually ended the breather with black eyes and broken noses in brawls over the Indian women fish packers.

In the 1870s a large fish cannery was operating just west of the Pillar, the locality called Altoona. In expanding its activities at the river mouth, the New England Fish Co. took over the cannery and enlarged it. For several years large numbers of Chinese were imported to gut and clean the salmon, their usefulness ending with the introduction of the Iron Chink, mechanical marvel that did all the cleaning and cutting.

As salmon runs diminished and canning became unprofitable, the company changed over to fish oil reduction and then in the late '40s closed down entirely. During these busy years the hamlets of Altoona and Pillar Rock were accessible only by boat, no great handicap when hundreds of gill netters swarmed the river and steamers made regular stops. But with the cannery closed, boats fewer and river steamers no longer running, the communities were cut off from the world. It was not until the early 1950s that a road was cut through to them — to all but Brookfield. The cannery there burned and the deserted town never did get more than a rough dirt track through the

timber. It is now used as a log dump by Crown Zellerbach, access not available to the public.

Just off Altoona Head, rocky point projecting from shore at the western edge of the village, lies the wreckage of the British steamer *Welsh Prince*. At 11:10 P.M. on May 28, 1922, she met the American freighter *Iowan* head on in a grinding collision. In the dense fog common to the lower river, neither vessel could see the other even after the crash until the British ship sent up an orange flare which showed her to be on fire. Her fore quarters were nearly severed, seven seamen crushed to death and she was settling fast. Responding to distress signals, the *Oneonta* set out from Astoria, feeling her way through the fog and removing the bodies of five men, two trapped in the sinking forecastle.

When the vessels were separated it was found that the *Iowan* could be towed even with her crushed bow and she was taken to Portland for repairs. When the fog cleared the upper decks of the *Welsh Prince* could be seen just above the water as she settled to the bottom. After several attempts to raise her, agents Frank Waterhouse and Co. notified the Furness Line of London that their ship was a total loss.

In that position close to the main channel, the hulk was declared a menace to navigation and M. Barde and Sons were employed to break it up. The firm brought ten tons of super-power gelatin dynamite from Olympia, Washington, blew off the top deck, then blasted the hull apart.

90

THE BLOOMS WERE A BEACON

*Baker's Bay (or
Chinookville, Wash.)*

A sailing ship bound for the shifting shallows of the Columbia River mouth was completely at the mercy of wind, tide and luck. Where was the channel? There were no markers, no lighthouses, no break to be seen in the low, timbered headlands obscured by fog or haze or spume from the sea pounding on the rocks and beaches. The skippers set their course by guess and St. John, put the sail gangs on point and sometimes escaped the sand spits and shoals to cross the bar into the river's yawning mouth.

The bark *Isabella* had no such luck. Out of England, bound for Fort Vancouver in the fall of 1829, she sighted the bar but lost headway in a lull, let her slack sails be caught in a sudden gale and was washed up on the sands. Capt. Thomas Ryan ordered her abandoned and all hands made shore through mountainous seas to watch the *Isabella* be pounded to kindling.

Her second mate and boatswain, Essexman James Scarborough, was one so stranded but being an experienced seaman found employment with the Hudson's Bay Co. and for ten years was master of the *Cadboro*. After his shipwreck experience he had deep compassion for skippers trying to enter the Columbia and upon taking up a homestead on the bluff above the bay where the *Isabella* came to grief, he immediately planted a grove of fruit and hawthorn trees. In succeeding years,

"THE CHINOOKS" wrote Capt. Lewis in his journal, "are low in statue, rather diminutive and ill-shapen possing thick broad, flat feet, thick ankles, crooked legs wide mouths, thick lips, nose moderately large fleshy, wide at the extremity with large nostrils, black eyes and coarse hair, their eyes are sometimes of a dark yellowish brown the puple black. The most remarkable trait in their physiognomy is the peculiar flatness and width of forehead which is artificially obtained by compressing the head between two boards while in a state of infancy and from which it never afterwards perfectly recovers" . . . (Photo Smithsonian Institution).

OLD PRINT of British ship **Tonquin**, anchored in harbor then called Haley's Bay, officially Baker's Bay, in 1811. John Jacob Astor sent out two parties, one overland led by Wilson Price Hunt, one by sea captained by crusty Jonathan Thorn. Latter was one of several to select site of what would be Astoria. **Tonquin** sailed from here to Clayoquot Sound, Vancouver Island, where it met disaster through attacks by Indians and explosion (Photo Smithson¹an Institution).

LEWIS AND CLARK CAMPSITE

MERIWETHER LEWIS AND WILLIAM CLARK WITH MEMBERS OF THEIR EXPEDITION, CAMPED IN THIS AREA FROM 16 TO 25 NOVEMBER, 1805 FROM THIS POINT THEY SAW THE BREAKERS OF THE PACIFIC OCEAN AND KNEW THAT THEY HAD COMPLETED THE MISSION ASSIGNED TO THEM BY PRESIDENT THOMAS JEFFERSON THEIR OVERLAND JOURNEY ESTABLISHED A NEW CLAIM FOR THE UNITED STATES TO THIS REGION.

STATE PARKS AND
RECREATION COMMISSION

MARKER AT BAKER'S BAY (Chinookville). Capt. Clark noted in his journal. "The tide meeting of me and the emence swells from the Main Ocian raised to such a hite that I concluded to form a camp on the highest spot I could find . . . in the upper part of Haley's Bay . . . This Chinook Nation is about 400 Souls inhabited the country on Small rivers that run into the bay directly below us . . . I directed all the men who wished to see more of the main Ocian to prepare themselves to set out with me early on tomorrow morning. The principal Chief of the Chinooks came to see us this evening." The "Chief" would have been one-eyed Concomly (see **Boot Hill**).

when the trees were in full bloom, the sheet of white blossoms on Scarborough Head was conspicuous for many miles on the lower river, a beacon seen even out at sea.

At the base of the Head near the beach was a Chinook Indian village of perhaps 300 to 400 natives, the community existing many years before advent of the white man. Among the first of these were men named Svipton, "One-Eyed" Skelly and Haley, an adjacent inlet first called after him, Haley's Bay.

When Capt. Bruno Heceta sailed up the Columbia about the time of our American revolution he indicated the bay as "Bahia de la Ascuncion". Thirteen years later Capt. John Meares named it "Deception Bay". Lewis and Clark had other ideas and it became "Rogue's Harbor". Later Capt. Baker of the brig *Jenny* anchored there and no doubt unaware that the water was topheavy with names, bestowed yet another on it—his own. And Baker's Bay it has remained.

By the custom of most white men alone in Indian country, Capt. Scarborough in 1843 married a Chinook woman, Ann Elizabeth, a member of the tribe in the village on the site of Chinookville, across the river from Fort Astoria. At one time the tribe was headed by famous one-eyed Chief Concomly (see *Boot Hill*).

The young couple took up a donation land claim of 640 acres which included part of Concomly's domain as well as Scarborough Head or Hill. Besides his fruit trees and shrubs the captain raised stock animals picked up on his voyages. He built a house shared with his Indian wife, contrary to custom, and to them were born four sons, only two surviving.

During these years Capt. Scarborough had his hand in many business ventures such as shipping fish to England and serving as river pilot. A mystery begins with the story of his having been paid for these efforts over the years in gold ingots amounting to $60,000, and that he buried the fortune somewhere on the hill. In February of 1855 the captain died suddenly without divulging the location of the ingots. James Burney of Cathlamet took the two boys in, one of them, Ned, living to be 80, dying at Cathlamet about 1925.

In 1864 the government bought the Scarborough estate as being a strategic location for defense of the Columbia. About 1894 Fort Columbia was built on the site, becoming a state park after the end of World War II.

Presumably the treasure is still somewhere about, apparently not discovered in the building of the fort or highway through the park. There remains a large area still undisturbed, too large for a search without a clue. Ruby El Hult, author of *Lost Mines and Treasures*, estimates the present value of the gold ingots to be about $120,000.

BLEWETT PASS, WASHINGTON

Blewett Pass in Washington was not so much a town as a continuous string of little towns, mines, mills and settlements, now faded away. There are many visible traces and in some cases a substantial reminder of those roaring days when thousand-dollar gold nuggets were not uncommon.

The most impressive of these is the Blewett Stamp Mill, north of the summit of the Pass. While much of the building is collapsed, enough stands to give a pretty good idea of what it once was.

An old gentleman lives in a tiny cabin across the road, his name is Anton Newbauer. Although the mill is completely useless now, he loves it still, having worked there as a young man. "You would never guess to look at the old mill now that there were hundreds of men working here in the 80's. Gold was what we mined here, and the lode was rich. There is still a lot of it down in that shaft and the tunnels that go clear back into the mountain. But the main vein pinched out about 1905, and the mill hasn't operated since. Now and then someone gets the idea of mining here again, but gold would have to be worth $200.00 an ounce to make it pay now."

Old Anton's estimate of a profitable price is far too high, according to later talks with other old hard-rock miners, but most are agreed on from $75.00 to $100.00. Everything depends on how much labor and machinery is needed for the amout of the yellow metal extracted. Simple, inexpensive placering operations are still paying off even at the present low price.

ORE LOADING chute is almost buried in rank vegetation typical of mountainous area. Even so, rainfall is much lighter on this east-facing side of Cascades. Timbers and logs would long since have rotted away on western rainy side.

OLD BLEWETT STAMP MILL reduced large chunks of rich gold ore into more manageable size for extraction. Weight was hauled to top of t o w e r (right), allowed to fall with crushing force on ore.

BOSSBURG, WASHINGTON

Although twice in the history of the State of Washington the annual value of silver produced has exceeded that of gold, the yellow metal has held first place in the dreams of prospectors and the imaginations of those interested in old mining camps. The mines of Republic turned out millions in gold, those of Blewett Pass some, yet fully half of the old camps and ghost towns of the state have histories bound up with metals of another color.

Old Trinity was strictly a copper producing camp. The golden product of the Swauk district, including the Blewett Pass, was so alloyed with silver its color was definitely paled to a light yellow. The Ruby silver mines near Conconully were going full tilt in 1890 and at least a thousand miners were working in the camp at its height. The lead-silver mines of Colville produced large amounts of ore, the biggest being the old Dominion. For lack of roads or railroads the output was carried to Spokane at a cost of $100 a ton.

Five years later the Young America and Bonanza deposits were opened up at what is now called Bossburg, its first name Young America. The galena ore here was so rich some of it was "specimen" material and for some time the mines were going at top speed. The village grew up a short distance from the mines, just off the banks of the Columbia River.

The summer of 1892 saw 800 people at Young America and a quartz mill was erected. There were also stores, a good-sized school, the inevitable saloons and honkytonks. The next year the town was formally platted and rechristened Millington. A Congregational Church and large meeting hall were added and again, in 1896, the town was

ROTTING REMNANTS OF VEHICLES of another day lie in grass and weeds around old town.

CRUMBLING FALSE-FRONTED store in Bossburg had living rooms upstairs. Columbia River is just beyond, hills once heavily timbered with Ponderosa pine now show sparse cover.

rechristened—Bossburg in honor of the first citizen, C. S. Boss.

After mining operations tapered off Bossburg attempted to recoup its failing fortunes by establishing a ferry across the Columbia. Fruit orchards were set out and produced apples and pears, vines growing top quality berries. A sawmill had been put in working order and some lumber was shipped. The prevailing limestone formations were tapped, stone was shipped in building blocks as were lime products.

None of these efforts lasted long. The old zip was gone, silver mining collapsed under the low prices and Bossburg died on the vine. Nearly all the old buildings are gone. A store, a few sheds, substantial schoolhouse still stand, the latter occupied by a family who had topped the old structure with a TV antenna.

CONCONULLY, WASHINGTON

It was high drama even for the raw West. Sheriff's deputy, Pete Barker did not like the looks of the stranger watching the L. L. Work Bank in Conconully. He told Sheriff Fred Thorp the fellow was far too interested in the bank's workings. Thorp took a good look at the man but could not get worked up over the idea of arresting him for doing nothing. By chance a man-wanted poster came in the next day depicting Frank LeRoy, wanted in the east for burglary. The face was that of the stranger.

Thorp found him in the Morris Saloon playing pool with his back to the door. With his .45 at the man's back, he said quietly: "I'd like to search you, if you don't mind." LeRoy swung around and said: "Sure." Then starting to open his jacket, he jerked a pistol from a shoulder holster and fired. The bullet went wild and LeRoy went into a fast dance, making himself such a difficult target Thorp's first shot also missed, his second taking off a finger, making LeRoy drop the pistol.

He broke for the door, drawing another gun from a second holster with his left hand. Another shot from Thorp caught the fugitive in the right shoulder. He spun around and dropped. While the sheriff was grabbing another gun, LeRoy gained his feet and ran staggering up Salmon Creek. He quickly collapsed, blood running from his mouth. He was carried to the jail on an old barn door.

While waiting for Dr. Polk, a search of the man and his belongings revealed two more guns, a set of burglar tools and some loot from a recent robbery in Brewster nearby. The doctor reported the patient would live but recommended he be locked up. The "maximum security" cell was without heat and as a bed patient, LeRoy was put in an outer room and given watchful care for about nine days. His guard was then lightened but in reality the burglar was feigning extreme weakness. Aware of tools in a closet, he got into the sleeping jailer's room one night, stole shoes, overalls and a blanket which he wrapped around himself Indian fashion and faded into the night. This was November 7, 1909.

LeRoy got safely to the nearby mining camp of Ruby, got a long-bladed butcher knife and at the home of Casper Miller demanded an outfit of clothes and probably some food. During the next three days Sheriff Thorp tracked him to a clump of sagebrush near the little community of Malott, leveled his rifle at the fugitive and gave him a choice: "Come out with your hands up or be blown to Kingdom Come." LeRoy stood with his hands high cursing: "If I had anything but this knife, I'd kill you right now!" Tried for burglary, he was adjudged a habitual criminal and sent to the state penitentiary at Walla Walla for 99 years. He was later paroled.

Although the Conconully jail later developed many weak spots, it was planned for strength. At one of the first county commissioner meetings careful details were specified for the detention of future prisoners. The jail was to be built of "two by six scantlings, spiked together—spikes to be not more than six inches apart." Orders were placed for 24 pairs of hand-

JURY PANEL at trial in 1906 on front steps of courthouse, photo owned by Helen Rice. Her brother George, top row, third from left, worked for freighting outfit, hauling logs on sled through town when load overturned on bridge over Salmon Creek, was tapped for jury duty while ruefully surveying wreckage. Standing at extreme left, top row, is Judge Hartew. Next, Mr. Gibson, then young Fitch, next to him, Bill Sproul. Next is unidentified, then Ham Pinkerton. Man leaning against post is unknown, next and final two are Ed Sayles and Bill Gamble. Of the front row only two are identified — at left, standing with hand on rail is Mr. Jay. At right, man with interlaced fingers is Joe Pinkerton.

"STREET SCENE ON SUNDAY," another of Frank Matsura's vivid pictures of Conconully in bygone era. Note raised sidewalk giving pedestrians some protection from mud and snow. No protection was possible when Salmon Creek flooded down main street. Wave more than 50 feet high was known to come down canyon after mountain cloudburst.

In May of 1892 one such disaster swept many buildings down street ending up as wreckage on huge delta of sand also carried by waters. Safe was washed out of one building, never found. One woman, safely out of home, missed her glasses, rushed back to get them, was swept away with house, body later found in wreckage, hand still clutching precious spectacles.

cuffs and three pairs of shackles complete with chains and 24-pound balls.

Nevertheless, from its building about 1891 to the time the courthouse was wrecked about 1915, the pokey suffered ridicule and abuse because of frequent escapes. Early one spring when snow was beginning to melt and the ditch under the lockup was filled with icy water, two thieves were incarcerated and told they could build themselves a fire in the stove. Instead, they built it on the floor and when the flames had eaten into the boards enough to weaken them, the men took a plank and poked out an opening over the ditch. The first man got down with no difficulty but the second was so fat he stuck midway. His friend came back to poke the hole bigger and pull the fat man down through.

One Sam Albright heard two of his friends were lodged in the famous calaboose and came to Conconully with another friend, Clint Williams, to have a chat with the prisoners. The visitors found the jailer absent, unlatched a window and climbed in. The reunited foursome had a friendly game of stud, after which the callers gave the inmates some books and candy and departed the way they had come, relatching the window.

Proprietor Gibson of the store of that name in Conconully tells of a jail break with a different twist, when Ben Snowden was jailer. "Old Ben had three fellows in there, one named Kallentyne. When Ben took their food in, one of the men was doubled up on the floor like he was sick and Ben set the food down to go and see what was the matter with him." It seems the jailer always kept a rifle hanging on the corridor side of the door and the prisoners knew it. When Ben bent over, the two on their feet ran for their gun while the one on the floor held Ben. The rifle came cracking down on his skull, almost killing him, and the three took off, hiding in the brush at the edge of the lake. Sheriff Thorp quickly organized a posse and surrounded the patch of willows and aspen trees.

When he demanded the fugitives' surrender, the man with the gun threatened to shoot anyone who moved closer. Thorp was a man of courage and strode forward, but there was no shot—the gun had jammed in the beating of old Ben. The three walked out meekly and were returned to jail.

Then there was the day in January, 1891, when Indian Steve was jerked from the same jail by a howling mob of drunken miners. They tied his hands behind his back, blindfolded him and forced him down the road to a large tree. A heavy limb stuck out horizontally about fifteen feet up and a rope was thrown over it, the other made into a noose which was

97

PICTURE MADE IN 1962 shows town in opposite direction of early-day photo. Historic courthouse stood in grove of pines at bottom center. Comparatively new church is at right on site of earlier one destroyed by fire. Indian name of Conconully meant "clouds" or anything threatening, in this case monster supposed to live in lake of same name. Sparsely pine-clad hills are typical of Okanogan Highlands, large section of north-central Washington, extending into British Columbia. Modern camp ground and State Park are at right of picture. Lake teems with regularly planted trout, mostly rainbows averaging 8 to 11 inches.

looped around Steve's neck. The lynchers hauled him into the air, jerking him up and down. The body swayed there a day or two and then the rope was cut off, the tied end remaining until the tree was cut down in 1938.

This lynching and other incidents were part of the "Conconully Indian Scare." The government restricting of the Indian population to the nearby Colville Reservation was difficult or impossible to enforce, the natives making sporadic forays into Conconully and neighboring Ruby, Tonasket and Loomis.

They were suspected at once when the dead body

of C. S. Cole, driver for the freight line between Okanogan and Conconully, was found near the road near the close of 1890, wagon rolled over the cliff and horses gone. There were no clues until a squaw who loitered around Conconully began spreading rumors that Indian Johnny and his friend Indian Steve had done the deed. Asked why she would inform on Johnny, her "fella," she said she had tried to get him to marry her but he would not. She said one reason he had picked Cole, aside from stealing the horses, was that the freighter had poked fun at the Indian about his feeble attempts to raise a mustache.

Deputy Ives took off after the pair of braves who he heard were at an encampment near Chilliwhist. Johnny saw him first, drew a gun and fired, the bullet grazing Ives' cheek. The deputy's shot was more deadly, hitting the Indian in the head and killing him.

During the gunfires a squaw was wounded, which further angered the sullen tribesmen. Bad feeling was so strong Ives decided not to look for Indian Steve and get out as soon as possible. He said later that as he rode away he could imagine guns aimed at his back, making his flesh crawl, but he escaped unmolested.

Word was soon sent to the camp that Steve had better give himself up before there was more trouble, and on January 5, 1891, he surrendered to the sheriff in Conconully. He was placed in jail and Judge Price, who knew Indian ways and thinking, started an investigation before trial. The next week the Ruby *Miner* was to print this ambiguous note:

"Last Thursday morning twenty horsemen galloped through Ruby, the soft white snow muffling the sound of their horses' hooves and the slumber of the camp was not disturbed by their movements. Death was in their hearts and they sped remorselessly onward." Jailer Thomas Dickson had been warned by the judge of the strong possibility of a lynching and when he saw the mob approaching, he hid the cell key under his mattress. The mob soon found it, opened the door and dragged Indian Steve to his death. This item appeared in the Ruby *Miner* the following week:

"Trouble is on foot and danger stalks abroad. It is principally owing to the lynching of Steve that this condition exists—but there are many supplemental reasons. George Monk accompanied by Smitkin started to convey the body to the Indian Mission. The Indians claim that Monk, when he started out, was sitting on the corpse which was wrapped in a blanket and carried on a single bobsled. The appearance of the body was the signal for the start of a big dance. For two days the body was kept while the Indians stimulated themselves at the bier."

The lynching did intensify matters. It was now rumored Indians were gathering in the mountains for mass attacks on Conconully. Another report had it that every man, woman and child would be killed and scalped in vengeance for the deaths of Johnny and Steve. Alarm grew to the point that citizens appealed to the U.S. Army for help.

In response, on January 17, 1891, Gen. A. P. Curry arrived with a detachment of soldiers and an arsenal for use of residents in case of attack. One hundred eighty rifles and 3,000 rounds of ammunition were stacked in the courthouse. When no raid developed, the guns were stored in an unused room where they gathered dust for many years.

In the beginning, Indians trapped beavers in the area, selling the pelts at a good profit and calling the valley Sklow Outiman or Money Hole. The first whites were prospectors who founded Salmon City on Salmon Creek.

In March of 1888 the newly organized board of Okanogan County Commissioners met in a log barn

OVERALL VIEW OF CONCONULLY taken about 1905 as shown in old newspaper, Conconully *Record* in real estate plug with list of merchants. Main business section is at lower right, courthouse at base of hill, left of center; public grade school at left. Salmon Creek is seen flowing parallel to road in lower right. Site of hanging of Indian Steve is along same road at extreme bottom center. Church shown here just below courthouse was destroyed by fire, replacement built on same site shows at lower right of modern photo.

on the farm of John Perkins at the head of Johnson Creek near the booming mining camps of Ruby City and Salmon City, four miles apart. George Huley, later mayor of Ruby City was one member, Guy Waring, pioneer merchant of Loomis, another. Next day, the 7th, another meeting was held at which members read petitions from both towns pleading the right to be the county seat. Ruby City won out and the committee left the log barn to meet in Ruby. By November, Salmon City had changed its name to Conconully and, the population of both towns having swelled enormously, an election was held to decide which city should now have the county seat. Conconully got 357 votes to Ruby's 157, and the commissioners again switched locations.

About 1900 there was a strong movement to change the seat to Riverside, that town doing the promoting and Conconully sitting back. The latter town had an elegant courthouse, built by the famous Steven Cloud and sheltering a safe that weighed a ton and a half with a time lock unequalled in the country. The Riverside effort failed.

One of the first county treasurers was Andrew J. Nickel, earning $125 a month, his wife having campaigned with him and getting $75 as deputy. Mrs. Nickel had spent several months driving around the county in a light buggy drawn by ponies Peter and Peggy, had talked to every man encountered on the road, passing out campaign literature and a card. After

the election, she related her embarrassment when the newspapers in 1914 with the local high school footponies continued to stop at the sight of every man on the road.

A freighter named Brown used a buggy with two horses when the load of supplies and mail was light. On the road steeply descending to Conconully by a series of switchbacks, his progress was blocked by a snowslide. As he unhitched his horses to lead them around, one struggled into the deep snow and vanished. Brown led the other one down the hill and just before arriving in Conconully, met the other animal which had floundered safely down.

A stage line ran between Conconully and Oroville with bearskin coats and foot warmers as standard equipment to keep passengers from freezing to death in winter. But in November of 1904 which had been deceptively warm, the driver did not take the coats and warmers along. A large group of teachers took the stage in Oroville for Teachers' Institute in Conconully, all wearing light clothes. During the meeting the temperature plummeted to below zero. On the way home men and women teachers had to huddle together under a few blankets and at each way stop to change horses on the eight-hour trip, they were taken into the stage depot and thawed out.

Disastrous floods and fires plagued Conconully as well as avalanches and Indians. Superstitious residents recalled the invective screamed from the knoll above town by a bitter miner who had been rolled in a bawdy house. "Curses on you, damned Conconully! May you burn, be drowned and burned again!"

In spite of the silver panic of 1893, the town kept going in a limited way. It made headlines in area newspapers in 1914 with the local high school football team called "Terror of the Okanogan" but other headlines the same year proclaimed the end of the old camp. The proud position of county seat was surrendered to the now more prosperous town of Okanogan.

The old courthouse was torn down, the lumber used to build a little city hall. The jail was removed, leaving on the site the two concrete and rock vaults—and now even these have crumbled to a large extent. One has visible evidence of bars which were used as added protection for legal documents. Visitors and prowlers for historical remains are usually happy in the delusion they have found the famous Conconully jail which actually was a frame structure.

A third substantial vault remaining near the present little post office belonged to the bank which bandit LeRoy was so intently watching before he was caught. The huge livery stable stood until about 1958 when it was razed. A tiny, false-front, one-room building which served as a plant of the Conconully *Record* was torn down about the same time.

The area is now a State Park with a fine campground having all modern facilities even to automatic laundry machines. It is situated in an aspen grove on sand brought down the canyon by Salmon Creek in flood times. In the center of a landscaped park is a replica of the little log cabin in which the original county commissioners met. Trout fishing in the lake and reservoir is rated among the best in the state.

FAMOUS HOOSEGOW in Conconully, long since vanished, was butt of ridicule because of frequent prisoner escapes but did keep many prisoners in custody. Was located near courthouse which can be seen in overall photo of town. Section at left confined prisoners; quarters for jailer, at right.

ORIGINAL PHOTO OF CONCONULLY COURTHOUSE was picture post card taken in 1905 by little Japanese photographer, Frank Matsura; property of Mrs. R. Brunke who still lives in old silver camp. View from balcony was superb, looking out over piney mountains and Conconully Lake. In winter, when frozen, lengthy stretch of water served as part of highway to "outside," eliminating difficult and dangerous avalanche-beset road.

STONE HOUSE dates from Conconully's early roistering days as does tenant. He walks down steep trail to tavern each day, wearing pair of six guns as he has for fifty years. These are checked at door, returned when old gentleman leaves.

COPPER CITY, WASHINGTON

Mr. Fred Eaton has lived in the area of Copper City for nearly fifty years, and the town was already old and abandoned when he came. There had been a good strike of gold and copper, creating great but short-lived excitement. The great "Yacolt Burn," an enormous forest fire in 1902, stopped everything for a time and the mine was never worked profitably again. Mr. Eaton surmised that the vein had run out.

Some years later, a Sam Pumpelly conceived a plan to revitalize the mine and sell stock. "Sam drank a lot and would do anything to make a fast buck." He hauled good, rich ore from another mine and scattered it all over the diggin's. But his reputation was his undoing and the scheme fell through. He died not long after. Since then, the mine has been completely abandoned except for a few fishermen who cast their flies on the tumbling waters of Copper Creek.

LITTLE GROUP OF CABINS is swamped in rain-nurtured verdure.

CURLEW, WASHINGTON

Always a bridesmaid, never a bride—that was the story of Curlew. It was named for a water bird and a lake where they abounded but it never had a name for gold.

Curlew had its beginings in a very modest way in the '80s with a few trappers' cabins. Since the soil was rich and comparatively free of trees and stumps, a few farmers built homes and fenced some fields. A school and a few stores were built.

During the early years life in Curlew was peaceful. Occasionally some prospector would come into town claiming he had struck gold in the hills and there was a flurry of excitement. The news was readily accepted each time since the wish was there and lots of gold had been found in Republic and other nearby camps. But alas, nothing ever materialized from these claims except grubstakes by the gullible storekeepers.

Curlew had settled back into a succession of naps when the actual bombshell exploded. "The railroad is coming!" The Spokane and British Columbia announced plans for a line through Republic, Kettle Falls, Curlew and Grand Forks in Canada. The Great Northern already had an option on the only logical right-of-way but that did not deter the S. & B. C. from making a great show of surveying another one alongside. An elaborate station was built on the hill above Curlew—then the long, empty pause. The investors

J. C. KIEHL who has lived in Curlew since before the days when the "Hot Air Railroad" made numerous false starts toward construction which never materialized. He stands here at side door of Ansorge Hotel where he now resides. Small false-front stood here first, erected by Ansorge and used as restaurant. To make room for hotel it was moved around to side, facetiously referred to as "Ansorge Annex."

COPY OF OLD PICTURE loaned by J. C. Kiehl shows Ansorge Hotel in days of first World War. Jitney service operated by Kiehl was in full swing, taxis shown here lined up and ready to go. Several loungers on porch seem not too interested in proceedings.

ANSORGE HOTEL at right, now more than commodious home for Mr. and Mrs. J. C. Kiehl, two of Curlew's oldest inhabitants. Mr. Kiehl remembers: "There were many times in the old days when the hotel was so full they had to put extra cots in the hallways. Those were the war days and I ran a jitney service for drummers and prospectors. It seems like they wanted to go everywhere, around town and out to the neighboring towns, even to Republic. Those boys were always good pay and sometimes gave me tips." Building at left was old Maxwell Meat Market.

MANY BOARDED UP FALSE-FRONTED STORES line streets of one-time flourishing Curlew. Most breaks in ranks caused by fires which took heavy toll in days when frame structures were tinder dry, water pressure low.

were wondering where their money had gone when more surveys were ordered and the "notch on the hill" was deepened to a more respectable cut. Now, everybody thought, we are really on our way to having a railroad through town. Real estate values advanced and property changed hands.

Again the interminable wait. The grumbling of citizens grew louder. "That new railroad is nothing but a lot of hot air!" was shouted and the Spokane and British Columbia was always called "The Hot Air Railroad" through the years, the line never being completed. Eventually the Great Northern exercised its option and Curlew did have trains, but it was too late. All hopes of a big gold discovery had long since vanished and Curlew was just a whistle stop.

ST. PATRICK'S CATHOLIC CHURCH built in 1903 and kept in good repair now has scant congregation. Barren hills surrounding town once had good growth of timber, were stripped to provide wood and lumber.

FRANKFORT, WASHINGTON

"Curiosity unveils marvels" and no one knows it better than Dr. Ralph Isaac of Portland, Oregon. He spends much time in the outdoors of his free days, eyes and ears open, feelers tuned to a sensitive pitch. One summer day in 1960 he and his son-in-law walked along the beach of the Columbia River, at Knappton on the north or Washington shore. The tide was going out and they looked for a trail to skirt the headland which appeared to block the way.

"We came to a group of weathered houses," the doctor told the author later, "some just above high water level, some well up the bank. At first we thought all the houses were vacant, although most of them were still furnished. We looked through one window into a kitchen and saw dishes and silverware still on the table, as if the people living there had just finished a meal. Exploring further we discovered the settlement wasn't entirely deserted, that it had two inhabitants, a German who lived alone at one end and a lonely Swede at the other. We talked to the latter, commenting it was fortunate he had company in the otherwise deserted place. His reply was: 'We got mad at each other a couple of years ago and ain't spoke since.' " Mindful of the returning tide which would block their return the two explorers were forced to leave, not relishing a climb over the intervening headland with its mantle of tangled vines and brush native to Washington's coastal regions.

Dr. Isaacs lead was tantalizing to this inquisitive photographer but—how to get to Frankfort with camera equipment when the light was right (all the buildings faced south and the Columbia) and not be at the mercy of ebbing and flowing tides? After several futile attempts to reach the spot, information came in the late summer of 1964 that the firm of Crown Zellerbach was logging on the bluff above Frankfort, that dirt roads had been knifed through the heavy timber to a point a mile above it. So an over-night camp was made and in the early morning a climb down an old overgrown trail.

Here was the classic deserted village—a small one almost isolated, never reached by road of any sort, without telephone, electricity or wheeled vehicle larger than a wheelbarrow. Frankfort's only exchange with the outside world was by fishing boats, the nearest towns mere settlements, the nearest city Astoria across the broad mouth of the Columbia River with its formidable bar and almost constant threat of storms. River traffic with Frankfort tied up at a wharf which extended out across the mud flats to deep river and which was now rotted and wrecked by heavy battering of waves, making Frankfort accessible only by small boats that could reach the bank at high water, or by foot. What was the story behind the desolation?

Early in 1890 two promoters, Frank Bourn and Frank Scott, took a long look at the small clearing they found on Gray's Bay. It seemed a likely spot to start a city, a river metropolis protected from fierce winter storms by a prominent headland. Maybe they could induce a railroad to build a line to the site or at least promise to. At any rate the two Franks could call their city Frankfort.

FRANKFORT RESIDENTS when Lawrence Barber visited isolated community in 1947. He found 11 people, 6 of them shown here. At left is Fred Hansen, who with 9 brothers and sisters, was raised in Frankfort, all attending one-room school presided over by teacher Ulrika Brandt, daughter of Swedish sea captain. She stands next in line, partly concealed by Hugo Claeson. Next is Mrs. Claeson, then Charles Lawrence and Mrs. Lawrence.

Rumors were soon spreading like wildfire, hinting that the Northern Pacific Railroad was actually surveying a route down the north bank of the Columbia to connect with ocean shipping points. Further, said the "overly Frank" reports, the line would pass directly along the edge of Gray's Bay, a station to be built where Bourn and Scott indicated.

The promoters built a flimsy landing float at the river's edge but its usefulness was limited, as lower reaches of the Columbia advance to the ocean only on the ebb tide, being forced backward on the flood. This meant that if prospective purchasers were dropped from boats on the wharf at low tide they were faced with a mile or more of oozy mud flats.

Yet buyers came on the heels of promises and the picturesque bay front seethed with activity. Bourn and Scott took in another partner, L. O. Chemault, and on May 15, 1890, filed the original plat of Frankfort, plans calling for 1226 lots. Streets and alleys were laid out with fine disregard of terrain, much of it swampy with only a narrow bench of solid ground, this terminating at the bottom of a steeply rising bluff.

Nevertheless many of the lots were sold. The promoters ploughed their increasing funds back into Frankfort's boggy soil, building a hotel, general store and sawmill, and all these signs of a city to be, encouraged more lot sales. A newspaper was soon in print, a saloon and then two more doing business. But it soon became apparent to the most

optimistic that with all this no railroad tracks were being laid. While a committee of inquiring citizens gathered at the front door of the real estate office, two of the partners faded away at the back, leaving Bourn to face the music.

Well, it was like this, he said—the railroad had decided against building the line. He had been informed of the change in plans only yesterday. However, nobody would regret his investing in the future of Frankfort. The site was perfect for a salmon cannery and think of that tremendous stand of timber at the very door of the sawmill. The committee went away and if its members were not placated, they grumbled without protest.

Bourn was still there ten years later when Axel Nelson arrived but the population had fallen to about 150. The salmon canneries were interested in Frankfort as Bourn had predicted but not to the extent of building plants. Two of the larger concerns, New England Fish Co. and Anderson Packing Co., had built substantial wharves where they could load fish netted by Frankfort fishermen and these companies had hired Nelson as agent to facilitate the buying and loading. He bought the long unused hotel built by Bourn and partners and rebuilt it as a substantial home.

At this time the *Mayflower, Pioneer, Julia B.* and other steamers plying the river made regular stops at Frankfort docks. When the *Mayflower* was condemned as unseaworthy she was replaced by the *Shamrock*. Five years later a smart new steamer, the *General George Washington* made its maiden voyage on the Columbia and began regular stops at Frankfort. The vessel had been built by its owners, William Anderson, Ed Simmons and Ed Shatto, was destined to be the most familiar steamer on the run, the best remembered by old timers.

Early in January, 1947, Lawrence Barber, marine editor of the Portland OREGONIAN, visited Frankfort and found only 11 residents, among them Axel Nelson. The community was even more isolated than in earlier days, having no mail delivery or regular boat service. Nelson complained that Frankfort was cut off from the rest of the world, that in case of emergency it had no way of getting word out. A man needing medical attention would die before any aid could be summoned. He said he had gone into the matter of getting the county to build a road, either from Knappton, a stretch of only three miles but over the steep intervening headland, or from Deep River to the north, three and a half miles over the mud flats. Either way the cost would be between $35,-

000 and $50,000 for a single lane graveled road and the county could not consider it.

Barber's story and pictures appeared in his newspaper January 12. On the 17th there was a news item from Astoria headed: "Navy To Help Isolated Area." The announcement read: "The navy Wednesday came to the rescue of Frankfort, Wash., the tiny community on the north shore of the Columbia." The item stated that Capt. L. B. Ard, commanding officer of the Tongue Point Naval Station would send a crash boat to Frankfort at the request of the Astoria Chamber of Commerce, and if any emergency condition was found to exist the navy would provide temporary weekly service until regular commercial boat service could be restored.

And a month later, on February 12, the OREGONIAN carried this dispatch: "Doctor Rushed To Isolated Area—The isolated community of Frankfort . . . called on the navy Sunday for assistance when one of its 12 inhabitants became suddenly ill. The navy command at Tongue Point dispatched a picket boat to carry Dr. J. B. Lund from Astoria to Frankfort to treat Leo Nelson who was seriously ill with intestinal influenza. . . . The navy has been sending a crash boat there occasionally as an emergency service."

Frankfort's ultimate usefulness was mentioned in the OREGONIAN's issue of January 14, 1953: "Logger Acquires River Townsite — The forest grown townsite of Frankfort, across the Columbia River from Astoria, has been sold at auction by Pacific County, Wash. for $74,918. E. J. Mell, Shelton, Wash. logger bought the bulk of the property . . . several independent buyers took lots on the waterfront that might be capable of development for resort purposes. The sale put an end to the dreams of real estate promoters of more than fifty years ago who platted the townsite in the hopes it would develop into the metropolis of the lower Columbia."

HOME OF AXEL NELSON, native of Finland, who arrived in Frankfort at turn of century. House was built of lumber salvaged from hotel made useless when plans for railroad collapsed. Most of furnishings remain, although badly damaged by vandals. Piano still stands in parlor but needle point settee dumped on front steps has been ruined further by rains which often total 15 inches a month in winter at near-ocean site. Moisture and mild climate foster heavy verdure which will soon engulf Nelson home and entire village.

VIEW FROM DESERTED VILLAGE of Frankfort across broad mouth of Columbia River. Early morning mists rise from water, partly obscuring Oregon coastal range in distance. Large public dock was wrecked in violent winter storm in 1933. Mud flats in center foreground are exposed by low tide which strongly affects Columbia here near ocean. Volume and power of water at flood are evidenced by stranded logs at shoreline.

LAST REMAINING RESIDENT of Frankfort was Swedish fisherman, Sven Hovic, who was taken to rest home in helpless condition in 1962. Sven had used most of his winter's wood, rest remaining to rot, as apples on tree. Wires were strung above fence to discourage marauding deer and elk, other residents using more effective fish net barricades 8-feet high.

HOME, WASHINGTON

"Home", said the indignant editorial headed "The Nudes and the Prudes" in the colony's newspaper THE AGITATOR, "is a community of free spirits who came out into the woods to escape the priest-ridden atmosphere of conventional society. One of the liberties enjoyed by Homeites was the privilege to bathe in evening dress or with only the clothes nature gave them, just as they pleased. . . But eventually a few got into the community and proceeded in the brutal unneighborly way of the outside world to suppress the people's freedom. . . ."

The community of free spirits included two who lived in a tree. Joe Kapolla and Franz Erkelems arrived in the idyllic colony on the shore of Joe's Bay in 1908, attracted by the well-publicized tolerance of Home's people toward ways of living that might be considered odd elsewhere.

The site Joe and Franz selected for a home had a ready-made water supply, a bubbling spring, but the same plentiful waters made the ground too soggy for a house. The problem was solved by cutting off the top of a large, forked tree nearby and building their domicile on the several high stumps. They put up a tent on the ground below for use as a kitchen and since it straddled the cold spring, a natural ice box was provided. Dish washing was eliminated, the dirty dishes merely placed in the flowing water where minnows nibbled off scraps of food. Among the many stories told about the partners is one about a "dinner party" given for two lady guests, one of whom brought her small boy along. He amused himself grabbing at the little fish swimming among the dishes and unexpectedly caught one. Joe Kapolla told him to put it back immediately. "That's our best dish washer."

Home's history of individualism, discontent and frustration is recorded in its series of newspapers or more accurately in the several revivals of the same one. Beginning as the NEW ERA, the little paper was successively brought out as the DISCONTENT — MOTHER OF PROGRESS, THE DEMONSTRATOR and the AGITATOR, all printed on a portable press. The NEW ERA, started in June of 1897 by O. A. Verity, stated in one of its first issues: "Liberty we have, so far as *we* are concerned, but the laws of the state — of course — the ever-present thorn in the flesh — are the great barriers to the realization of Liberty. Now, one may, at Home, keep within the pale of the law or completely ignore it, just as he pleases. Most of us prefer the latter course and teach others to do the same." An issue or two later came forth with the illuminating premise — "The love principle of our nature is a natural one, and to defy it is to defy nature."

More exciting was the coming of Halley's Comet, the arrival scheduled for four o'clock in the morning. Joe and Franz were out scanning the heavens and Joe spotted a glow at the brow of a hill. "There it is!" he shouted but Franz said it couldn't be, that the comet was supposed to appear over a hill in the opposite direction. In the next moment they realized they were looking at Joe Brewster's cabin and it was ablaze. They were eager to help put the fire out but the only source of water was a deep well and neither of them knew how to operate the windlass. Joe managed to get the bucket down and excitedly wound the handle as fast as he could, the full bucket coming up with a jerk and banging against the head of the open-mouthed Franz. The water spilled out and by the time more concerted team work brought up another bucketful, the fire was hopelessly out of control. Halley's Comet had meanwhile made its fruitless trip across the sky.

The paper attracted plenty of attention but costing only a dollar a year, with most copies being mailed free to outsiders as propaganda, the NEW ERA soon died. One of the last issues fell into the hands of an alcoholic printer named Charles Goven in a Barbary Coast saloon in San Francisco. He recruited friend James F. Morton Jr. to go with him to Home with the idea of improving the paper and at the same time enjoy the purported freedoms. They arrived to find the NEW ERA defunct and Goven set about to revive it.

Volume 1, No. 1 of the new paper, dated May 11, 1898, was headed: "DISCONTENT — MOTHER OF PROGRESS, Successor to NEW ERA —Dedicated to Anarchist Communism — Price 50¢ Yearly." On the 29th a summary of Home history was included. "Our progress in the two years we have been here has been slow. The Mutual Home Association was started by three comrades whose combined cash was one $20 gold piece each. They came from the Socialist Colony at Glennis in a boat they built themselves."

The three referred to were George Allen, O. A. Verity and F. F. O'dell who had indeed built their own boat, toured the maze of waterways adjacent to Tacoma and made their selection of Joe's Bay, a small intrusion from Von Geldred Cove, which in

VIEW UP TINY JOE'S BAY, roughly twenty miles from Tacoma. Life in Home was tied closely to waterways, only means of transportation and access to outer world, which though scorned in theory, supplied many of daily needs. Wharf housing totters precariously on barnacle-encrusted, rotting piers. Other structures in background also date from colony days. Long dock was later convenience, ship passengers for Home in first years landed unceremoniously on small raft and ferried ashore. Low tide here has given access to beach for low angle photograph, exposing oysters in plenty, many 7 inches long. They are escapees from those planted commercially in Dabob and Quilcene Bays. For about ten days after hatching, larval form called "spat" floats freely in water, may drift long distances in free-swimming stage. Early Home settlers likely would have welcomed added item to meager food supplies but they were many years too early.

turn is an arm of Carr's Inlet. There were twenty-six acres of land there, available to the colonists at a price of $2.50 per acre. The trio and their families set to work digging clams and cutting wood, selling these products to neighboring townspeople. In the spring of 1897 they bought the land and for-

mally set up the Compact of the Mutual Home Colony Association.

O'dell continues the story in DISCONTENT: "We came here, got our land on time and went into debt for the lumber, $100, to build houses, unable to pay freight entirely on our goods. Allen (an honor stu-

112

dent of Toronto University) taught school and with the proceeds we lived while the other two built houses and cleared land for the gardens. After the short space of 16 months we were practically out of debt. Incoming members aided us with payments for land and membership fees. Today we have 22 members, 14 adult male workers, have 11 houses erected and another cost $300 well under way; bought and paid for two teams of horses, but sold one recently. This success is the result of our labors as none of the incoming members had means to aid them."

Allen went on working hard said the item of January 1, 1899: "Comrade Allen has his hands full these days teaching singing classes, writing copy for advertising in DISCONTENT, all voluntary and without pay. Yet, there are those who say that in Anarchy where money is eliminated there would be no incentive to labor." In another issue was this bit: "Comrade C. W. Fox has rheumatism. He says it is nobody's business, though, that he can be sick if he wishes." And every issue carried this note: "How to get here. Parties inclining to visit us will come to Tacoma and take steamer *Tycoon* for Joe's Bay, leaving Commercial Dock every day except Saturday and Sunday at 2:30. Ask Captain to let you off on Joe's Bay raft." Presumably, someone in the colony would row out and bring the visitor ashore.

By 1900 Home's population was seventy-five, including thirty school children. DISCONTENT had claimed a circulation of twelve hundred, it being obvious the paper was intended for outside propaganda. One of these readers was Emma Goldman, feminist radical, who wrote essays for the publication on free love in which she invariably blamed the organized church for prostitution.

Although Home was getting a reputation for being a retreat for those who advocated free love, sin and anarchy, there was no serious focus of attention on the doings there until the assassination of President McKinley in 1904. Home could not be suspected of harboring the actual assassin, Leon Czolgosz, but it was a known refuge for anarchists like him. In the hysteria following the President's death, a group calling itself Loyalty League held a mass meeting in Custer Hall in Tacoma. Members formed a Vigilante Committee whose express purpose was to go to Home and "subdue" the colonists. The Tacoma LEDGER reported that the Committee should charter a steamer, go to Home, run off the members and burn their town.

While the excited Committee members were discussing ways and means, the pastor of the German Evangelical Church of Tacoma, Rev. J. F. Doescher, made a trip to the colony, interviewed members in their houses and preached a sermon in their Liberty Hall. When he returned to Tacoma he went straight to the LEDGER office and demanded that the paper see to it that any raid on the colonists be prevented. "They have made clearings", he said, "planted orchards, made gardens. The people are sober, industrious and friendly. Their neighbors give them good witness. They are better citizens by far than those that have been shouting 'Exterminate the vipers!' "

The newspaper did discourage the raid, possibly because destruction of the colony would ruin a good news source. But Home was not out of the woods. The postal authorities took over, sending the United States marshall over to arrest Goven and his helpers for "depositing obscene matter in the U.S. Mails."

As a gesture of passive non-resistance, Home members greeted the marshall at the gangplank, made him a guest of honor at a dinner and later at a dance. The marshall dined, danced and next morning escorted his prisoners to the Tacoma jail. The LEDGER had a large type heading next day to the effect that the intrepid law officer had single-handedly attacked, subdued and arrested the miscreants at great personal danger to himself. The DISCONTENT cried out at the injustice, attempted to have the LEDGER retract the statements and when it failed to do so, the newspaper was branded in the colony's own as "not being interested in simple truth."

The trial was held on March 11, 1902. Goven and his associates were acquitted but authorities held one more trump. In April the Home post office was removed by order of the Postmaster General. Shortly afterward the DISCONTENT was deprived of its mailing privileges and that finished the paper.

Following a new established pattern, another new publication was created from the old, THE DEMONSTRATOR, with Morton listed as publisher and Goven as printer. The appearance was familiar and so was the approach. It also reminded outsiders: "If you should consider coming to us to live you should consider several things. There is much hard work to be done. We have cleared rough streets but still lack sidewalks. While there are eleven cows here now, there still is not enough milk for our needs. Most important consideration however, is that you will be able to live under the anarchist plan, that you may do just as you please as long as you do not infringe upon the natural rights of others."

Indicating some satisfaction in the way things were proceeding, was this item: "How does a com-

EARLY COTTAGES built by colonists stood in open, old growth trees having been cut for wood. Lusty, brushy second growth has all but covered some houses falling into decay through abandonment. This house provided excellent view of harbor entrance, is not now visible except to searchers of relics of colony days.

munity of eighty people, with two newspapers, one weekly, one monthly, a school with two teachers, no saloons, no churches, no policemen and no jails compare with what you have been used to?"

But now transportation troubles beset the colony, the newspaper reporting: "The steamer *Tycoon* has been laid up for repairs and our sole communication with Tacoma has been by means of the Dadisman and Adams launches.". . . "Our path along the shore toward Tacoma is being extended and improved and it is beginning to take on some of the aspects of a real road."

Morton did very well with THE DEMONSTRATOR for a time, as long as he paid strict attention to business. He was susceptible to outside interests, such as helping promote his friend, Henry George,

for mayor of New York. While in that city Morton neglected his newspaper and it died like the others.

What bothered Home the most or what gave the Tacoma LEDGER the most ammunition to fire at Home was nude bathing. The reports that the colony's beaches were filled with assorted human forms cavorting gaily in the altogether caused more than raised eybrows. Hundreds of LEDGER readers visited the place "just to make sure the truth or falsity of the reports."

What started most of the rumors was Henry Dadisman's purchase of two hundred acres adjoining Home. He opened the land to settlers, the first of whom were a number of Dukhobors from Russia. Members of the sect were accustomed to being undressed at home and naturally the same when

114

bathing. Home colonists who had enjoyed such bathing privileges but had been discreet or in semi-seclusion, were now emboldened to the same openness. But there was a complication. A small neighbor village named Lake Bay did not share in these liberal views. Residents there protested that four people, two men and two women, were bathing in the nude across the bay. Arrested for indecent exposure, the quartet was brought before Justice Tom Larkin in Lake Bay court. One witness was asked how she could be sure the bathers across the bay, nearly half a mile from her home, were nude. She replied: "I have a good pair of binoculars and I know how to use them." Worst of all, it turned out the complaining witness was a resident of Home.

By this time there was a new newspaper in the colony, the AGITATOR, run by Jay Fox and it was he who wrote the editorial mentioned earlier—"The Nudes and the Prudes". The Tacoma LEDGER made much of the editorial and drew attention to the various "atrocities" committed in Home in recent years, implying that Home was capable of allowing anything. In the winter of 1910-11 the plant of the Los Angeles TIMES was bombed by anarchists, Home was immediately suspected of harboring the guilty men. William J. Burns, head of his detective agency visited the colony under the guise of a book salesman. The evidence he picked up there led to further investigation and eventual arrest of two of the men involved in the bombing. One, Matthew Schmidt, had actually lived in Home at one time. The other was David Caplan, apprehended in New York on information given Burns by a boy named Donald Vose living in Home.

Burns later wrote a book enlarging on his experiences. The volume had a wide circulation and it did Home no good. It included such distorted paragraphs as "Home Colony is the nest of Anarchy in the United States. There are about 1200 of them living there without regard for a single decent thing in life. They exist in a state of free love and are notoriously unfaithful to the mates thus chosen, and are so crooked that even in this class of rogues there does not seem to be a single hint of honor."

A few months later Fox's editorial boomeranged. He was arrested for "tending to encourage or advo-cate disrespect for law or for a court of justice. The trial, held in Pierce County Courthouse, excited much comment in newspapers nationally. Every detail of life in Home Colony appeared lurid when reported in the LEDGER. Nothing was said of the industry, frugality and general peacefulness of the settlers.

Fox was convicted, the jury recommending leniency. He was sentenced to two months in the county jail and while serving the time, the State of Washington elected a new governor, Ernest Lister, who pardoned Fox unconditionally. The editor returned to Joe's Bay, but things were not the same. Unfavorable publicity had been too much for the colony. The Association was broken up and people began to move away.

Jay Fox and his wife remained with a number of other faithfuls. Fox died a few years ago but his wife still lives in the old home across the bay with an interest in painting. The colony area is again populated, sparsely enough, by summer residents and a few permanent homes. Home's post office was never reinstated under the same name but the area is served by another at the crossroads about half a mile away. It bears the name of the colony's old antagonist, Lake Bay. In retrospect, all things considered, there was no place like Home.

SOME COTTAGES closer to water front have been kept in repair, are occupied by summer residents. Apple trees, here in full bloom, attest agricultural proclivities of settlers. Venerable specimens are small remnants of orchard of seven hundred assorted fruit trees planted on this bench above Joe's Bay. Beach below was site of many stories told of residents in days when reputed nude bathing caused big furor in Tacoma press. One was about two young girls called to mother's knee. "You're getting to be big girls now and shouldn't go swimming without your bathing suit." Girls, later observed sun bathing on sand in nude, protested: "We **did** wear our suits while we were swimming."

LOOMIS, WASHINGTON

The first question the judge asked the mammoth lady was: "Did you intend to kill these men?" Her answer put an end to the proceedings. "Hell, no! If I had wanted to kill them, they'd be dead."

It all came about because sheepherders were anxious to get their woolies to summer pasture. Just above Loomis was a regular route by which the animals were moved but obstructing it were several ranches from which permit of access had to be obtained. One of these ranchers was a lady reputed to weigh some four hundred pounds, with a temper to match. One band of sheep moved too slowly across her property and she told the herders to hurry them along. When they still didn't go fast enough to suit her, she got her .30-.30 and sent several shots over the men's heads. They filed a complaint of attempted murder and the sheriff, unaware of the lady's bulk, went after her in his little buggy only to return to town for a dray wagon. After she was released, it was used again to take her home.

The first settlers in the Loomis area operated a large cattle station owned by Phelps Wadleigh and Co. in the early 1870s. In the bitter cold winter of '79-'80 their entire herd of 3,000 head perished, wiping the enterprise out of existence.

While the cattle station operated, helpers had started small farms on the side and when the station was gone, some of them stayed on. One was Alvin Thorpe, a man of experimental nature, a unique type in a day when harsh realities forced pioneers to take the accepted course. He got his supplies the hard way like everybody else, freighting them in, and one bad spot on the route was the crossing of the Columbia River. At this point a "ferry service" was operated by one "Wild Goose Bill," a fleet of three canoes conveying passengers and mail, cattle and horses swimming. On one of his trips Thorpe bought some peanuts to put in a crop. He planted them carefully but none ever came up and he later discovered the nuts had been roasted. He tried it again with green ones, grew several crops at a profit.

A rancher who made a more lasting imprint on history and gave the town its name, was J. H. Loomis who started what became a trading post and then a large general store in a somewhat accidental way. Seeing that many of the ranchers ran out of supplies before fresh shipments came in, he thought he would help them out by laying in extra goods for himself. When his shortsighted neighbors ran out, he would let them have what they needed at cost. Later, when joined by a partner Gus Waring, he was induced to

raise the selling price a little and buy larger amounts next time. The system proved the beginning of a long and profitable business.

Waring was a man of many talents. Educated at Harvard, friend and contemporary of Theodore Roosevelt and Owen Wister, author of *The Virginian*, he tried making a success at architecture in his father's office, gave it up and left for Portland, Oregon, with wife and three children. He worked on a railroad there for a short time and then headed for the Okanogan country, working first as a cowman, then barber, cook and carpenter before settling down as successful partner of Loomis. Their trading post became the largest business in town. Many "characters" of the Okanogan range were customers, two of the most famous being friends of Waring—"Okanogan" Smith and a missionary, called saintly by many, Father de Rouge.

Between Loomis and Oroville are the remains of a home, built in 1860, and orchard of Hiram F. Smith. He was prominent in local affairs, friendly with the Indians who gave him the name, "Okanogan." Elected to the legislature in 1865, he had to go through British Columbia, down the Fraser River by steamboat and cross Puget Sound to reach Olympia, the territorial capital. Returning to the Okanogan, he brought apple and other small fruit trees and peach seeds. These trees still grow at the site, are over forty feet tall, were the first orchard trees in an area now world famous for apple production.

During the early period of ranching in the area, various mines were discovered which gradually preempted farming in importance. A variety of metals was found in the hills around Riverside, the Solomon group working on a "huge body of ore" yielding as high as 50 percent lead with silver 25 to 70 ounces per ton along with some copper and gold. Tungsten was also found but ignored until the first World War when that metal came into demand. Other mines included Black Diamond, Whiskey Hill, Bull Frog, Golden Zone, Kit Carson, Six Eagles and Why Not?

Among the more famous was the Pinnacle which had a strange beginning. Original discoveries were made at the site in 1880. The first men to work it got out a lot of gold, took the metal outside to have it melted so it could be sold and never came back, leaving foreman James O'Connel to wonder about them. He waited a decent interval, then relocated the mine. When it was legally his, he named it the Pinnacle and he was soon called Pinnacle Jim. He was a strange, stubborn man. Where others carried six-shooters,

he carried a bowie knife and occasionally brandished a heavy gold-headed cane.

John O'Hearne was a close friend who became Pinnacle Jim's partner and they got along well except when drinking. One of their bitter arguments started in the saloon of the Wentworth Hotel and Jim rashly asked John outside to settle it. The latter carried a gun and it proved superior to the knife, Pinnacle Jim lying dead at the end of the battle. O'Hearne was tried for murder but freed as having shot in self-defense. Shortly after this came inquiry from a lawyer as to James O'Connel's whereabouts, an uncle having died and left him a large sum.

Such affrays were not uncommon in Loomis. Children sent to the grocery store had strict instructions to walk down the center of the street, not on sidewalks where they would encounter drunks weaving out of saloons and "those terrible painted ladies." They were to continue in a straight line until opposite the grocery and then to make an abrupt turn and go straight in.

Walter Allen who still lives in Loomis tells a story of those early days. "When I was a young man there was a district at the foot of the hill where there were several 'houses.' One of them, the best known, was called 'Big Edith's'. I had a friend who dared me to ride my cayuse right into the parlor and in those days I never backed down from a dare. We went down there on our horses and I rode up the front steps and through the front door with no trouble. Then I rode through the hall and came to a sort of screen of strings of beads hanging in front of the parlor and started to ride through. When my cayuse felt those beads swishing across her shoulders, she bolted. We went on through the parlor and through the back door that wasn't even open. There was a porch in back, quite high from the ground. My horse turned a somersault and I landed partly under her. Didn't break any bones, but was pretty shaken up."

Mail service encountered some difficulties getting started. The last distribution point was Marcus and when anyone left there for the Loomis area he was given what mail there was and was expected to carry it to town and dump it where it would be claimed by addressees. One young man made the trip rather often and went to the trouble of personally delivering letters, collecting 25 cents for each. It was soon noticed a large amount of the letters were worthless advertisements and inquiry revealed the enterprising youth was furnishing a mailing list to advertisers in Marcus.

Loomis had an official post office after 1888. Judge H. Noyes, who had come out from Springfield. Massachusetts, and bought an interest in the trading post of Waring and Loomis, was first postmaster. A branch office was established for ranchers on a farm owned by Jess Huntley. He was a busy man, abrupt and irascible, and although holding a mail franchise he was unwilling to take the time to wait on people

GAUNT CONCRETE SHELL identified as early power generator for mines, sawmills and crushers, incongruous in now unpopulated area near Loomis. Water provided ample power, was carried down to plant from mountains above by flume, remains showing above structure. After passing through generators inside building, water was carried away through now yawning hole in floor. Small settlement grew up around plant, even a jewelry store operated by Bill Kepp. A laundry was established by Henry Decent so close to the stream it was washed out in the first heavy spring freshet.

or deliver letters. When a bag of mail came in, he would dump it in a large box on the counter and let everyone dig through it. One day he was getting ready to plow and a man asked him to look for a letter he was expecting. Jess retorted sharply—couldn't any damn fool see he was busy and couldn't he look for it himself? The man took offense, reported the incident and the postal authorities wrote a caustic letter to Huntley, ordering him to deliver all letters to patrons and give no back talk. Gathering all mail and equipment into a bag, he drove to the office at Loomis and angrily dumped the contents in the middle of the floor. "There's your damned post office!" he fumed.

There was social life of an elevating sort in Loomis and one cultural influence was a fine band. It was made up to a large extent of men employed in the Palmer Mountain mines. The Company provided tailored uniforms, the band practiced in the Eagles' Hall and performed at affairs in neighboring towns as well, being paid $100 per performance.

While all the mining excitement was going on, there was a steady amount of ranching in the surrounding hills. This did not provide the same sort of thrills that mining did but it had its compensations. There was young Joseph Rice in Spokane who yearned to be a rancher and had ideas of homesteading on Palmer Mountain. He hesitated to ask his sweetheart Helen Fitch to marry him and go to such a wild country but she was willing. They were married in 1903 and homesteaded on Palmer Mountain four and a half miles from Loomis.

At first Joe had to work in Tillman's Sawmill to get started but this was a stroke of fortune as he fell heir to a lot of cull lumber and with it built their first home. Later the couple got enough money for a more pretentious place and the first home became a chickenhouse. Funds for improvement came slowly but Helen and Joe were hard workers, determined to make a success. They planted wheat and in the fall a thresher crew would arrive at the farm on its rounds, the threshers' wives in at the big dinner and carrying

DECAYING RUINS OF CABINS built in 1890s high on Gold Hill above Loomis. Great excitement prevailed when first discoveries were made but cooled somewhat when difficulty of moving ore to mills became evident. John Reed and "Irish" Dan McCauley found gold in a piece of quartz on the steep mountainside about 1890. They had no capital for hard rock mining and sold out to a company naming itself Gold Hill Mining Co. It started operations, had great difficulty getting ore down mountain to mills at Loomis. Road was constructed but washed out at every rain or when snow melted. First enthusiasm generated building of small settlement just prior to turn of century. Gold return was finally judged too small to justify better road or building of mill at site, entire project abandoned around 1910. At present, steep winding road to ruins is badly washed, long hike required to reach remnant of short-lived gold rush. Almost all trees are second growth; virgin stand cut when mining was carried on, was spruce, larch, pines with scattering of Douglas fir.

LOADED FREIGHT WAGONS pulling into Loomis from Oroville — photo in collection of Walter Allen of Loomis. On driver's seat are Mr. and Mrs. Frank Schull. Dick Sutton says: "Frank did a lot of freighting, mostly of ore to Spokane. On the return trips he carried lots of whiskey and wine for the saloons. Some of the saloonkeepers were Jack Long, Jimmie Kenchlow, Johnnie Woodard and George Judd." Man on ground holding dog is identified as Al Carroll. Perambulator is mounted on rear wagon.

away tales of the Rices' baked beans. Helen had her own recipe and grew her own beans from a "start" brought along from Spokane. The variety name for these succulent beans, a little larger than ordinary, was never known. They were just "Helen's Beans."

After wheat was threshed, Helen and Joe made frequent trips south to Tonasket with loads of grain, starting about four in the morning to get to market early. And Helen made thirty loaves of bread at a time, selling them around the area. She kept a large flock of chickens, a six-foot fence protecting them from marauding coyotes. The eggs and churned butter also helped out in income.

The water supply was a spring at the bottom of a very steep slope from the house. After staggering up the bank a few times, Joe rigged up a contraption to ease the situation. He equipped a large wheel from a broken washing machine with a cable to which a bucket was attached. When the wheel was turned, the cable took the bucket down hill and overturned it in the spring. Continued turning of the wheel brought the full bucket back.

The distance to Loomis was usually covered by buggy in summer, sleigh in winter. If the snow was frozen hard, the latter with no brakes could not be used on one steep hill. So Joe would have to walk for the mail. He carried a shovel to open the trail below and to put it to good advantage on the steepest pitch, he sat on the scoop and slid down.

There were other breaks from drudgery. In winter, a little lake higher up Palmer Mountain froze practically solid. The couple cut ice and stored the harvest in an icehouse they built. In summer, ice cream parties were often held, either at the Rice home or neighbors.

Sometimes Helen took horseback rides around the country when she felt the need to get away for a change. Her favorite mount was a mare named Tootsie, brown with three white stockings, and no one else could ride her. The two would have a wonderful time, leaping over logs and low fences.

And the dances at Loomis were the best of all. They danced the favorites like "Black Hawk Waltz" and "Three Step" but there were enough Swede loggers wanting some Hambos and Schottisches. Helen says when one of these Norsemen with a few drinks in him would whirl her around in a Hambo, she could hardly stand for dizziness at the finish.

Once there was a masquerade and she wanted Joe to dress as an Indian. There being no costume rental in those days, she cut a picture of an Indian suit from a mail order catalog and copied it as best she could. She insisted he have long black hair and she achieved this by cutting off the luxurious tail of a white horse, dyeing it black and sewing it to a skull cap. Joe won first prize.

But the homestead was increasingly a burden and after both Joe and Helen had long spells of sickness, they abandoned the old place in 1914. Long years later they realized $120 by selling the property to a sheepman. By then the buildings had fallen into decay and Loomis was declining to the point where all property values were next to nothing.

The last ores were taken from the Palmer Mountain Tunnel mine in 1927 and this marked the finish of Loomis as a going town. It is quietly peaceful today with only a handful of people. Helen Rice, now a widow, lives in Portland and furnished the author with much of the information about the Okanogan area.

MARYHILL, WASHINGTON

In its journey to the sea the Columbia River makes its final turn west through timbered mountains and then a desert of barren rocks and cliffs. No spectacle could be more astonishing than the immense gray castle sprawling high on one of the river's bordering palisades.

The pile is best viewed from across the river on the Oregon side. The observing traveler up the Columbia gorge may well ask: "What, for goodness sakes — is that?" That, the traveler's guide will usually say, is Maryhill Castle. "It was built by Sam Hill, son of the railroad tycoon, Jim Hill, as a monument to his mother." However, Samuel was not the son of the "Empire Builder", James Hill, but his son-in-law. He was a trusted employee of Jim Hill at first, then in 1888 married the oldest daughter of his boss — Mary Hill. Jim did have a son Louis, but the brothers-in-law were not overly compatible. The unanswered questions are — did Sam Hill build the castle as a memorial for his wife, as a palace-residence, or did he foresee its ultimate use as a museum?

Samuel Hill majored in law at Harvard and was admitted to the bar in 1880. Jim Hill engaged young Sam to help him fight some legal battles, then admitted him to his giant railroad combine, allowing him to carry on his own legal practice and make some profitable investments. He traveled extensively, making friends in high places everywhere. One of these was Queen Marie of Roumania, who would later dedicate his castle on the cliffs.

Samuel Hill was personable, shrewd and eccentric. Shortly before the end of World War I, he bought some 7,000 acres of rock and sagebrush which surprised no one who knew him but did intrigue them. When Sam announced he was going to set up a colony for Quakers from Belgium, he raised more questions than he answered. Was the project a purely benevolent gesture or was he planning to add more millions to his coffers with cheap foreign labor?

The ground planned for the colony on the Washington side of the Columbia was opposite Biggs Junction in Oregon. The site included a long established village called Columbus, an agricultural center, the gently sloping ground on the river's shore deep and fertile — a bench extending about half a mile to suddenly rising cliffs of barren rock and scanty soil only a little less arable. A wagon road wound up a steep gully to the summit and along this the colonists would be quartered in cottages Hill would build. On both sides of the steeply sloping valley rose vertical cliffs, partly separated into palisades, each surmounted by a rounded dome of rocks, soil and sand. On the top of the highest one, Samuel Hill, in 1913, started construction of what would be the most conspicuous structure anywhere along the Columbia, an imposing feudal-type castle, such as those that stand along the Rhine.

LITTLE CHURCH was serving community of Columbus when Samuel Hill appeared, turned town into supply center for building of Maryhill Castle, changing name of town to Maryhill. Tycoon kept church in good condition during "occupation" but it has deteriorated. Building is set on low bench of river bank, grass and trees showing fertility of narrow band of soil, barren hills making up background.

SIMULATED STONEHENGE—one of Sam Hill's projects in connection with castle—"exact" replica of mysterious place of ancient worship or astronomy near Salisbury, England. In original only few of pillars retain connecting slabs, only two of original five gigantic trilithons surrounding central altar or sacrificial stone. Hill sent engineer, astronomer, other workmen to England to measure and make plaster casts of original rocks, bringing back molds for duplicating them. Hill's interest in Stonehenge stemmed from visit to original where guide informed him flat rock in center was used for human sacrifice. As a Quaker, he was particularly impressed, comparing such useless slaughter of human life to that of war. It was then he conceived idea of erecting similar structure as memorial to war dead. Legend on horizontal slab in center reads: "In memory of Soldiers and Sailors of Klickitat County who gave their lives in defense of their Country. This monument is erected in the hope that others inspired by the example of their valor and their heroism may share in that love of liberty and burn with that fire of Patriotism which death alone can quench."

During the next several years parcels of Quakers came from Belgium and other European countries to look at the rocky ground, searingly hot in summer, swept by icy winds in winter — looked briefly and went away. A scant few did settle for a while, making some effort to coax a crop from the stark land, but they also departed.

While the Samuel Hills lived in a stately mansion in Seattle, construction of the castle went on

regardless of the failure of the colonization plans. It was known almost from the start that it would be called Maryhill. Was it named for the wife, Mary Hill? One point seems a fact — although Mary never saw the pile at any time, even from a distance, gossip had it she was a resident, almost a prisoner, a woman with a failing mind.

While the exact purpose of the vast building was never known, possibly even to Sam Hill, it was almost completed by 1926 and in the fall of that year came Queen Marie to dedicate Maryhill Castle. Before leaving Portland for the ceremony, the Queen attended the International Livestock Exposition, sitting with her royal party in a special box. The group made a worthy subject for the newsreels and the royal lady was not above making pin money by endorsing beauty products.

And at Maryhill she found ready a platform erected in front of the gaunt, gray shell. From it one could look east up the Columbia, south into the gorge and down many miles of the river's westerly flow. After the outdoor ceremony everyone hurried indoors for more convivial celebration, then departed to allow workmen to continue plastering walls.

Construction went on a few more years and when completed the interior included electricity,

SAM HILL'S CASTLE dedicated by Queen Marie of Roumania on a dreary, gray early winter day as indicated here. This is conventional rear of structure, more ornate facade commanding almost limitless view of Columbia gorge, shown dimly in background.

plumbing and other refinements foreign to the traditional castle. Samuel Hill died February 6, 1931 in Portland, his ashes taken to Maryhill and deposited in a tomb on the rocky cliff. It was supposed he had not made up his mind to what use the castle would be put, yet in his will he left a handsome endowment in the hands of trustees of the state to perpetuate the building as a museum.

In 1940 Maryhill Museum was opened to the public. It attracts an increasing number of visitors each summer, offering extensive and varied exhibits of painting, sculpture and Indian artifacts. The Throne Room is displayed, complete with furniture including the royal throne itself, all transported from the now vanished Kingdom of Roumania.

PEASANT SHELTER at Maryhill. It was Samuel Hill's wish that the countryside surrounding his feudal castle be filled by Belgian Quaker immigrants. Many did come, a few remained to eke out miserable existence on stony, dry soil of hillsides. Then even these were forced to go elsewhere. Land affords few near-level spots, bluffs in background descending to Columbia River in giant stair steps.

HE WENT DOWN WITH HIS SHIP

Young Jimmy Kyes seemed to feel a great compassion for the small seedling. He loved to spend his summers roaming the snowy-peaked Cascade Range in northern Washington and this day in the 1920s he stood at the edge of a tarn, a tiny high country lake, snow still mantling its fringes. Growing there was a little alpine fir, its foliage displaying the blue coloring sometimes found in this species.

Jimmy wanted to nurture the struggling little tree and he lifted it from the earth very carefully so as not to disturb the roots, carrying it down to the old mining town of Monte Cristo where he was staying. He planted it in the garden of the hotel there and it was his to care for. In 1923, while in the U.S. Forest Service as lookout on the summit of Mt. Pilchuck, he met Mr. and Mrs. H. A. Annen of Everett, Washington who would later carry on Jimmy's protective efforts by building a fence around the tree.

James E. Kyes was born in Everett and educated in grade and high schools there. He studied at the University of Washington, specializing in mining engineering, and a year later was appointed to the U.S. Naval Academy at Annapolis, graduating in 1930.

After serving on the carriers *Saratoga* and *Ranger* he returned to Annapolis to complete a two-year postgraduate course in engineering and then assumed command of the U.S.S. Destroyer *Leary,* taking it on convoy and patrol duty. On Christmas eve 1943, the vessel was returning to port where Kyes would be given a new command. A message was received that an aircraft carrier in the North Atlantic was under attack by German submarines. The *Leary* was ordered to go to her assistance.

As the destroyer drew near the carrier she was struck by two torpedoes fired from the enemy wolf pack, the vessel breaking into three sections and sinking rapidly. Commander Kyes was donning his preserver when he saw his negro messboy was without one. Kyes put his around the boy and went down with his ship as it foundered.

James Kyes, who held the rank of full commander for two years at the time of his death, received posthumous honors including the Navy Cross for heroism displayed during the sinking of his ship. Already held were the Purple Heart, Bronze American Defense Service Medal, European-African Campaign and Middle East Area Campaign honors. Another mark of recognition for his courage was the naming of the destroyer *Commander James Kyes* in 1946, which was christened by Kyes wife Frances, their son David beside her. An even more enduring memorial is the 7,239 foot mountain seven miles west of Monte Cristo named Kyes Peak, Jimmy and a companion making the first recorded ascent of the rocky spire in 1920.

And the alpine fir still grows in the old hotel grounds.

NEAR FLATTENED RUINS of hotel on Dumas Street in one time mining camp of Monte Cristo, stands fir tree planted by James Kyes in boyhood. About time of his death picket fence was placed around tree and later this monument erected memorializing heroic death of Commander Kyes at sea.

OLD TIME PHOTO of Monte Cristo. Extensive mines, mills were served directly by railroad. Present day Monte Cristo, while no longer important as gold mining center is mecca for campers, fishermen, mountain climbers.

ALPINE PHLOX, botanically Phlox Douglasii, forms dense mats of deep pink to white flowers, spreading color over large areas of Cascade Mountains at altitudes of from 4,000 to 7,000 feet.

LETTER IS FRAMED and secured to picket fence around tree.

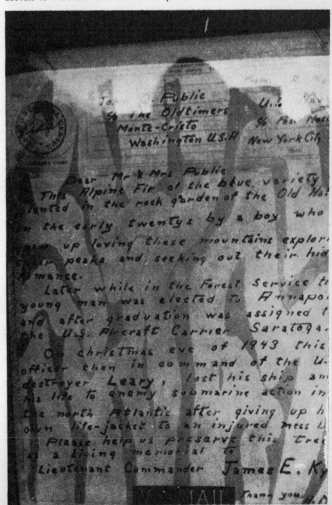

TIDEFLAT TABLEAU

Nahcotta, Wash.

"Folks, you are now in Oysterland, U.S.A."

"I don't care about oysters. I can't eat the slithery things."

"Well, I'm sorry, lady. If I was anything more than the conductor of this train I'd get you some crepes suzette."

"When does this train get to Nahcotta? It's over an hour late and my sister will be frozen to death waiting for it."

"Oh I don't know. She's probably keeping warm and happy eating oysters. They're fine for the blood."

Some such spirited conversation might have taken place on the Ilwaco and Shoalwater Bay Railroad or was it the Ilwaco Railway and Navigation Co. or maybe this week the Oregon and Washington Railway and Navigation Co.? Sometimes the "noon" train would come puff-puffing into the tiny station at Nahcotta on time but more often it would arrive at 11 or perhaps 1. While travelers got nervous, residents understood that schedules depended upon the ocean tides at the mouth of the Columbia River since the main reason for the existence of the narrow-gauge line was its connection with the ferry from Astoria, Oregon.

The Chinooks were the original settlers at Nahcotta, their villages once dotting the entire North Peninsula. An ample food supply was guaranteed them by the millions of oysters growing wild on the flats of the harbor. Innumerable food middens still evident today show oyster shells their main content. No primitive tools are found with them as oysters require only to be picked up at low tide and pried open.

The abundance of bivalves and fish attracted whites too, the first to arrive at Nahcotta as a resident being J. A. Morehead in 1890. He was shortly joined by James R. Morrison and eight other men, some with families to form a fair-sized village. With later settlers came a store, Morehead building one to contain the post office, Morrison being the first to handle the mail. There was unanimous agreement in naming the town for old Chief Nahcotta who was still camping on the outskirts. While lacking the power of Chief Concomly at nearby Chinookville, Nahcotta displayed the same friendly attitude toward the whites.

In 1899 the town became the terminus of the short line railroad running on narrow-gauge tracks which over the years had so many names the Nahcotta station master A. P. Osborne sometimes forgot just who he was working for. By 1908 the train was running on a regular schedule and continued to until 1930. Until recently traces of trackage were visible in places along the line.

Once boasting a weekly newspaper edited by John Phillips, Nahcotta is today a resort settlement with two small industries—a sweater knitting "factory" and one punching and stringing oyster shells for nurturing baby shellfish.

OLD OYSTER BARGE, one of once large fleet at Nahcotta beached away from water except during flood tides. Flat-decked vessel took large empty baskets to anchorage over oyster beds. Baskets were filled at low tide and reloaded on barges which floated at high tide and were towed to oyster plants. In background is Willapa Bay, early termed Shoalwater Bay. In middle distance are rotting pilings, all that remain of large railroad terminal dock. Body of water, considered to be prehistoric channel of Columbia River, offered exact condition of alternating fresh and salt water demanded by oyster. While tide is out bay is freshened by flow from many rivers. Returning tides obstruct streams temporarily providing high salinity. Sometimes strong offshore winds and high tides force in oversupply of salty water, preventing breeding, even killing some stock.

OLD POSTCARD shows Nahcotta when narrow-gauge railroad had terminus here. Hotel at end of rails was important then, has vanished now. Water supply was pumped by windmill and stored in tank left.

NIGHTHAWK, WASHINGTON

Hiram Smith, called "Okanogan Smith" by friendly Indians of the Similkameen Valley, was elected to the territorial legislature of Washington in 1860. After serving one term he settled on his ranch near Chesaw, tended his orchard for 40 years and died peacefully, surrounded by his many white and Indian friends. He left a considerable estate with no will in evidence and his affairs were in such a confused state a lawyer was engaged to untangle them.

He did and made a good thing of it—attorney James M. Haggerty of Portland, Oregon. He completed the legal work, established headquarters at Loomis and started a systematic search for mineral prospects.

Not a man to work with his bare hands, Haggerty planned to become a wealthy miner by his wits and he was right. Newspapers of the day stated: "Haggerty appropriated three mining claims which turned out to be good producers." These mines were strung along the Similkameen in an area where nighthawks, sometimes called "bull bats," were very prevalent and the supply center that sprang up here was named for the birds.

The Ruby, Kaaha and the more famous Six Eagle mines were among those developed by Haggerty. Had

he confined his activities to them and not let his tongue wag so much when he was drinking, he would have been spared some grief. He had moved from Loomis but liked to visit his former haunts and brag about his success as a mine operator. And if he had only stopped there, accepted some scorn and let it go at that, he would have gained some stature. But he made a fatal mistake one evening in his cups at a Loomis saloon, an ill-timed comment about a mine on the hill above Loomis.

The Palmer Mountain Tunnel mine was of more than doubtful merit and all the local gentry were aware of it. In spite of this, the owners had sent a John Wentworth to Portland to cajole innocent investors into sinking money into the property. The population of Loomis and the mine owners rationalized that selling this stock was not really dishonest, that further development so financed would certainly turn up a rich vein that might be the making of everybody in the town. Gilbert Alder was one of the residents who, while waiting for this to happen, had put in his time farming and raised a crop of sugar cane. The long hot summer matured it enough for Alder to make some molasses and he proudly brought a jug of it to the saloon to show it off.

OLD BARN, says Leo W. Andrus of Nighthawk, was built by father known in community as "Daddy" Andrus. Dating from 1900, venerable structure still serves purpose. International road runs past barn, crosses Similkameen on bridge close by.

RUINS OF OLD NIGHTHAWK MILL are composed, in general, of rusting machinery. Town itself lay in valley in middle distance beside Similkameen River. Surrounding hills are typical of Okanogan Highlands, those near town are sparsely timbered, with heavier stands farther away.

This night he stepped up to the bar, ordered a drink and displayed his jug of black molasses as an example of what the area could produce. Haggerty felt a great urge to push his importance into the conversation and pompously declared:

"Well, it's a good thing Loomis can produce molasses. It'll never turn out any gold from that damn mine."

It would have been better for Haggerty if he had tried to shoot somebody. At his words several men jumped up, threw him to the floor while Alder poured the contents of his jug over the spread-eagled form. Another man rushed upstairs to the business quarters of one of the girls and grabbed her pillow. The cotton slip was quickly split and the feathers shaken in snowy humiliation over the sticky coating of blackstrap.

OLD PICTURE reproduced in Okanogan *Independent* shows group dressed in Sunday best gathered outside Log Cabin Saloon in Chesaw, few miles from Nighthawk. Sign on Chop House at right advertises meals at all hours, 25¢.

Chesaw was mining and farming center, never very large. Main feature was hostelry Bungalow run by hospitable Chinese who gave town name. Bungalow was open to all travelers, owners respected in a day when Orientals were generally despised.

Log Cabin Saloon in Chesaw

128

NIGHTHAWK HOTEL was built by Ed McNull for drummers in boom days. Later when Nighthawk Mill was running "full blast" Ewing family took it over as boardinghouse for mill workers. It stood vacant for many years near the little grocery store operated for 25 years by Mr. and Mrs. Lynn Sullivan who now live on Palmer Lake a few miles south.

Haggerty was allowed to slither to his feet but was jerked off them and put astride a hitching rail that had been yanked loose and given a rough ride out of town. His face was never seen again in Loomis. Whenever he had business in Spokane, he avoided the town and went by way of Oroville. When he died years later, he asked that he be buried at Nighthawk—"But don't take me through Loomis."

Nighthawk had been built where the ground was level but the main producing mine was across the Similkameen. A footbridge was good enough for the early traffic but when it became inadequate, a ferry was put into operation by William Berry, an observing and enterprising man. After several passengers had asked him: "Where can a fellow get a drink in this town?" he started a saloon with financial help from his brother Joe. It was a success in summer when the dry and dusty wind blew, a success in winter when at forty below a man needed warming.

About the turn of the century the Vancouver, Victoria and Eastern ran its line through Nighthawk and the town looked forward to a rosy future. For a time it seemed to be coming true as all heavy equipment for the mines including that for twelve-mile-distant Loomis, was rail shipped to Nighthawk. This meant freighting lines were based here, large livery stables maintained, as well as hotel, store and several more saloons.

When business of transporting mine equipment and passengers was flourishing, the rail line, a branch of the Wenatchee, Oroville and Great Northern, ran from its connection at Spokane through Danville, Molson, Chesaw, Nighthawk and Hedley, B. C., terminating at Princeton where it connected with the Canadian Pacific. By 1950, the line had been cut to a spur fifty-odd miles long from Oroville to Hedley. Freight was limited to a small amount of farm equipment and produce with a passenger or two now and then, the train coming to Nighthawk twice a week, the engineer always on the lookout for a flag signal that someone wanted to get on. A tiny one-room customs office stood beside the single track.

Now even the Tuesday and Friday arrivals of the train have ceased. The tracks are gone, so is the customs house. There is only one business in Nighthawk now—the little general store.

ORIENT, WASHINGTON

Gold had been discovered on the shoulder of First Thought Mountain and there was a certainty something big would come of it. Alec Ireland platted the town of Orient in 1900 and Mr. and Mrs. George Temple drove a wagon there from Bossburg which was then a thriving place, establishing a homestead the following year.

Gold hopes were slow being realized. There were no loose placer grains in the stream and it took time to interest big money for hard rock mining. Ireland, Billy Stiles and the Temples were at first the only residents of Orient, the latter proving up their claim and in 1904 receiving their ownership papers signed by President Theodore Roosevelt. They worked hard on the farm and Temple started a stage line from Bossburg to Republic, and up to Greenwood and Phoenix—a big mining camp in Canada—and Grand Forks, also across the border.

As the mines developed in a big way, Temple got much business hauling machinery, particularly for the Easter Sunday and Little Gem Mines. There were several other prosperous operations, one named after the mountain looming over the town—First Thought. This mine was also the main course of the economic development of Orient although its name came from another mine, the Orient.

Two quartz mills were set up, one at the First Thought, the other at the Gold Stake. By this time Orient had grown into a bustling town. "It was a very lively place," says Mrs. Leslie Gourlie, daughter of the Temples, "We had five saloons, two big livery stables, several stores and three hotels. These were whipsaw-shacky places, called by their owners names—Mrs. Reynolds, Mrs. Hayes and Mrs. Arnold. All three were pretty good cooks, doing the best they could under the circumstances. The best food, however, was available to the men at the mine cook houses. Most of the single ones ate there, slept in the bunk houses and lived quiet lives during the week. But on Saturday nights they'd come down to town and cut loose. What wild times they had, spending most of their money just that one night. There were plenty of loose women and lots of hard liquor to help them do it, too."

When the Great Northern Railroad made plans to run its line to Republic, George Temple ceded the right of way through his land, as he did later for the highway. During the hectic days of railroad construction there was a boom, the hotels full and Mrs. Temple feeding many of the men in the tiny homestead cabin.

When asked if Orient is permanently finished, Mrs. Gourlie replied: "Oh, no. There is lots of gold in the mines yet. They have barely scratched the surface. Most are down only about a hundred and fifty feet, none more than three hundred. All we need is an advance in the price of gold. Of course the machinery is getting all rusty and likely will be badly out of date. But the people who are still living here are hopeful that something good will happen to the town. We really haven't had any activity since the first World War."

ORIENT FIRE DEPARTMENT did its best when fire broke out in Orient but best was often not enough. Many buildings burned because of tinder dry condition and insufficient water pressure. Fancy tower in background is crowning glory of school which once held several hundred pupils. Structure was fixed up several years ago and is in good repair but now serves only handful of children.

THE TOWN THAT OYSTERS BUILT

Oysterville, Wash.

The pilot of the river steamer looked with disdain at all the industry displayed in harvesting the flat, curly-edged shells in the low tide mud. "It's sure a good thing I don't like oysters," he said, "or I'd eat 'em and I hate the damn things!"

There are deeply etched opinions about the succulence of oysters but the early workers on the Pacific Ocean beach cared little about that. They had a tide flat gold mine in millions of the bivalves lying there defenseless in the oozy muck just waiting to be picked, shipped to market and opened before eyes bulging in anticipation. "Too good for Indians," they said.

When the white man first came to Willapa (then called Shoalwater) Bay he found its south arm one vast field of oyster beds. The native marine bivalves were the small, delicately flavored *ostrea lurida.* For them and the later introduced Pacific oysters, the bay offered perfect conditions for reproduction and growth. The oyster requires an almost exactly formulated mixture of fresh and salt water and the saline content must vary at specific intervals. Willapa Bay, like very few harbors on the Washington coast, offers the right mixture, an inflow of fresh water supplied by the Naselle and other rivers while the tide is at full or receding, supplying an alternating flood of salt water from the ocean. Native Chinook tribes had long made the shellfish a major item of food but this local consumption had hardly dented the supply.

The first white to see commercial possibilities here was very likely young Virginia-born Charles Russell. For several decades the United States had been on an oyster binge, consuming huge quantities in all forms, appetite whetted by rumor that oysters would enlarge or resuscitate the libido. Russell was aware that during the time the non-ambulatory oyster was exposed by outgoing tides it closed its valves tightly, excluding desiccating air. He also knew this normally short hibernation period could be extended.

The only entrance to Willapa Bay was at the north end, some 30 miles north of the Columbia River from which Russell would ship his oysters to San Francisco. In prehistoric times the Columbia had at least partially emptied its waters into the now separated northern estuary, the old channel now low and watery or marshy in spots. This route was used by Indians for centuries as a portage connection from the Columbia. In the summer of 1851, with a partner, Russell took a canoe over this route to the bay and at low tide walked over the flats, easily collecting a load of oysters which he took back to Astoria. The cargo reached San Francisco in good condition and was sold at a good price. When gourmets there clamored for more they expanded the life purpose of *ostrea lurida.*

Heartened by visions of success Russell put into action ambitious plans to improve the southern access route to the source of supply. Meanwhile he learned that a Capt. Fielstad had run a schooner direct from San Francisco to Willapa Bay, entering

OLD POSTCARD version of Oysterville's famed courthouse, forcibly entered by rival residents of South Bend across bay to remove county records.

PACIFIC HOUSE, Oysterville's largest hostelry of which no trace remains. Likely not all people in old photo were patrons though hotel did big business while town flourished.

131

LINES OF PILING, weathered to silvery gray, indicate location of wharf where sailing ships loaded live oysters for San Francisco markets. Here also were tied barges that placed empty picking baskets, later retrieving filled ones at next high tide. Long unused baskets now rust away, half-filled with sand, oyster shells. Willapa Bay is in background.

by the easy but farther north entrance south of Cape Shoalwater. Hard on his stern were the schooners *Sea Serpent* and *Robert Bruce*, other ships following. One was delayed by a storm when sailing south, the cargo spoiling, and one burned to the water's edge by a mutinous cook. The oyster rush was on.

In 1854 R. H. Espy of Wisconsin arrived at the bay to locate and supply logs for pilings. A man of strong religious principles he invited I. A. Clark, of similar background and who had some money, to become his partner. While scouring the shores of the bay they became enthused with the possibilities of commercially canning the abundantly available oysters. Abandoning the piling venture Espy and Clark built a log house on the spot where the town of Oysterville would develop, the location between sea and bay near the northern tip of the peninsula.

Then came the brothers John and Thomas Crellin to share in the oyster profits, John establishing a mercantile store. With rapid growth the little town was demanding mail service and got it in 1865, the post office set up in a corner of Crellin's store. Mail had to be carried over devious Indian trails from Chinookville.

After a few years of such primitive service Lewis Loomis, who was to become a big man in Oysterville's history, secured the mail contract. In 1875 he and his partners built the 110-foot, screw-drive *General Canby* at Willapa at the northern end of the bay, the vessel undoubtedly named for the ill-fated army officer who died at the hands of Captain Jack in the still fresh Modoc War (see *Tales the Western Tombstones Tell*). As soon as launched, the ship was put into service carrying mail and passengers from Astoria, Oregon, to Ilwaco, Washington, where they were dumped on the beach.

132

OLD ANCHOR AND BUOY are few of marine items in machine repair shops of near-defunct Columbia River Smokery.

If time and tide were right, a stagecoach that was humanely called "clumsy" picked them up.

Powered by eight broncos the wooden vehicle was closed at the ends, passengers admitted from one side. There were seats inside for five but what was that when twenty people climbed in? Two would cling to the mail-loaded boot at the rear, others perched on top and when all were aboard the coach bumped and swayed onto the wet sand recently vacated by the Pacific, then headed north.

In recent years the North Jetty at the mouth of the Columbia River has diverted river-born sands northward, building up a beach far-famed for length and width. In the 1870s the beach was narrower and the stagecoach was sometimes forced to take to the dunes, humping itself over the sandy hillocks and small pieces of driftwood. The region has a heavy annual rainfall and when frequent ocean storms lashed the coast those unlucky passengers on top must have deeply regretted embarking for Oysterville.

The village had become seat of Pacific County some time before the first schoolhouse was erected, lumber for which was California redwood shipped north on a schooner that returned with canned and smoked oysters. The arrival at Oysterville of the ship was celebrated by a general holiday. When all sobered up the entire town joined with the hired carpenters in putting up the little schoolhouse and painting it bright red. The first teacher was James Pell.

Ten years later, with growing pains subsiding, residents began to think of social festivities, something more dramatic than box lunch suppers and community dances. With all that water around why not stage a yacht race? After several small but successful annual events, the town went all out in 1876 with a well advertised regatta that attracted such famous racers as the sloop *Artemisia* owned by wealthy Ed Loomis. The affair attracted the entire population of the coastal area, and a large contingent of "city folk" arrived from Portland on the specially-chartered steamer *Gussie Telfair*.

Shortly after Oysterville became a village much of Washington was being harassed by rampaging Indians, the troubles threatening to explode into a full scale war. Towns and settlements along the west coast were thrown into panic, most of them erecting blockhouses. Oysterville did so, hastily building a log fort near the water. While the structure still lacked a roof, townsfolk realized their placid, friendly Chinook neighbors were laughing at their efforts and sheepish carpenters left the project unfinished.

In the expanding community by the bay the main street was called "Front," built largely on rocks brought in as ship ballast and piled along the edge of the harbor to be close to canneries and vessels. The village so near the water was vulnerable to extremes of high tides which all too often demolished whole buildings when high winds combined with high water. One storm took away the roofless fort.

Oysterville was the seat of Pacific County very early but for years no actual courthouse was built. In 1860 a man named Dupenny was accused of murdering the Indian wife of a neighbor, William McGunnegill. Constable Espy was forced to board the suspect in his home temporarily before transferring him to the more secure Army barracks jail at Fort Vancouver. Even so nothing was done about the situation until 1869. Then the county erected a substantial two-story structure set on a foundation of squared logs.

During the decade of 1880-1890 Oysterville enjoyed its greatest days of glory. The first really adequate wharf was extended into deep water in

'84, another built in '88. A newspaper, first in the county, was established in 1887. Called the *Pacific Journal*, it was edited by "Alf" Bowen.

The 1890s were not "gay" for the oyster center of North Peninsula. The shellfish were found elsewhere on Willapa Bay and rival town South Bend had grown up on the shore opposite. The upstart had the unfair advantage of being on the mainland at a strategic point in the stagecoach system, and close to forests, it soon had a large lumbering industry.

In the fall elections of 1892 South Bend was declared the new seat of Pacific County and all records were ordered delivered there. Oysterville ignored the summons, the town's hardy, brine-soaked citizenry refusing to give up the honor of county seat, claiming the South Bend electorate had illegally included residents of all surrounding communities. Authorities were successful in obtaining an injunction but before this could be put into effect, ambitious promoters of the rival town forced the issue.

On February 5, 1893, a cold day dawning over a snowy scene unusual for the peninsula, two steamboats docked at Oysterville. Eighty-five men swarmed off and converged on the courthouse. Auditor Phil D. Barney was the first to assess the invasion and when South Bend leader John Hudson kicked in the courthouse door, the enraged Barney broke off a chair leg and valiantly attempted to defend the records by cracking several enemy skulls. A witness to the fracas was 6-year-old C. J. Espy who says, "I hid behind the door and was scared to death but I saw the action." Overpowered, Barney was forced to watch the removal of all paper except that in his vault, the key to which he steadfastly refused to give up. Later, however, other Oysterville authorities persuaded him that further resistance would be futile.

Although later investigation proved the South Bend election was highly irregular, counting ballots of transient loggers and other non-registered voters, the situation was by now irreversible. Staggered by the blow Oysterville mourned the loss of the courthouse for two years then decided to put the

LITTLE BAPTIST CHURCH was built in 1870s by Oysterville's founder, R. H. Espy, photo made some years ago. When author returned to Oysterville in 1967 to make more recent one, he found church being restored. Repairs are being made by son C. J. Espy who reported that services were held until "community interest dwindled to a point that continuance of regular services seem inappropriate. Sunday School was maintained until about 1942. Since then occasional funerals and weddings have been held there. There seems to be no immediate or early rejuvenation of service activities, only a hope by the writer and his family who, for sentimental reasons are giving some attention to the upkeep of the physical edifice."

INTERIOR of Baptist Church in Oysterville. No one, including builder's son C. J. Espy can explain why pews are divided in center. He does report structure never had electricity except temporarily in recent years when church was lit for wedding by extension cables powering borrowed light fixtures. Original light came from two large chandeliers with circles of lamps, suspended from ceiling on ropes, lowered for filling with kerosene and wick-trimming. After years of faithful service one crashed down on pews. Though accident happened in midweek, potential danger to worshippers caused removal of chandeliers and use of small wall lamps seen here. When founder-builder R. H. Espy died his casket was squeezed into tiny sanctuary leaving little space for passage.

OLD COLUMBIA RIVER SMOKERY is now mostly idle, small crew operating part of equipment in winter, smoking and canning limited catch.

empty building to practical use. In 1895 a brash sign announced it was the new "Peninsula College." Courses scheduled studies in grade and high school subjects, the initial enthusiasm bringing in forty students. Tuition was $30 for nine months. A faculty of six was hired and the institution opened. At the end of the first year the student body dwindled to half, the second showed fewer. The college closed and the building suffered ignominy as a cow barn, in recent years collapsing through heavy weather and neglect.

Little is now left to indicate the existence of a town large enough to support several hotels, saloons, stores. In addition to being remotely situated, Oysterville's prosperity was based on a single industry. When the once ample supply of oysters vanished, so did the economy.

The few present residents of the town are mostly descendants of pioneers, notably C. J. Espy. He recalls that during the period of prosperity every out-of-town visitor was sooner or later regaled with a bit of doggerel:

Said one oyster to another
In tones of pure delight,
"I will meet you in the kitchen
And we'll both get stewed tonight."

BEAUTIFUL HOUSE might be termed Victorian, displaying uniquely elaborate barge boards. Built in 1869 as home of pioneer Tom Crellins, it became home of Harry Espy, elder son of founder, who grew up here and was father of Dr. R. H. Espy, Gen. Sec. of Nat. Council of Churches, N.Y.C. Next door is 1871 house built by town's founder and birthplace of C. J. Espy who, now in his 80s, sleeps in room of nativity.

PORT BLAKELY, WASHINGTON

When the Port Blakely Mill was put into operation in 1863, the fir and cedar forests seemed to stretch endlessly behind it. But the saws chewed their way through the logs so fast it became obvious that the island on which the mill was located could not supply enough trees for very long. Then the mill men got Sol Simpson out of Nevada with a reputation for railroad building. He took over the Puget Sound and Grays Harbor line which had been built across the neck of the Olympic Peninsula from Grays Harbor on the ocean, cutting through "enough timber 'til kingdom come" as the saying went.

Simpson extended the line into Port Blakely and to several other mills that needed logs. The official name of the railroad was the G. S. Simpson and Co. but it was familiarly referred to as the Blakely Line and its rails were the first to be extended so far east in Washington.

Simpson did not confine his activities to railroad building, making many improvements in yarding logs, cutting time and cost in getting them from woods to mills, waterways or his rails. Ox teams had been the only method used for pulling the big logs along the greased skid roads but Simpson said horses would be better and proceeded to prove it over the opposition of the old timers. But his satisfaction was short lived as along came that revolutionary new contrivance, the Dolbeer donkey engine, that ousted both oxen and horses as log dragging power.

WHEN PORT BLAKELY WAS A PORT. Sailing ships jam the harbor in days when Washington lumber was number one cargo. The **K. V. Kruse, Malahat, Mowtor, Oregon Fir, Forest Friend, Conqueror** were a few of the old lumber carriers that tied up at the big Skinner and Eddy mill dock. The **Alice Cook** and **Commodore** were two of the sailing vessels built at Port Blakely.

HERE WERE DOCKS that fronted town of Port Blakely and its mill. Rotting stubs have replaced wharves once covering acres of tidelands. Gone also is imposing hotel which fronted on dock. Tide is shown here at low ebb but at flood, water line reaches nearly to trees at left. Town no longer exists, is replaced by scattered suburban cottages and permanent homes. On clear days view of city of Seattle is seen between headlands marking entrance to bay.

Of prime importance to every sawmill is the log pond. Its function is to corral the logs in live storage, to hold them until the selected logs are conveyed into the mill, kicked onto the carriage which moves forward to meet the saw. Port Blakely's narrow bay was usually so cluttered with sailing ships from all over the world there was no space for an undisturbed log pond. But the mill owners had their eyes on the extreme end of the bay which was a mucky flat of mud at low tide.

The problem was neatly solved by throwing a dam across the bay, trapping a quarter mile half-circle of water. Near the center of the earth-fill dam, gates were installed which would admit the flood tide from the outer bay, then close to prevent the filled pond from emptying. The log spur of "The Blakely Line" was built alongside the pond so logs were dumped into it.

During the heyday the Port Blakely mill was said to be the largest in the world. It employed 1,200 men and cut 400,000 feet of lumber a day. A shipyard was built on the bay not far from the mill and constructed among other ships was the largest stern-wheeler in the Northwest, the *S.S. Julia.*

When the United States bought Alaska from Russia, it acquired a few bonus items, one being the gunboat *Politokofsky*. Offered at one of the country's first "surplus sales", the vessel was purchased by the Port Blakely Mill Co. Its guns were removed and the ship put into service as a cargo carrier to ply Puget Sound.

OLD BLACKSMITH SHOP built of bricks from local kiln. It was established early to construct first "permanent" buildings, all of which are now gone except this one. In cool, moist climate of Puget Sound, English ivy luxuriates, thriving like native plant as shown here.

Until '79 the importance of Port Blakely seemed to be ignored by some of its neighbors. Tacoma, for example, suddenly became aware of lost opportunities when its LEDGER spoke up in an editorial February 29, 1879: "Blakely is the smartest town of its population in these parts, and a little trade with it would help New Tacoma immensely. Olympia now furnishes the bulk of the beef that goes in there to supply ships, steamers and townspeople, a new trade, by the way, gained by that city at the expense of Seattle." Also of Tacoma, the item conceded three inches later.

The port reached its peak period during and shortly after the end of territorial days. By the beginning of the World War it was almost dead, picking up somewhat during that conflict, then again lying back never to recover except as a suburban area for ferry commuters to Seattle. All shipbuilding and sawmill structures are long gone. Rails have been taken up, short sections being used for gate posts. Except for the stubs of teredo-eaten pilings, remains of the old dam and a brush-concealed brick smithy, few signs of the once booming town remain.

The town was described in the late '70s as being long and narrow, confined at the rear by the steeply-rising hills, on the front by the bay filled with so many sailing vessels it sometimes had the appearance of a "woods of killed and bleached trees". While the townsite had been cleared of timber, stubborn stumps remained and wagons going down the one "street" had to meander around the obstacles.

Other than the post office, school and several saloons, the most imposing building in the village was the new hotel. It had two stories and was proudly claimed to be painted. The gay structure faced the bay, fronted by a roomy "porch" which was really a dock built on pilings over the edge of the bay and connected to the wharf where passenger ships tied up. Disembarking passengers were easily influenced to walk the few remaining steps to the hotel where they could promptly alleviate thirsts and sign the register.

RUINED FLOOD GATES once controlled ebb and flow of tides to create stable log pond of small bay at right. With gate gone, all water flows out on extreme low tides, final dregs seen here spilling into outer part of bay. Dam has nearly disappeared, was built along lines of pilings seen in background, constructed mostly of soil, mixed with bricks from early kiln. Walls of gates are of cut stone, iron gates long since vanished, perhaps salvaged for metal during first world war, by which time Port Blakely was nearly defunct as town.

PORT GAMBLE, WASHINGTON

When Captain Talbot and Cyrus Walker left the schooner *Junius Pringle* in June, 1853, in small boats, after sailing all the way from Maine, their object was to find a suitable site for a sawmill. It had to have its back set against many years' cut of timber and it must be flush to deep water instead of the mud flats prevailing along most of these inner shores. When they came to a small bay edged by an Indian village called Teekalet, "Brightness of the Noonday Sun", they knew they had found the place.

The oval-shaped harbor about two miles long had a narrow entrance to protect it against winter gales and many other advantages. Knowing the first white men here had been members of the Wilkes Expedition who had visited the waters in 1841, they named it Port Gamble in honor of Robert Gamble, naval officer and veteran of the War of 1812 in which he had been wounded.

Talbot and Walker recognized the value of the location immediately, and with the same dispatch returned to the *Pringle* which speedily sailed into the bay. Hardly had she dropped anchor when a crew of ten men was sent ashore with tools to construct cook and bunkhouses and other buildings, the lumber for which had been brought from California. The first native materials used were the cedar logs cut from the site to clear it, and squared for mill foundations. By a quirk, almost unbelieved by later sawmill men, the first lumber actually sold from the mill was white pine, brought from Maine by the *L. P. Foster* which arrived in September. There were 60,000 feet of the imported, "coals-to-Newcastle" lumber and the lot brought over $100 a thousand. This was the first profit made by Pope and Talbot in Washington, although their families were cutting trees and shipping lumber from their home area in East Machias, Maine, as early as 1767.

The *Foster* also carried to Port Gamble the machinery for the mill, which by that time was almost ready to be outfitted. It was 45 by 70 feet in size, built just above the high-tide mark. The boilers were fired and saws started turning not long after the *Foster* was unloaded and the first boards were "plowed back", being used to side up the mill until then open to all breezes.

The mill was not the first in the area. Mentioned in the Port Ludlow account is Captain William Sayward's little mill at that point. There was a sawmill at Fort Vancouver, owned by the Hudson's Bay Co., one run by Michael Simmons at Tumwater, Henry Yesler had one on the Seattle waterfront and there was a small operation at Port Madison on Apple Tree Cove owned by J. J. Felt. But these were all small businesses, the Pope and Talbot mill at Port Gamble being the real start of the Sawdust Saga in the Pacific Northwest.

Port Gamble's first little "muley" saw was able to cut about 2 thousand feet a day, that being eleven and a half hours. Logs were hauled into the mill by cable and drum, then hand-spiked onto the carriage to be pushed up against the up-and-down saw. In another year production had been increased six times by improved machinery. Four years later there was a new mill with modern twin circular rig having 56-inch saws which could cut logs up to 9 feet in diameter. It was soon producing ship spars and timbers 60 feet long.

LOST TO TIME and vandals is surname of young man buried in old cemetery at Port Gamble. Tombstone shows Indian name of town, Teekalet, was then in use, also that Washington was still territory, not achieving statehood until 1889. March of year 1863 when stone was erected did see reduction of area which previously included Idaho Territory, to present size.

It was dark inside the mill early in the day and toward evening, especially in winter. Illumination was by "teakettle lamps" which had spouts for wicks on both sides and burned dog fish oil bought from the local Clallam Indians. Results were a small amount of light, plenty of smoke and smell.

The monotony of long work days, broken only by Sundays, Christmas and Independence Day, was relieved by the "Indian War" in November of 1856. In the dusk of November 18, seven high-prowed, black war canoes entered Teekalet Bay. They were filled with Haida warriors from the Queen Charlotte Islands who made camp on the opposite shore, ostensibly preparing to attack the next morning. The sawmill crew hastily threw together an eight-sided fort of planks and at dawn waited inside for the expected raid. The 19th and 20th went by with nothing happening. In the late afternoon of the second day of "siege" the U.S.S. Massachusetts entered the bay. It sent a few shells into the Haida camp and the Indians departed as quickly as they had come. The next morning the sawmill workers were back on the job as usual.

Most of the white men came from Maine, a few of the crew being Indians. They were undependable workers, unused to discipline, with a habit of working only when the salmon were running, when they needed deer meat or when berry picking was good. Even with a steady job at the mill an Indian could be expected to take off for the woods or streams when he felt like it. Being expendable they were replaced when more Americans were available. Pay was $30 a month for eleven and a half hours, six days a week and the men got it weekly, in silver half dollars.

In 1858 the company announced it would "have the town surveyed and laid out into lots for the accommodation of all those who wish to make permanent residence here." In 1860, with a population of over 200, another notice was posted on the big bulletin board. The company planned "to erect buildings for all those who desire Public Worship, social enjoyment or fraternal communion".

1870 saw 326 people in the town. By now a hall had been built for dances and public meetings. In two more years Port Gamble ranked fourth among cities on the Sound and for the first time attracted a circus, in the summer of 1872. That same year the PUGET SOUND DISPATCH reported: "The town, which is owned almost entirely by the Mill Company, includes beside the mill and warehouses,

many neat and tasteful residences and presents quite an attractive appearance. There is the Masonic Hall and a school house. The only real estate in town owned outside the Mill Co. are the houses of A. S. Miller and John Condon and two large, well furnished and well kept hotels owned by John Collins, The Teekalet House is kept by Miller and Condon who minister to the necessities of the thirsty traveler."

By this time the school had about 40 pupils being taught by two teachers. The "exhorbitant" salaries paid the "principal" teacher, $90 a month, and his assistant, $50, were the cause of a bitter controversy. One resident wrote "There is much ire over this expenditure. It is thought by many that the school board faces bankruptcy, and that the school directors are trying to give their children a college education at the expense of the poor man's children who, because of lack of funds, will not be taught even to read and write. The large salaries are attracting many teachers to Port Gamble, there being 30 applicants in 1872 as against 2 in 1870."

Luella Buchanan in her History of Kitsap County, records that "February, 1874, a library was established through the agency of the preacher, school principal and Cyrus Walker and on Christmas of that year it received a gift of 200 books. Also the Amateur Theatrical Club gave a play which netted enough to buy an organ for the Hall."

That same year Port Gamble's steady growth faltered somewhat in a business depression when many men "left for the mines" but soon steadied and went ahead until by 1876 it was reported: "The Exchange Saloon and Lodging House has 25 rooms and the grist mill is now chopping 60 tons of grain a month, enough for use of the mill and logging camps. There is also a good barber shop. Though not the county seat, the Superintendent and Justice of the Peace live here. Traveling dramatic companies find this a good place for shows." 1879 saw Port Gamble hailed as the largest sawmill town in the county, a position it held until 1885 when all had to admit the place was "fading somewhat".

The mill still operates, although on a greatly reduced rate. The main company buildings still stand, much as they did at the peak of operations. They are well kept and painted a neat, "New England white", still retaining the appearance that justifies the reference to "Little Boston." The structure prominently labeled "Port Gamble Post Office" houses also the barber shop and library which opens only on Tuesdays.

ST. PAUL'S EPISCOPAL CHURCH in Port Gamble was built by mill owners as duplicate of Congregational edifice in home town of East Machias, Maine. All imported was original landscaping. In face of abundant verdure offered locally, New Englanders brought from Maine various trees such as eastern maples. Most of these, planted near church grew crowded, were replaced by others.

PORT LUDLOW, WASHINGTON

"At Port Ludlow a man could be sure of $30 a month for a twelve hour day. He could have a roof over his head and hot meals. But he would have to work for them. The mill whistle split the foggy gray chill at twenty minutes past five. Twenty minutes later it blew again and the men sat down to a breakfast of boiled beef, potatoes, baked beans, hash, griddle cakes, biscuits and coffee. At six o'clock whistle saws were turning, logs and boards booming along the rolls in the wet, sawdust-filled air. And twelve hours later — every day — the men were paid spot cash at the company store." Thus does Ralph Andrews vividly describe a day at Port Ludlow in his HEROES OF THE WESTERN WOODS.

The first sawmill at Port Ludlow seems to have been that of red-headed Captain William Sayward and J. F. Thorndyke who had come out from Maine in the fall of 1853 and built a simple mill overlooking Admiralty Inlet. In June of the following year the schooner *Junius Pringle* arrived off Cape Flattery with Captain William Talbot and A. J. Pope who had organized the Puget Mill Company, and a Maine surveyor, Cyrus Walker, hired on a temporary basis. Pope remained on board. The other two explored the shorelines of the waterways to locate a suitable site for a sawmill, Talbot in the ship's longboat, Walker in an Indian dugout canoe.

They stopped at Captain Sayward's mill to exchange Maine pleasantries and marvel at the great expanse of fir forest, then found among the coves and inlets an ideal mill site at Port Gamble. But they did not forget the advantageous location Captain Sayward had.

By 1862 the big Pope and Talbot mill at Port Gamble was underway with a will. The partners were planning expansion when their manager, Captain J. P. Keller died. Cyrus Walker, still on the temporary basis, was offered the position on a permanent salary. He accepted only when offered the opportunity to buy a one-tenth interest. The operation grew rapidly with mills at Port Gamble and on Camano Island and in 1878 the company decided to build one at Port Ludlow. Captain Sayward's interests were purchased and a huge plant replaced the small one. It measured 65 by 394 feet and could turn out 100 thousand feet of lumber every day it operated.

With this mill well established Walker set about buying up immense amounts of standing timber, known as "stumpage", never more than a mile or two away from tidewater. The problem in logging was not in cutting the trees but in getting the logs to the sawmills. Much of the timber was acquired by taking advantage of the Timber and Stone Act,

REMAINS OF DOCK on which Cyrus Walker, Pope and Talbot's manager, welcomed visiting dignitaries who came on sailing vessels to the mill town. Much larger docks were located quarter of a mile to right adjoining giant sawmill, long since wrecked. Port Ludlow was situated on small deepwater bay on Admiralty Inlet, waterway providing access to Puget Sound and Hood Canal. In foreground lies twisty-grained log resembling stranded sea lion.

passed in 1876, which enabled any person declaring his intention of becoming a citizen to buy 160 acres of timberland at $2.50 an acre. The Pope and Talbot men, as well as other mill owners, made a practice of having sailors from their ships walk into the timber, then each making a legal purchase of 160 acres. They then sold it to the company at a nominal profit. It was a standing joke along the waterfront that the seamen never bought land very far

from their ships for fear of getting lost in the woods.

For several years Cyrus Walker had been paying court to Emily Foster Talbot, daughter of the captain. She finally accepted him and in 1885 they were married, the couple setting up housekeeping in the manager's house at Port Gamble. When the building caught fire and burned to the ground, Walker laid plans to build the fabulous mansion at Port Ludlow.

FOOTHILLS OF OLYMPIC RANGE (opposite page) look down on old log pond of Puget Mill at Port Ludlow. Trees are mainly Douglas fir making up "second growth" which has sprung from slash of early logging. Bound groups of piling, termed "dolphins" in marine parlance, remain from sawmilling days, floating logs shown being stored temporarily in today's "contract" logging.

The new home, called Admiralty Hall after the inlet it faced, was nearly a block long, built of the material so readily available, red cedar and fir. The bathrooms set the scale for all else — said to be "as big as kitchens". During the fifty years Walker was a power in the Puget Sound lumber industry three generations of Chinese cooks held forth over the enormous kitchen range at Admiralty Hall. There was a well-stocked wine cellar for the benefit of guests, Walker himself abstaining.

For most of the years Walker reigned at Admiralty Hall, Port Ludlow was the lumber capitol of the world. The position was attained after a shutdown, when lumber was being over-produced and causing prices to drop to unprofitable levels. Walker accepted a subsidy of nine hundred dollars a month to keep the mill closed and the company town had its first experience at being near a ghost during the several years when almost all employees moved to other mill towns. When prices rose, the mills again rolled and Port Ludlow gained a new and greater prestige. Its lumber and shingles were shipped to every corner of the world including South Africa where Cecil Rhodes was building a grape arbor.

Industry at Port Ludlow was not confined to sawmilling. A large shipyard was kept busy building such vessels as the three-masted schooner *Courser*, barkentine *Katherine Sudden* and the *Moses Turner*. Built for the Hawaiian trade were schooners *Waehue*, *Lihuluho* and *Luke*. Among steamers built were *Augusta* and *Hyack*.

Cyrus Walker and his associates cut trees from purchased stumpage as long as it lasted, then started cutting into their own extensive holdings, kept for years for the purpose. When at last that source of trees was exhausted, the mills were dismantled and many of the houses barged over to still operating Port Gamble. The colossal, soft wood mansion was turned into a hotel, at first elegant, then increasingly shoddy as time took its toll. Forced to close for lack of patronage it stood idle, transients "camping" in the once plush rooms. Then one night it caught fire and in hours little but ashes was left. Today the ghost town hunter searches in vain for any sign of the building itself. Still growing where the lawn used to be are old holly trees, maples and shrubs brought around the Horn to grace the grounds of a lumber baron's castle.

ENORMOUS MANSION built by lumber baron Cyrus Walker stood on slope immediately above docks and mill. Grounds were landscaped with shrubs and trees brought on ships from Maine, centered by brass cannon, veteran of War of 1812. It boomed on 4th of July and whenever company's ships sailed into Admiralty Inlet. Visitors welcomed into the huge center hall found walls paneled with native fire and cedar. House was filled with massive pieces of furniture also brought from New England. Highboards of carved bedsteads reached almost to ceiling, every bedroom having marble-topped dressers. Sideboard in main dining room was of walnut, hand-carved in Germany. Room and closet doors slid back and forth like those on ships. Widow's walk surmounting cupola afforded Walker unobstructed view of domain and access to flagpole of Sitka spruce. House was used as hotel in later years and became completely covered with ivy. After abandonment it burned to ground. (Photo courtesy Stewart Holbrook.)

REPUBLIC, WASHINGTON

John Welty was discouraged after a whole summer of prospecting along the streams in northeastern Washington. When winter snows covered the ground he got a job for the winter, glad of a respite from clawing over the rugged mountains. But wanderlust and the ever-present hope of a good strike pulled him out along the streams at the very first break in the weather. In the middle of February, 1896, he did make that strike, and in the same stream he had worked the fall before —Granite Creek.

The resultant boom was such that by the first of May that year, Republic had a name and newspaper—the *Republic Pioneer*. On the 14th of the month it reported with a glow: "Here is a little city that is moving right along. Large quantities of whiskey, flour and other necessities arrived during the week."

By fall the camp had fifty log and canvas shacks, five stores, three blacksmith shops, four restaurants, two hotels, two fruit and cigar stores, two meat markets, three livery stables, three bakeries, three assay offices, tailor, shoemaker, doctor, jeweler and the usual lot of saloons. The Miners' Union sponsored big dances held in Patsy Clark's big boarding house. No cemetery existed until a young woman was found strangled "by persons unknown" and her body was the means to a permanent burial place on the steep hillside. The first school was a tent in the brush of the creek bottom, soon replaced by a log building. Indians were welcomed in the school and at first outnumbered the white pupils.

By 1900 a large part of Republic's growth was in the direction of brothels and saloons, the latter numbering up to twenty-eight, with six dance halls going strong, night and day. As late as 1940 an elaborate Opera House remained from those days. It was described as having an "elegant false front, copiously ornamented with balconies, each of which had a railing supported by fancy turned spindles." Republic now serves the surrounding farmers and vacationers, the days long vanished when the roistering miners found many easy ways to spend their money.

ORIGINAL ALTAR is intact in old Church of the Immaculate Conception in Republic, Wash. Edifice stands on steep hillside, conspicuous for miles around.

RIVERSIDE, WASHINGTON

Gun-toting, cattle-rustling Frank Watkins rode at the head of a string of stolen horses. He had run away from the rope in Oregon, chased by a mob and now, in 1903, was arriving in fresh territory and headed for Williams' Saloon in Riverside.

What Watkins liked was hot toddies such as Tom and Jerrys and he had heard how good Jack Williams could make them. He stomped in, pounded on the plank bar and demanded one of Williams' specials.

Watkins' reputation, not for consuming hot drinks but for confiscating hot horses and cattle, had preceded him. The tea kettle was steaming away but the bartender thought it was out of the cowboy's line of vision. He was not about to indulge cattle thieves' whims. "Ain't no more hot water," he sang out. But Watkins had heard the simmering kettle even though he couldn't see it. "Well," he drawled, "no more use for that thing then." And he moved out to sight the kettle and shoot the spout off.

The rustler hung around Riverside all winter. He seemed to think he rated the protection of the law, unaware that the townspeople were wary of him. Twice he went to the sheriff with complaints he had been shot at, once exhibiting a hole in his hat to prove it. "Too high," the sheriff may have said.

One evening the next spring he rode into Riverside, bedded his horse in Kendall's Livery Stable and after supper climbed into the loft to sleep in the hay. As other sleepers in this early day flophouse were wak-

ing and shaking the grass seeds and nits out of their ears, they noticed Frank Watkins was not stirring in his nest. He was dead with a bullet in his head.

At first it was called suicide but Watkins' gun was found beside him unfired and there were no powder burns on his skin. Nobody cared much how the cowboy had died and the questions asked of the other sleepers and witnesses at the inquest were desultory. No one appeared to press further inquiry and the business was settled. Watkins was buried without ceremony beside the road entering town. The grave can still be seen and may even have the little fence around it.

Richard Sutton tells this story, especially if you call him "Dick." His father, Robert W., brought the family to Riverside from Genesee, Idaho, in a covered wagon in 1890 and Dick grew up here, marrying in 1908 and rearing a family of five boys and five girls.

The early prosperity of Riverside was due entirely to its road position, freight teams and boats using it as a convenient stopover for loading or unloading. The actual year-around head of navigation was Brewster, where the Okanogan River meets the Columbia. Most of the year the former, which flowed past Riverside, was too shallow for steamboats, even the shallow draft paddle-wheel vessels, but in spring it swelled with melting snow from the mountains. That was a period of feverish activity and a fleet of loaded steamers brought a steady stream of supplies to Riverside, the center for a vast area of mining and farming communities. Merchants stocked up for the whole year and mine owners replaced equipment parts. As soon as flood waters subsided, river traffic was finished for another year and shipping activities began. Goods were moved to outlying points and Riverside was the headquarters.

At the turn of the century, the town decided it deserved the honor of being the county seat. Growing pains were about over and things were booming. A large store operated by C. E. Blackwell and Co. stood proudly on the waterfront near a big hotel, the Occidental. A bank was doing a flourishing business and the interest was 12 percent on loaned money. For a while it was squeezed in one corner of Pat Carney's saloon but the enterprising banker, Arthur Lund, quickly expanded into a separate building and even established branches of the bank in neighboring towns. With all this the populace thought Conconully had been on the top of the Okanogan heap long enough.

Heading the ensuing county seat fight, one-sided with Conconully sitting smugly on its prestige, was the fiery editor of the Riverside *Argus*. Outspoken, vituperative, Wallace Struble spared no dirty words in supporting the proposed shift. This was the same

period county elections for officials were scheduled and although most candidates were vigorously for or against the change, all kept their opinions buttoned up for fear of losing votes. When the election was over, Riverside was right where it started. Conconully held the county seat until 1914 when it went to Okanogan.

Struble put up another good fight but another losing one over the matter of a bridge over the Okanogan River—at Riverside or Okanogan? Final disposition was made in secret and editor Struble sounded a bitter blast in the *Argus* of Dec. 8, 1908. "On Monday last the retiring board of county commissioners awarded a contract to the Puget Sound Bridge Co. for the sum of $10,500 for the erection of a 'steal' bridge across the Okanogan at the village of Okanogan. The contract price does not include approaches which will probably swell the total $500 or more making the cost of the structure at least $11,000." The next paragraph was set in capital letters. "The awarding of this contract was done, the *Argus* is informed, with extreme secrecy. In a star chamber session at which only the commissioners and one Harry J. Kerr, 'Mayor' of Okanogan village, were present. Even the people of Conconully, except those in on the deal, were not aware of the proceedings and expressed surprise that

LIVELY SCENE ON WATERFRONT about the turn of the century — photo copied from calendar of Dick Sutton, pioneer resident of Riverside, showing large shipment of wool arriving from ranch of Clay Fruit to be loaded on sternwheelers tied up on Okanogan River bank.

Driver of wagon at left is Bert Winnick, his lead team Baldy and Jake; on next wagon is driver William G. Reeder, owner of freight line with headquarters at Brewster. Reeder had small terrier which nipped at heels of out-of-line or laggard horses. On driver's seat of third wagon is "Six-Shooter Andy" Southworth who habitually carried gun and bowie knife. Standing on ground at Andy's right, sporting boiled shirt, is ship's captain of Griggs Steamship Line. Loose horse in foreground is Nespelum, privileged race animal which didn't have to work and turned rump to photographer.

such a high-handed course should have been taken by a retiring board of commissioners."

The Okanogan *Independent* of Oct. 10, in a resumé of the historic battle said it had remained independent but did point out the advantages of the Okanogan site, prophesying that "the pendulum of development will swing in favor of Okanogan, that the bridge will have marked convenience in the transportation of trade to the growing communities of the Tunk Creek and Omak Creek areas," further pointing out that the railroad would be coming along in a few years and would likely bypass Riverside.

Riverside and the *Argus* editor must have sensed the truth of the prediction but to see it in the public prints was a punch below the belt. And Struble must have felt a certain satisfaction when the bridge was finished and proved to be eleven feet higher than needed to clear the tallest stack on any sternwheeler, which made the cost excessive and the approaches too steep to use in icy weather.

Riverside settled down to enjoy what it did have, its famous week-end dances in the big hall at the south end of town. These were held on Friday nights instead of Saturday because of the Sunday races at a fine track near the river. And also due to the Sunday racing, Authur Lund reaped a harvest by keeping his bank open.

True to the ominous prediction, the railroad did bypass Riverside when it came through in 1914, a blow to the town depending on road and river traffic. It was left sitting on the banks of the Okanogan to grumble and nurse the stray wagon freight. And the final stroke of destiny came when a modern highway was built to the north of the town.

In 1958 Stanley Hixon, a rancher in Tunk Valley, with "a small fortune tied up" in a museum on his ranch, decided something must be done about Riverside's retrogression, pointing out the 1896 population had dwindled to 186. He put over the plan of selling the town as a ghost town, building on its heritage to attract tourists the way the two famous Virginia Cities had. He enlisted the aid of the two grocers, tavern, dairy and roofing companies, about the only merchants remaining, and formed the Riverside Historical Association. Memberships were sold for $5, ground broken and plans made for a fine museum town utilizing the large collection of Hixon's ranch.

Mrs. De Tro, of H. De Tro and Co., general merchandise, said, when interviewed in 1963; "Oh, that all fell through. The thing was too optimistic. They planned too big. They spent all their money but couldn't do enough and no tourists came. Mr. Hixon and his wife separated and he moved to Arizona. The ghost town venture is a thing of the past."

OLD RIVER SCENE is often attributed to Riverside but structure showing in right background is Bureau Hotel in Okanogan. Owner Capt. Charles Bureau, more efficient as shipbuilder, constructed steamer *Enterprise* shown at right, piloted by Jack Brown. Other boat is *Chelan*; pilot—Capt. Grey. This picture, as most other old ones in this group, was taken about 1907 by Frank Matsura. He was pathetic little Japanese, arriving in Conconully in 1905. Developing a knack for photography, he gathered simple equipment, recorded hundreds of happenings. He moved to Okanogan in 1907, expanded interest into livelihood, was a lonely figure under racial prejudice. Early one cold Sunday morning about 1913, he was walking down street when he saw open window at back of store and was suspicious. Alerting sheriff, was told to fetch owner living some distance away. Storeman, responding to knock at front door, found Matsura dying on step. Suffering from tuberculosis, he had run all the way and had hemorrhage. Little photographer left behind invaluable heritage of historic pictures.

OLD KING COAL IS DEAD

Who ever heard of a coal rush? Yet Roslyn had several—the sudden influx of miners in 1886, rushes in and out of town when it was beset by fires, strikes, explosions and competition from nearby Ronald. There was "never a dull moment" in this coal center of the pine woods.

The railroad set off the first blast. The Northern Pacific needed a west coast source of good coal and this area was only four miles north of its main line. The first coal was packed out of outcroppings by horses in 1883 and three years later the Northern Pacific Railroad sent a corps of experts in to probe the protruding black ledges along Smith Creek east of Stampede Pass. What they found was coal of a quality and quantity that encouraged a survey for a branch line up the creek bed from Cle Elum. By act of Congress the company already owned every other section of land in the region which included this coal and within weeks more than a hundred men were working at the outcropping veins. Some brought their families and the result was an almost instant town.

Logan M. Bullitt platted it and with a romantic gesture named it Roslyn after a sweetheart in a Delaware town of that name. Dedication papers were filed in Minnesota September 22, 1886, with local legalities for Kittitas County taken care of six days later. Most streets were laid out sixty feet wide with Pennsylvania eighty. By December 13, it was evident an addition would be needed and this was platted at the northeast corner of the original townsite. Almost immediately still another became necessary to accommodate all the new arrivals.

The first iron horse brought a wave of them, mostly miners from Italy, followed by others from Austria and Slavic countries and Negroes in quantity. That first winter saw some four hundred men congregated in camp.

Company officials were well aware that a percentage of them would be rascals, male and

SPIRALED STRIPS OF STEEL are long undisturbed shavings from machine shops at lower edge of Roslyn.

female, and since it was a company town they were determined to keep it as peaceful as human nature would allow. Gambling dens were strictly prohibited and officially absent for many years but that did not prevent some clandestine poker games and cock-fights.

To curb excess drinking the company set up its own saloon, which with a general store were the first business structures in town. One individual lot buyer erected a building across the street from the company enterprise, getting little trade until the word "Saloon" was painted on its false front. Then the owner got the Sunday punch and a padlock on the door. He was instructed to read the fine print in his deed, a clause strictly forbidding manufacture or sale of intoxicating liquors.

Inevitably another saloon went up, but on private land just outside the town limits in the "tall uncut." Two more followed it and then another, so labeled but actually a spot where a lonely coal miner could find a warm embrace for a price.

Rumor had it several men not reporting for work had been rolled and dragged into the heavy forest. All this forced the town bosses to allow legitimate saloons within town limits where they could be regulated.

Other pioneer buildings were the hotel (corporation owned) that housed a hundred men, boarding house and two livery stables. All were built of lumber cut in the company owned sawmill from company owned timber.

The first half of 1888 saw a briskly flourishing Roslyn with some 1200 population. On June 22, about four o'clock in the afternoon smoke was seen coming from a building between First and Second. The alarm was sounded, a futile gesture with so little fire protection available, for within two hours all buildings were in ruins. Loss was about $100,000 and that meant loss for most property owners felt the 10% insurance premium was exhorbitant.

In a few months Roslyn was on its way to recovery, many new buildings springing up from

NO. 3 MINE, altho part of Roslyn complex, warranted separate town of Ronald for convenience, businesses, rooming houses, saloons. Although later mines like No. 9, 10, were fairly good producers, none ever surpassed production, importance of old No. 3.

PARTLY OCCUPIED, partly boarded up house is typical of many old homes in Roslyn, once flourishing coal camp, deterioration now well under way.

the ashes and an era of prosperity prevailed. Then in August came the first of several labor uprisings, An organization called the Knights of Labor was organizing unions all over the country and in July of 1888 almost all Roslyn miners were made "brothers," the few dissenters made miserable. The town was fertile ground in which to plant and cultivate seeds of strike against the Northern Pacific mine owners. Wages were small, working hours stretched to ten, miners working under constant threat of explosions and collapsing tunnels.

The ensuing strike was long and bloody incidents frequent. Most workers had little or no backlog on which to subsist and some had to leave town. Mine officials imported crews of Negroes as "scabs," many remaining after the settlement to account for much of Roslyn's population to its very end. Among scanty details of the strike is the item that officials called for martial law but the settlement was reached before soldiers were sent in.

By December of 1890 all miners were working full time, the monthly payroll $84,000. Then when the owners lost the Union Pacific contract the payroll shrank to $63,000 and lean days came until new contracts were secured. Then the famous producer, Mine No. 3, one mile away, was opened and all was rosy again, the town of Ronald growing up around the new mine, named after Alexander Ronald, a mine superintendent.

In the midst of happy prosperity came the disastrous explosion of May 9, 1892. A noontime underground blast took the lives of forty-five men. A relief committee was quickly organized and gathered $7,000 from outside communities, $2,000 from Roslyn citizens, the fund aided by supplies collected by Knights of Pythias and other organizations. 36% of it went to widows, the remainder to the fatherless children.

That same year on September 24, bandits got away with a small fortune from the town's bank, Ben E. Snipes Co., and more money was spent in a futile attempt to solve the crime. The bank may have been thinly financed for on June 9 of the next year its doors were closed in the face of a clamoring mob of depositors who lost $100,000. The blow was a crippling tragedy as the sum represented all savings in the community. Some depositors eventually received certificates of indebtedness, "good for framing," as one man said. The next year saw a strike in May over wages which lasted several months, greatly depressing business and working hardships.

Yet things brightened up at the end of 1896. One reason seems to be the progressive ideas of B. F. Bush who came to Roslyn as manager of the coal company's operations that year. He put into practice a more liberal policy which increased the number of working days to six per week which was still not enough to supply the coal in demand. For the next seven years the town enjoyed the full dinner pail, fat pocketbook and comfortable home.

OLD MINE CAR stands idle with others in lots once occupied by business buildings, long made empty by series of destructive fires.

A murder shocked the town on the morning of Friday, March 20, 1896. The brutally bludgeoned body of the well-liked company doctor, J. H. Lyon, was found a few feet from his own doorstep. The apparent weapon was a table leg lying a few feet away, covered with blood and hair, pocketbook and jewelry untouched on his body. The last person to see Dr. Lyon was his long-time friend, merchant Samuel Isaacs. Enraged townspeople collected $400 as reward for the murderer's arrest and conviction to which was added $500 by the state governor, $300 by Kittitas County and $300 by the city of Roslyn.

Suspicion eventually fell on two brothers known to have made threats against the doctor, accusing him of what amounted to malpractice in treating a third brother. The evidence was slim and they were released after a preliminary hearing, the record stating, "Mystery still enshrouds one of the blackest crimes ever committed in the history of the State of Washington."

In the same period the town was struck down by an epidemic of diphtheria. After several deaths all schools were closed, all public gatherings banned. On the heels of this came another. Smallpox spread rapidly, blame placed on admitted poor sanitary conditions in the town. When this scare subsided, Roslyn again went forward.

In 1904 the population was some 4,000 made up mainly of Slavs, Negroes, Italians and Germans. By this time the mines were privately owned, 1898 legislation denying railroads the right to operate mines of any kind. In 1909 another mine explosion took ten lives. By 1930 the population was down to 2,289, the decline continuing steadily. Today the town, not entirely dead, displays many examples of Victorian elegance in its surviving buildings, some of them still occupied.

POWDER HOUSE building solidly built of stone and iron-shuttered, still stands at Ronald, "suburb" of Roslyn. It held large supplies of blasting powder for coal mines but stored well away as accidental explosion might collapse mine shoring.

153

RUBY, WASHINGTON

At the height of Ruby's success as a boom town, the Ruby *Miner*, on June 2, 1892, editorialized: "As Virginia City is to Nevada so is Ruby to the State of Washington. Ruby is the only incorporated town in Okanogan County. It is out of debt and has money in the treasury. Public schools are open nine months of the year and are under the management of competent instructors, these furnishing unsurpassed advantages. LET US MAKE SOME MONEY FOR YOU IN RUBY. THIS DISTRICT IS APPROPRIATELY TERMED THE COMSTOCK OF WASHINGTON."

Ruby's first butcher, W. A. Newcomb, was a jolly, friendly man who was popular with the citizens, a fact that served him well later. He was known to have an ample supply of fresh meat and one day somebody found out why. The butcher was a rustler on the side and when cattlemen came into his shop with a rope, he was put under protection of the sheriff and hustled off to Conconully for trial. The guards were friends and being friendly, all got drunk as lords and on the trip Newcomb made an easy escape.

County commissioners held a special meeting, the second in Ruby's history, to vote a reward of $500—and hoped the townspeople would match it—for the capture of the butcher-rustler. Notice of the reward was posted in Ruby, advertised in the Portland *Oregonian*, Seattle *Post-Intelligencer*, Walla Walla *Statesman* and Victoria (B.C.) *Colonist*.

Whether or not the reward was responsible, Newcomb was apprehended and brought back to Ruby. Tempers of cattlemen had now cooled enough to try him in a local court, where he was judged not guilty and freed, jurors being friends of the affable Mr. Newcomb. His experience apparently chastened him and he afterward bought his beef.

As a silver town Ruby had a series of booms and relapses as new discoveries were made and old ones faded out. It was a raw-edged town with little regard for law and order. On one occasion a few town toughs were idling on a bench outside Billie Dawson's hotel when the stage pulled in with a stranger on top. He was wearing a white plug hat, the like of which had never been seen in these parts. Lounger Len Armstrong bet Al Thorpe, considered a crack shot, that he couldn't put a bullet through the trick top piece without hitting the head under it. Without hesitation Thorpe drew his gun and fired, putting a neat hole in the upper crown. When the visitor protested at the violent reception to Ruby, Thorpe apologized and set up the drinks.

The same hotel was the setting for another shooting incident when Jonathan Bourne, who had spent half a million in his silver mine which was currently in low production, found he couldn't meet the payroll. A crowd of irate miners assembled outside the hotel and, not knowing which room Bourne lived in, shot out all the windows.

Bert Comstock ran a saloon in Ruby; John Bartlett, a store. The former had eyes for Bartlett's wife and she responded. The pair left town together; in a few days Bartlett's body was found in his store, dead apparently by suicide. The fleeing couple had take the Bartletts' baby daughter with them and when she reached fifteen, Comstock deserted the mother and married the child.

Ruby shared Indian troubles with Conconully. Walter Brown had a dairy between the towns, delivering milk to both. He attended a Fourth of July celebration in Ruby, arriving just in time to witness an atrocity. An Indian brave name Pokamiakin, as handsome as he was bold and brash, came into the crowd with a fast horse he had stolen, well-known race horse, Nespilim. Sheriff Bill Tiffany ordered the Indian to dismount and submit to arrest but the brave refused and spurred the animal into a spurt. Tiffany galloped alongside him, grabbed Pokamiakin by his long, black hair and dragged him along the ground. Dairyman Brown, in telling the story, said the crowd was sure every bone in the Indian's body was broken but he got to his feet running. In the hail of bullets, both he and the horse were killed.

Winter snows were cruel to towns in the area, avalanches frequent and crippling the mining camps situated at the bottom of steep slopes. One such slide in Ruby crashed down on an engineer named Magee and his two helpers who were pinned under a flume, which fortunately allowed them to breathe and saved their lives. Not so lucky was a young Ruby man who taught school in Conconully. He was buried in a slide on his way to the school, found dead in the big snow pile.

Richard Price, later scheduled to preside over the never-held trial of lynched Indian Steve, was sent into the area by the Indian service to make a survey on all white men who had Indian wives. He was to determine nationality, tribal connections of women, number of children, wealth and social standing of couples. It was never revealed what purpose the survey was to serve, but it gained good results for Price. He was justice of peace in Ruby and a well-versed counsellor on Indian affairs.

HOTEL BUREAU in nearby, hated rival city, Okanogan, was long time in building since builder, Charles Bureau, described as "handsome Frenchman," was too busy with many girl friends in Portland. Started about 1900, hotel was still unfinished in '20s when Bureau died. Four-horse stage regularly covered route from Oroville to the north, calling at Riverside as last stop before Okanogan.

BANK ROBBER LEROY, alias Charles Ray or Andrew Morgan, shown in newspaper photograph with Sheriff "Baldy" Charles McLean after capture by Sheriff Fred Thorp. Prisoner shows desperate gleam in eyes even in poorly reproduced photo, also wounded finger. Likely LeRoy was even then planning escape which took place soon after.

LOG CABIN ON JOHNSON CREEK, where in 1888 first Okanogan county commissioners held meetings under confusion due to fact county seat was undetermined. Delegations from Ruby and Conconully gathered in separate camps outside cabin to carry on campaigns, Ruby delegation promising office space free from taxes, Conconully five acres of land for county buildings. Stimulating refreshment caused boisterous demonstrations, Ruby people forming circle around cabin, dancing and shouting —"Ruby for County Seat!" Decision went to Ruby, lasted for 11 months, then to Conconully until 1914.

OLD RUBY pictured in only known photo, has been completely ravaged by time, fire and vandalism. No building remains in lusty, boisterous town called "Babylon of the West." Ruby was early county seat, had no office buildings or safe. County treasurer found himself in tough town with county funds of $1,800, placed money in can, buried it at his ranch. Although some gold and considerable copper were mined here, Ruby depended on silver and silver crash of 1893 sent camp rapidly downhill. Remaining residents moved to one-time rival, Conconully.

ONCE THERE WAS LIFE

SKAMOKAWA, WASHINGTON

Until the year 1915 the town of Skamokawa had no land connection with the outside world. Surrounded on three sides by rocky cliffs and dense virgin timber, on the fourth by the broad lower Columbia River, the inhabitants took to the water.

Situated in Wahkiakum County in the state of Washington, Skamokawa is less than 80 miles northwest of Vancouver, yet is unknown to many Portlanders. It will repay the one-day tripper with its blend of Ghost Town atmosphere and live fishing and farming community.

It would be hard to say exactly when the town got started. Since there have been Indians, there has been some sort of village there, made up of fairly permanent aborigines. Fishing then, as now, has always been good along the lower river, the most desired fish being the Chinook Salmon, because of its delicately flavored red meat. The earliest whites found the peaceable Chinook Indians catching their staple food in the most primitive of nets and weirs, made of willow stems bound together with twine of twisted cedar-bark fibers.

Shortly after the Hudson's Bay Post was established at Fort Vancouver in 1825, other posts were strung along strategic routes. One of these was less than three miles from Skamokawa. A labyrinth of waterways, sloughs and creeks intersect the area. A peculiarity of the waterways funnels fog into the place, causing the Indians to give it the name, meaning "Smoke-on-the-water." (Pronunciation is Ska-mo'ka-wuh.)

The natives built up a steady trade in supplying the new Hudson's Bay Post with fish. Up until then they had always dried their catch (a dubious accomplishment in this damp atmosphere), ground the result into powder and stored it for the winter. A deerskin full of this stuff must have been a hard thing to live with, especially if the shelter grew warm and the air close. But now the post introduced the method of salting down, an only slightly less odoriferous method of preservation. The casks full of fish were sent up the river to Fort Vancouver, from whence they were shipped to England.

156

All went well until one day the Factor was found murdered and everything of value at the post stolen. Soldiers were sent down from Fort Vancouver to deal with the culprit, who, it was naturally assumed, would be found among the Chinooks. But these people were not given to deeds of violence, and were outraged. In effect, they said, "We didn't do it, but we know who did, and we'll bring him in" and they did, too.

Some time previously, a ship had been wrecked on the shores of the Olympic Peninsula, to the north. The crew had chosen a bad spot to be shipwrecked, because here lived the savage Hoh Indians. The entire crew was slaughtered, the ship pillaged. It was a member of this rapacious tribe who had wandered south and committed the crime at the post. He didn't enjoy his ill-gotten gains long; the indignant Chinooks, eager to prove their innocence, tracked the luckless Hoh down and returned him to their village. On the spot where one day the present schoolhouse would be built, he was tried and summarily hung. The noose had been knotted before the trial was finished. This headlong rush of justice was in striking contrast to later laxity among white settlers on the site.

Mr. L. E. "Les" Silverman, who was born in Skamokawa in 1897 and lives there still, provides much information.

When Mr. Silverman's father, C. L., arrived there in the 80's, there was quite a little town along the inner waterway called Skamokawa Creek. The creek is submerged in tidal water backed up from the river and is actually more like a canal. Along this waterway for perhaps a quarter mile stood a line of small buildings on each side. One side held most of the business structures; at least two of which, a saloon and a meat market, still stand precariously. In those days elk steak "tender and juicy" sold for eight cents a pound. The saloon, soon eclipsed by a fancier one, became the office of a tiny steamboat company called "Bobbidge & Holt." The name along with the words "Steamer Efin" are still faintly discernible on the front of the little building. The

FALSE FRONTS line this watery "Street." Many of the buildings are the original ones included in a painting of this scene made by T. S. Weedell, along in the 1880's.

name *Efin* was made up of the initial letters from the given names of the owning family. These were Edmond, Fred, Ida and Nellie.

All these structures faced the water, their rears the wilderness.

No man was ever tried for murder in Skamokawa since Indian days. This was in spite of not a few killings. One man, standing on the dock, whipped out his pistol and shot to death a man approaching in a boat. Presumably there had been bad blood between the two. The killer fled to the county seat, Cathlamet, gave himself up to the Sheriff, who turned him over to the Justice of the Peace. That worthy extracted 500 dollars from him as bail and pointedly suggested that he fade away for a while. He did so, moving to the Oregon side of the river. Every few weeks he came back to town on the early boat, visited his relatives and departed next day. He was never molested.

Skamokawa reached its peak in the first years of this century. About 1910 there were about 400 to 500 people, a fine schoolhouse had been built and three large shingle mills operated full tilt. The first co-operative creamery in the state was operating. A

PICTURESQUE HOTEL stood partly on wharf, partly on bank: was home to travelers who came to Skamokawa by river steamer. In times of high water in spring when snow in upper reaches of Columbia melted, hotel and wharf were surrounded by flood.

TIDAL EFFECTS ON LOWER Columbia are strong, as are fluctuations in seasonal levels of water. Walks on hinged connections and floating docks keep fishing boats accessible. Vat in foreground holds "blue vitrol" cupric compound in which nets are soaked, killing algae which would rot twine. Note roller, over which long gill net is fed into tank.

newer section had sprung up closer to the river itself. New docks, an imposing store and a three-story hotel faced the water. To them came, several times daily, the steamboats of the day. Sidewheelers and sternwheelers they were; the *Lurline*, the *Harvest Queen*, the *T. J. Potter* and all the rest.

But when river traffic died, so did something in Skamokawa. The big hotel emptied and faded, the store windows now stare on a sagging dock, the planks of which are rotting away and returning to the river. Empty, gray and weathered residences line a once busy steamboat slough, and the old school is forlornly a meeting place for the Redmen Lodge.

Mr. Silverman hopefully maintains the town is not dead and it never will become a true Ghost Town because there are still the fish and the fertile farmlands. Many docks are still draped with drying gill nets. Fish boats still ply the canals of once busy "Little Venice." A modern school stands at the edge of town where the guilty Hoh once swung at the end of a rope.

EARLY DAY FALSE FRONTS built during boom days looked down on wild mining and railroad construction camp.

SULTAN, WASHINGTON

Sultan, as were many Washington towns in the heavily timbered Cascades, was a combination mining and lumbering town. Some industry still persists, but the place doesn't begin to enjoy the color of the early days.

Sultan is now about as accessible as a town could be, barely off the highway. But in 1870 when prospectors found scattered flakes and a few nuggets of gold in the Sultan River, no roads existed, and timber as heavy as anywhere in the world covered the area. Indian trails made their way through the woods, and beside one of these John Nailor and his Indian wife established a claim ten years after the first discoveries.

Their place became a rough and tough hangout for all sorts of undesirables, thus setting the tone of Sultan's earlier days.

Prosperity was well established when the first light-draft river steamer, the *Mama*, reached the place in 1888.

Sultan really boomed when the Great Northern built its tracks on through the Cascades, one of the most staggering jobs in railroad history, and a separate story. The effect on Sultan, however, because of basing the men and materials there, was to expand an already rowdy mining camp into a sprawling mass of shacks housing all the hangers-on of a construction camp.

Sultan now is a quiet, respectable town. The buildings remaining from that wild, early period are on a back street.

TRINITY, WASHINGTON

Trinity is situated on Phelps Creek, in a wild, remote section of the Cascades. Heavy virgin timber crowds close.

Before the turn of the century there was prospecting, then placering nearby. Later, a rich vein of copper was found about five miles from the present site, and the first mine sank a shaft into the side of the mountain about 1900.

About 1914 the Royal Development Co. was formed and the town was built. A power plant was erected near the upper end of the main street. Large frame buildings followed; a mess hall, commissary, rooming houses and all the other structures necessary to a booming mining camp took shape. Another lesser street ran at right angles, fringed with smaller houses and cabins for the married men and their families. Above the power plant was the large mine building with the usual huge pile of tailings extending from it. On the older section of the latter was built a sawmill. Narrow gauge tracks led everywhere, and the dump ore cars ran back and forth between the openings of the shafts and tunnels and the mill.

Copper was the mainstay, although enough silver showed to pay actual cost of mining, 80 cents to the ton of ore. As costs increased and returns did not, operations began to slow down. There had been about 275 men working in the mines and the mill, but the number dwindled until at last everything stopped and everybody moved away, except one old man, a Mr. Foster, who stayed as watchman. Now even he is gone and the buildings stand silent and deserted. Many are crushed to the ground by the weight of winter snows totaling 30 feet some years. Dump cars are rusting on little rails, which look as if they were made for a long-gone toy engine. The skeleton of a deer lies inside the mill where the animal must have taken shelter in a winter storm and starved to death. The stream rushes through town, taking first one path and then another as the flushes of melting snows in spring urge it on.

OLD ORE CARTS stand rusting near mill.

OLD CABLE SPOOL reveals details in cross lighting.

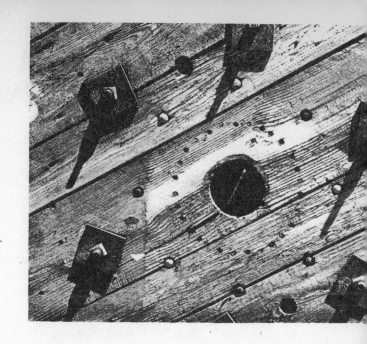

THESE WERE MESS HALLS and dormitories for single miners. Structure at right has been crushed by weight of snow.

SPECTACULAR PEAKS of some of wildest parts of Cascades rise behind remains of Trinity as backdrop. Dense timber covers hills. Fuel and lumber were never problem here.

UNION, WASHINGTON

Lumbering has been of prime importance in the Puget Sound country of Washington since 1788 when Captain John Meares left it with his sailing vessel loaded with spars for China. The load never reached there, the ship running into a heavy storm and the cargo jettisoned. Several years later when Captain George Vancouver's ship lost a spar, he had his men cut a tree in the Washington woods to replace it. Then fur trading became well established and the need for log cabins created a new industry. Millwright William Cannon set up a whipsaw platform at Fort Vancouver in 1825. He sawed boards with this crude hand-device for a year, replacing it with a sawmill built with machinery from London.

The Fort Vancouver mill operated until about 1847 when the machinery was sold to Colonel Michael T. Simmons who set it up at Tumwater, bringing sawmilling close to Puget Sound. In 1852 residents of the Alki Point settlement, later to be part of Seattle, cut trees on the hills back of the village for use as pilings. They brought oxen from the Puyallup Valley to haul the logs to the water, this probably being the first operation of its kind. A sawmill owned by Nicjolas De Lin in Tacoma sawed 2,000 feet a day. De Lin's boards sold only while there was no competition for his saws invariably cut them "on the bias", tapered from end to end or in both directions from the middle.

Henry Yesler's first steam sawmill in 1853 at Seattle was the beginning of the big time in the lumber industry and mills now spread along Hood Canal, actually a natural inlet from the Strait of Juan de Fuca. The Olympia COLUMBIAN reported in 1853: "There are now no less than fourteen sawmills run by water power and one steam sawmill in process of construction on Puget Sound. A large number of our citizens are getting out cargoes of hewn timber, piles, shingles and cordwood faster than the number of vessels engaged in that trade can carry them to market."

The shores of Hood Canal were becoming dotted with logging camps and small sawmills, with no central source of supplies. In 1858 partners Wilson and Anderson set up a trading post on the south shore of the Canal at the narrow neck of land connecting the Kitsap Peninsula to the Olympic Peninsula and the mainland. This strategic situation commanded a view of Hood Canal and ships in both northeasterly and northwesterly directions, the Canal making a right angle bend at that point.

As soon as the trading post was well established, the Rush House was built. It was a grand affair, two stories high with six bedrooms (guests supplying their own bedding) and most important, a bar where all sorts of potables could be had. The dining room served "elegantly complete" meals. To make sure no guests were absent when dinner was served, the cook went out on the balcony and sent out a couple of blasts from a cow's horn fitted with a shrill-sounding reed.

After a few years Anderson tired of keeping up his end of the trading post work and sold his share to F. C. Purdy. In a few more years the enterprise was transferred to the ownership of John McReavy, until then a lumberman. By 1876 there were at least fifty logging camps in the area, most of them buying all their provisions at the trading post. By 1889 the land around the store and hotel was becoming so well settled it was platted as a town and christened Union City. Growth had been slow but steady yet Union City was to regret things could not stay that way.

Around 1890 rumors were rife that Union City would be at the crossroads of several railroads — the Grays Harbor and Puget Sound, the Union City and Naval Station, and Port Townsend and Southern Lines. As a consequence Union City boomed so fast lots that had been worth next to nothing now sold for $1,000 each. So many people moved into the town there was no place for them to live, in spite of earnest efforts of the one sawmill, brand new, to turn out enough lumber for new houses. Tents blossomed everywhere, even along the beach. More than one greenhorn from the midwest pitched his tent when the tide was out, only to find his domicile flooded a few hours later. Meals were cooked over communal fires until stoves could be obtained.

Further inflation came with the arrival of construction crews, horses and Union Pacific equipment. On the very day work was to start came devastating news. Baring Brothers Bank of London refused further payments on its outstanding debts

HOME OF JOHN McREAVY who bought and operated town's early day trading post, platted and named Union City in 1889. Sawmill built by McReavy cut cedar boards lining interior walls of house. Building, erected in 1889, was once painted bright yellow, is now mellowed by age. It has ground level basement at rear where hand laundry was once operated by Indian women. House is now home of Mr. and Mrs. Lud Anderson. Mrs. Anderson was Helen McReavy, daughter of John, has written history—**How, When and Where on Hood Canal.**

of twenty-one million pounds, obligations assumed in a fantastic web of international finance. The panic of 1893 was on and all railroad work was immediately canceled. Union City's dream of becoming a rail terminus at salt water skittered away, the boom at an end. In embarrassment the town quickly dropped the "City" from its name and as plain Un-

ion, settled back to the simple existence it has since led. In recent years, with rapid transportation available, summer residents have built cottages along the shores of Hood Canal. Restaurants, stores and other small businesses have sprung up at Union, causing small scale prosperity, likely to prove more permanent than the first.

VADER, WASHINGTON

Vader, in the heart of the great Washington logging area south of Olympia, where Swedes and Finns and bull teams were trying to "get daylight into the swamp," had its share of shooting scrapes and murders. But while old-timers, including keen-minded Norman "Pat" Hitchcock, have trouble recalling the full details of them, sharp and clear is the memory of Husky Dog. Everyone who lived in Vader around 1906 will tell you about the town's most proficient alcoholic.

George Gale, now of Olympia, heard the story from Bill Dickenson who lived in Vader for several years. Husky Dog was brought down from Alaska by some prospector who wandered on, leaving his sled dog as a public charge. Bill Dickenson adopted the animal and always took him along when he had one or two in Vader's several bars. One evening as he stood up to the bar in the Spangler Hotel, Bill thought Husky Dog might be thirsty too, ordered an extra glass of beer and set it on the floor. Husky Dog sniffed but turned his head until a little of the brew was poured on the floor. He eagerly lapped up the sample and the rest in the glass when it was poured out. The husky's several admirers "set 'em up" for him all evening and when Bill left the dog walked as he never had at "40 below in the Arctic snow."

The next evening bartender Pat Hitchcock opened up and who but Husky Dog was waiting

VADER'S OLD CITY HALL is crowded by trees, grass, brush. At left are council chambers and shown under cedar tree barred windows of two-cell jail. Most occupants of hoosegow were drunks but it also held murderers. At right is fire station once sheltering two-wheeled hosecart pulled by hand by volunteer fire-laddies, sometimes in 4th of July parades. Hose-drying tower was surmounted by belfry, fire bell weighing more than 800 pounds. Present Vader resident John Groleau remembers when supporting timbers were judged unsafe and bell was removed. He says: "We attached ropes to it and pulled. It made a big crash when it came down, the belfry along with it. It landed behind the building. We always intended getting it out on the main street and mounting it some way as a momento, but never did."

OLD VADER HOTEL, last one to go and was under wrecking hammer when photo was made in 1962. Vader had at least five saloons, two housed in hotels. Near this building was newspaper office where GAZETTE was published.

at the door. Pat poured him a drink on the floor before serving anyone else, recognizing the hangover. The dog stayed in the bar all evening and when it closed he had to be ejected — but not like the men. The "cork-booted" inebriates had to be helped or carried out but Husky Dog was cooperation itself, letting himself be gently guided out. Then his aplomb deserted him. He headed for Bill's cabin but collapsed beside the road to sleep it off.

And so in truth Husky Dog became the furry face on the barroom floor, his progress downward being rapid because of an amiable nature that could not say "no." Several years of guzzling, says George Gale, "soon ruined Husky Dog's beautiful physique, turning him into a 300-pound monster with a gut like a beer barrel. His meaty jowls meas-

ured 24 inches from ear to ear. He became famous as the only dog in the country who could smile" . . . and that was about all. When forced to leave any bar at 2 a.m. he usually tried to make it to the nearby livery stable or blacksmith shop, Bill's cabin having long proved out of range. If he fell short of either he simply slept there, carrying his own blanket against the coldest weather.

And alas, retribution reaped its reward—Husky Dog fell seriously ill. His many friends came to his aid, guaranteeing care by the local doctor who immediately placed his patient on the water wagon. The dog lived a few months, then died in his sleep. Again quoting George Gale: "For Husky Dog the cork had been pulled, the bung knocked out of the barrel."

In the early 1850s flat-bottomed boats nego-

NEAR NEIGHBOR was town of Olequa, named for nearby stream. Was mostly farming community, depending largely on production of hops. With increasing expense of growing and lessening demand for hops, industry declined, most residents moving away. At one time several buildings stood at crossroads, center of Olequa, grocery store last to go. This photographer found only ruins of recently wrecked structure, settled for only remaining evidence of Olequa's one-time lively industry, fast-decaying hop drier.

tiated the Cowlitz River as far as Toledo, a land route, "military road," roughly paralleling the waterway. Near the small falls on Olequa Creek, a Cowlitz tributary and conveniently near the highway, the small village of Little Falls came into existence by the early 1880s, thought to be an outgrowth of an earlier Indian village, with post office, one-room school, general store, hotel and several houses.

When the Northern Pacific Railroad came this way it stopped not at the hamlet but at a point about a mile south, advancing no reason for naming the stop Sopenah. One old-timer in the area says a shipment of soap addressed to the general store in Little Falls, Wash., was sent instead to Little Falls, Minn., and the railroad wanted no more such mistakes. In any event, for many years mail came to the town addressed "Little Falls," rail shipments tagged "Sopenah."

Businesses found it more convenient to move closer to the rail point where others were already established, and took the Little Falls name along with them, the station alone retaining the word Sopenah. The community boomed in the latter part of the century, one large industry the Little Falls fire clay factory, using local high quality clays, and the Stillwater Logging and Lumber Co. Several hotels did a thriving business — Bannon, Spangler, Stillwater, the latter a three-story structure as was the school house. The town was also proud of its Opera House where thespians emoted from the heart to audiences of the bustling metropolis, then the busiest between Portland and Tacoma.

Among employees in the Stillwater mill was a Kentuckian. He liked his job on the edger so well and wrote home so glowingly many of his friends in the Blue Grass State joined him, resulting in a formation of a clique at the plant. Member stood by member on any and all occasions, as the time one of the southerners got into a quarrel with Ed Bertrand in one of the saloons. The two exchanged a few blows, the man from Kentucky getting the worst of it. He backed out the door vowing to get even, borrowed a gun at a friend's house, returned to shoot point-blank at Bertrand.

The killer waited for trial in the City Hall jail, facing almost certain conviction since the shooting had been witnessed by many. But his fellow Kentuckians collected a purse large enough to hire a clever lawyer to defend the prisoner. At the trial, self-defense was claimed with the contention that Bertrand attacked first, was even wearing brass knuckles. The accused was acquitted and released.

During Little Falls' best years there was continuing argument about the name of the town and station, railroad steadfastly refusing to conform. Finally a conference between townsmen and railroad officials brought the positive promise that the line would change the name, but not to Little Falls. So citizens huddled at City Hall and decided to call the town after a long time resident—Mr. Vader. The railroad went along with that.

Vader is today a near ghost. Gone are the hotels, saloons, industries. Quiet streets see little movement — of live people, that is.

168

CALIFORNIA
GHOST TOWNS

MINE-RIDDLED BUTTES LOOM above Sierra City. From these heights slid devastating burdens of snow, often burying portions of town. Alarm bell is mounted in tower beside comparatively young Sequoia. It announced disasters such as slides, fires, also arrival of stages and mail. Clapper is actuated by twin pull ropes while bell remains stationary. Several bells of this type persist in gold country, such as one in front of old firehouse in North San Juan.

AMADOR CITY, CALIFORNIA

A small group of Argonauts detached itself from the hordes swarming over the Sierra foothills and started panning the sands of Amador Creek in 1848. The tiny band had great faith in the chosen location even though little gold turned up in their pans to justify it.

Pickings grew ever smaller until the claim was exhausted and the men ready to fold their tents and fade away. Then in 1851 came the big strike. The original miners had been trying to get their gold the easy way, out of the creek gravels, but the bonanza was found in the quartz vein of the Mother Lode itself at the point where it intersected with Amador Creek.

The find was not made by an experienced miner but by a Baptist preacher, a Reverend Davidson. Not being able to do the hard work or handle the finances he took in other members of the cloth as partners. The popular name for the workings was naturally—"The Ministers' Claim." The mine

was later consolidated with six other workings, the combine called the "Original Amador," a complex of more than nine miles of crosscuts, drifts and raises. They opened up from a 1,238 foot inclined shaft. Total production was almost $4 million.

Better known and far more productive was the Keystone Mine. It was first dug in '53 and for several early years the ore was crushed in the primitive quartz mills called by the Mexican name of arrastres. Later more modern stamp mills were built and as their capacities increased the underground workings developed a shaft 2,680 feet deep. A large portion of the ore was of an unusual sulfarsenide type but it yielded $25 million.

Amador City is two and a half miles northwest of Sutter Creek and is similiar to it in history and general background. Sutter Creek was named for the man who had once operated the vast agricultural domain of Sutter's Fort where Sacramento stands today. Sutter had set up the sawmill at Coloma to supply lumber for his buildings. Instead, gold was discovered in the millrace and the subsequent rush of gold seekers destroyed Sutter's dream by depleting his help and overrunning his farms. He made a pitiful attempt to follow the "If you can't lick 'em, join 'em" school but failed utterly, principally because he had no aptitude for handling his help along the lines the American miners demanded. They claimed his system was "slave labor" and Sutter was forced to quit his claims at Sutter Creek.

More spectacular was the career of Leland Stanford in the same area. Having made a little money in Sacramento as a merchant he bought into the Lincoln Mine. At first there was nothing but trouble and at one time he was ready to sell out for $5,000. His foreman, Robert Dowes, persuaded him to hang on, the strike at last was made and Stanford was established as a tycoon. With his partners he then built his railroad, became U. S. Senator, then Governor of California and founded Stanford University.

OLD IMPERIAL — finest hotel in Amador City. Bar section operated until fairly recent years, barkeep in fancy vest pouring drinks for fewer and fewer patrons until forced to quit.

171

ALTAVILLE, CALIFORNIA

The question is: Does Altaville owe its place in history to the producing of its gold or its fossilized relic? For here, down 130 feet in the Matison Mine, was found the "Calaveras Skull," subject of controversy and confusion.

When gold in the Mother Lode's easily worked placer streams began to run thin in 1850, miners found more of it in gravel beds above and then in ancient deposits far below the level of active stream beds. This was mighty old gold, as evidenced by the fossil leaves and riffles found with it. Near Altaville several drift mines were developed with shafts as deep as 300 feet.

The Matison Mine was one of these and the finding of the old skull put the Mother Lode in the news more than the gold did. Scientists saw irrefutable proof that man was far more ancient than formerly believed, the public laughed at it as a gigantic hoax and Prof. J. D. Whitney became the man of the hour.

Out of the tangled web of tales about the skull finding is the clear fact that this gentleman, then State Geologist, in January of 1866, had exposed a wildcat scheme of a local financier to foist worthless stocks on the people of Altaville. His act made some bitter enemies but their wrath was blunted by the uncovering of the skull "dating back to Pliocene times."

The whole world heard about the discovery that July. At a meeting of the California Academy of Sciences at San Francisco, Prof. Whitney read a paper confirming the authenticity of the Pliocene Skull. From then on for years the press was full of stories on the subject, many scientists eager to accept the age of the relic, others scoffing. One newspaper reported, "The unscientific public hailed the story as a huge joke on the state geologist perpetrated by the fun loving citizens of the camp." Bret Harte covered the subject in one of his later contributions to the "Californian", the poem "To The Pliocene Skull." In 1903 the American Anthropological Society accepted the skull as a genuine relic but questioned the extreme age which admitted the presence of prehistoric caves in the Sierra Nevada.

And for the light touch is the story that about the time the skull was found, Dr. Kelly, nearby Angel's Camp dentist, failed to find something—the skull of his laboratory skeleton.

HEADSTONE in old section of Altaville cemetery which contains many interesting monuments from gold rush days. Unique in shape, headstone memorializes Alfredo Ribero by portrait cemented to marble. Picture remains unfaded through long years of strong sunshine, was made by converting photographic emulsion to enamel then baked on porcelain base. Uniform is likely that of local Militia during Civil War days.

RABBITS MADE HIM RICH

Angel's Camp, Calif.

Beside a name which strained credulity Bennager Rasberry had a worked-out placer claim, a cranky old muzzle loading shotgun and he was hungry. The rocky rises around Angel's Camp supported a lot of jackrabbits and if the miner could not find gold he could spend time gnawing away on the stringy meat of those sagebrush broncos.

Rasberry shot several and then had trouble with the ramrod. It was jammed in the barrel tightly and neither curses nor muscles could get it out. Losing his temper completely he fired the weapon at a rock a dozen feet away. The ramrod came out right enough and Rasberry saw it had scuffed off the weathered crust of the rock and exposed the yellow gleam of gold.

It may be assumed Mr. Rasberry forgot all about rabbits since it is recorded he picked up nuggets to the value of $700 before it got dark. Come daylight he returned with pick and shovel and that day returned with $2,000. When the following day's work netted $7,000 from the vein he made up his mind he had a gold mine and filed claim to it. Bennager Rasberry soon became the richest man in town and his name is perpetuated in an Angel's Camp street called Rasberry Lane.

George Angel was a veteran of the war with Mexico and went with other footloose, gold-hungry ex-soldiers to the Sierra foothills. He found a likely spot to camp on the bank of a small creek tributary to the Stanislaus but he also found throngs of other hopeful prospectors already working the gravels. Playing it safe, he set up a trading post before picking up shovel and gold pan. So although mining proved a spare time sideline for Angel, he was still able to sift out as much as ten ounces of gold on a good day.

The men Angel joined at the location that would bear his name proved to be the advance guard of the big rush. In those first months every man was friend with an equal chance and there was no need for formal claims. But when reports of the rich harvest reached the outer world and hordes descended on the peaceful community many a prospector found "a snake in his tent." When the solid citizens caught strangers working their favorite locations there was trouble and some killings resulted. Civilization had arrived and it became necessary to legalize claims. Yet this period, loosely called the "Age of Innocence," quickly came to an end when the creek sands gave up the last of the gold flecks.

By 1855 Angel's Camp was "law abiding" with wrong doers duly arrested by a legally appointed sheriff, tried in regular court proceedings varied according to the crime. At least this was supposed to be the procedure and sometimes it did work out that way. Among variations was the case of a miner killing another who called him a "hog thief." Although he had "sort of borrowed" the pig in question, he said, and although he had "et some of it," the slur had irked him to the point of drawing his gun and killing the porker's legal owner.

Some Angel's Campers thought the culprit should be strung up pronto and when lynching rumors spread the law sent to nearby San Andreas for aid in protecting the prisoner, at the same time rushing trial procedure. To a packed courtroom came the word that the San Andreas sheriff and emergency posse were nearing Angel's Camp. As if by pre-arrangement each court officer was seized and bound, the prisoner hustled to the hanging tree and was dangling from the end of a rope when the horsemen of the law rode up.

Today Angel's Camp is better known to the tourist than almost any other town in the Mother Lode. And this is not due to George Angel or the muzzle-loader of Bennager Rasberry or to any other bit of verified history, but to an incident nothing more than trivial, if indeed it happened at all.

The area around Angel's Camp was a hotbed for California folklore, nurturing over-fertilized stories about Joaquin Miller, Black Bart, salacious doggerel by anonymous miners and more classic tales by Bret Harte and Mark Twain.

It was in 1865 that Twain toured the Southern Mines. By that time they were "decaying" as a contemporary critic wrote it and it would seem the humorist found little of interest in the mines themselves, preferring, in Angel's Camp, the salubrious atmosphere of the Angel's Hotel bar. It is legend that bartender Ben Coon related to him a local anecdote which Twain jotted down in his notebook—"Coleman with his jumping frog. Bet stranger $50. Stranger had no frog and C. got him one. In meantime stranger filled C's frog full of buckshot so couldn't jump. The stranger won." Twain wove the fragments into a story which he later called a "villainous backwoods sketch" but which was printed and reprinted across the country and beyond in several languages.

BALLARAT, CALIFORNIA

The names of our old towns, and why they were selected, are interesting facets of history.

Cornucopia is often used, signifying the horn of plenty. Bonanza, Fairview and White Hills are obvious in origin. But Ballarat?

Research shows that gold was discovered in Australia two years after California's big find of 1849. The discovery was made in Ballarat, Victoria, in the southeast part of the country down under. And it was at Ballarat, Australia, in 1869, that the largest nugget in the world was found. It weighed an incredible 2,284 ounces.

The hopeful founders of this California desert town must have baptized it (with whiskey, of course) "Ballarat" for the famous one in Australia. Prospectors, in the 1890's, discovered the yellow metal in several of the canyons leading out of the western flank of the Panamint Mountains.

HOUSE MELTS SLOWLY into earth from which it sprang. View is away from mountains looking east across blazing desert. Dry lake shows as white streak behind shack. Tiny tin-roofed house was home of lonely prospector until fairly recent years.

The Panamint Valley, mostly a glaring white, dry lake bed, butts up against the steeply rising Panamints. These culminate in Telescope Peak, 11,045 feet high above the townsite. There were no trees anywhere, so there was no material for lumber, and consequently Ballarat was literally created out of clay. Its buildings were built of adobe bricks baked in the sun. Some residents added suitable ornaments and additions of corrugated iron, bottles, etc. Enough timbers were imported for lintels, doorframes and sills. In this barren, waterless waste there grew no little flower gardens, or yellow roses, as in other camps, only skimpy sagebrush and greasewood.

The town was actually a center for several mining camps, including the almost inaccessible Panamint City which hardly provided a level spot large enough for a dance floor. In Ballarat were found several dance places as well as the necessary adjuncts such as refreshments and ladies.

After the town died, it had a solitary inhabitant for years. This was "Shorty" Harris. In 1934 he died and Ballarat and he became ghosts together.

The adobe buildings are nearly melted away, but the remnants are well worth visiting, a monument to man's persistent search for gold in the face of almost insurmountable difficulties.

LONELY, WEATHERED REMNANT of business building strikes note of pathos against Panamints. Land is harsh, offering no timber, water, food. All supplies had to be hauled long distances. Yet Ballarat was scene of many gay times, even advertised a "Fancy Dress Ball."

BEAR VALLEY, CALIFORNIA

Col. John C. Fremont was no man for hard work but he knew what his head was for. When he shifted the boundaries of his 44,000-acre grant to cover the newly discovered gold country from Mariposa to the Merced River, he was very successful in getting others to work the extensive and rich placers on his claim. The many experienced Mexican miners in the area who were unwilling to work for wages were given a grubstake and "share" in a claim along the stream. On this basis they would wade into the water and slosh a pan or shovel gravel into a Long Tom like everybody else.

When the placer workings were going good, Fremont discovered the veins scattering loose gold into the creek bed. In 1851 he started hard rock mining in the lode itself and built several stamp mills to crush the ore. Of his operations he favored those at Bear Valley, first called Simpson-ville, and decided to build his home here. It was an imposing structure, called "The White House" by the people in the settlement.

A building boom now set in. Fremont's enter-prises erected an elaborate two-story wooden structure with wide, gingerbread balconies, the lumber brought around the Horn in 1850. The hostelry served as headquarters for the Fremont Company and shelter for travelers including Ulysses S. Grant, its formal name being Oso House. Also going up in this period were a number of saloons, a large livery stable and several stores including the huge general mercantile business of the company.

In 1858 Fremont brought to "The White House" his wife, Jessie Benton Fremont, and the children. In June of that year the famous "Mariposa War" came to a head, threatening for a time the lives of the little family. But Col. Fremont was above all a soldier and had seen trouble coming. He had been fortifying his best-known mine, the Pine Tree, against attack by men of the Merced Mining Co., which firm had taken over two other units of the Colonel's properties by force.

The Merced men surrounded the Pine Tree and prepared to stage a seige. Fremont was wily enough to slip a rider through the solid line

ADOBE STORE BUILDINGS are melting away. This is rear section of walls facing street. Door at left opened into estab-lishment of Nicholas Pendola, an Italian who built structure in 1850. Pendola was expert bootmaker, doing repair work as well. Most prominent custo-mer was Col. Fremont himself who had all his boots made here. Iron doors, shipped around Horn are still in place, $800 for the pair. Walls have unusual con-struction, adobe c o u r s e s are alternated with schist slabs, quarried in neighborhood. Gar-barino Store, General Merchan-dise adjoins at right.

around the mine who carried a message to the Governor, a desperate plea for help. This was answered in five days by a detachment of state troops which forced both sides to break up, the belligerents were admonished when maneuvered into court.

In 1859 the Supreme Court confirmed Fremont's title and the Mariposa War was officially ended. Later that year Horace Greeley visited Bear Valley, reporting: "The Colonel is now operating two stamp mills and netting $100,000 a year." Whatever the amount, Col. Fremont decided in 1863 it was not worth more gray hairs and sold the entire grant for $6 million. He came out considerably ahead since the original price in '47 was $3,000.

Bear Valley is a ghostly place now. Fremont's fine hotel with its balconies and pillars is gone, set on fire in 1938 by careless campers. Gone also is "The White House." Remaining are many ruined adobe buildings, several schist structures including the roofless jail and a few false fronts on the main street that breathe the atmosphere of the days when Fremont "owned" the town of 3,000 people.

ROOFLESS JAIL stands near schoolhouse on hillside. Built solidly of schist rock set firmly in mortar, structure would seem escape-proof, but further restraint was secured by fastening prisoner by leg-irons to heavy ring of iron in center of floor—common practice when town flourished. Hill behind jail is sparsely forested with digger pines.

BIG OAK FLAT, CALIFORNIA

White women were scarce in the early days of the West and particularly during the first several years of California's gold rush. So it was natural for a lonely white miner to take an Indian wife, not necessarily in legal fashion. James Savage—the same Savage who explored the Yosemite Valley while the head of a party pursuing renegade Indians—is assigned a vast loneliness, for he took five aboriginal wives to his bosom. And more, he retained most of their relatives as servants and laborers.

Savage was prospecting the gulches between Deer Creek and Moccasin Creek in 1849 and he and his retinue camped one night under an enormous oak tree on a wide flat. Next morning found the party panning the gravels of the creek and the showings convinced the leader that here they would stay. News of this kind could not be muffled and in a few months hordes of the gold-hungry, disappointed elsewhere, moved into "Savage's Diggings."

Before it was all over the placers of the immediate area had yielded a total of more than $25 million—one of the richest diggings of the Mother Lode. The name of the spot was changed to Big Oak Flat in honor of the gnarled patriarch standing alone on the only level part of the camp. The tree was of dimensions out of all proportion to other oaks of the mountains and was thought to be the largest in California, with a diameter of thirteen feet at the base, eleven at a man's head.

The oak was still monarch of the flat when the town grew to 3,000 but was succumbing to a man-made cancer. The miners could not resist the temptation to dig closer and closer to the roots until many branches died. Fire in 1862 which destroyed most of the frame buildings caught the dried or dead limbs and finished the life of the old tree. Unrestrained digging around its base at last toppled it in '69 and in 1901 a fire was set against it, burning most of the trunk and all the limbs.

In 1932 the Boys' Service Club of Union High School in Sonoma gathered the remaining fragments of the old oak and built a monument over them beside the road. In a few years this memorial was so decimated by the hackings of vandals that it was necessary to protect them with iron grillwork.

BIG GENERAL MERCANTILE is one of the finest examples of architecture in entire Mother Lode country and one of the best preserved. Built of dressed schist slabs set in lime mortar, the door frames are made square by the use of bricks. Heavy iron doors, characteristic of gold rush style, were shipped around Horn, had bars and hasp inside for securing at night. Not only did doors afford protection against bandits but kept fire out, or contained within.

THEY REST IN PEACE

BODIE, CALIFORNIA

As early as August, 1865, Bodie attracted such nationwide attention by its wickedness and flagrant disregard of law and order that *Harper's Monthly* sent out a man to "case" the town for a story. He was I. Ross Browne. Having at last arrived there tired and dusty, he was encouraged to sit up and take notice by a slug of snake medicine. His eyes having thus been opened, he looked around him and found the place "destitute of vegetation" with the exception of sagebrush and grass. Mr. Browne missed a few details. There were also Argenomes, a prickly "poppy" and an iris.

For some Fourth of July celebrations trees and shrubs were imported for the day. These "Fourth of July" affairs were indeed important. The entire population turned out, many ladies were in formal gowns. As the day wore on lubrication progressed, and by the time the Grand Ball started in the evening things were really lively even if the imported verdure had wilted.

Dances were held in the Miners' Union Hall which still stands today. Many fights developed and combatants were ejected to continue the often fatal fracas outdoors. If a corpse resulted no one worried too much about it, but the next day a question had to be settled. On the hill close to town there were two burying grounds, one for the "decent respectable folks," the other, larger and more populous, for all the rest, so which one should properly hold the newcomer?

The "Bad Man from Bodie" is a well-founded legend. He is a compounded figure, made up of real-life rascals who infested the town. Among these were two Mexicans who had learned of the planned movement of $30,000 in bullion. They waylaid the coach on the stage road between Bodie and Carson City and got away with the loot. They were caught shortly but the gold was missing. One was killed in the capture, the other died in the Bodie jail overnight. Presumably the bandits cached the gold in the short time between hold-up and capture, but the secret of the location was buried with Pedro on Boot Hill. This was in 1880, but the gold is still there.

Maiden Lane and Virgin Alley were the two streets comprising the "red light" district. Houses ranged from mere cabins with one girl to the elegant high grade salon. Whereas loggers in the northern woods towns brought their girl friends pitchy wood for starting fires, the miners of Bodie filched nuggets of gold for theirs.

As much gold remains under Bodie Butte as was taken out, some $75,000,000 worth, but the vast labyrinth of tunnels and shafts under the Butte and town are collapsing into one another, and water fills the lower levels.

One day, when the price of gold advances, life may return to Bodie. But it is not likely to be the same violent, rowdy and lusty force which once animated the place and its 10,000 people.

The main street, named for *Harper's* Mr. Browne, once lined solidly with commercial buildings, has dwindled to a few blocks of sparsely spaced structures. Some of the most historic ones remain; the Firehouse with its old hose cart, Assay Office and Miners' Union Hall. On side streets are the Methodist Church, the jail, the school and a good many others.

SIDE STREET LEADS to Methodist Church. Funds for building quaint structure were solicited from redlight district, bordellos, saloons and opium dens as well as more legitimate business. The former contributed bulk of necessary funds. Metal roof added in later years has prevented total decay of charming little building.

CALICO, CALIFORNIA

Calico is unique among ghost towns, a reconstructed and restored replica of the original. The man responsible for the feat should know what it looked like, for he worked there in the mines in 1910. He is Walter Knott, who now owns the whole town. The job has been no small project and is not finished yet.

The reason for the name is strikingly evident. The mountains forming a backdrop for the old camp are as brilliantly varied in color as any fabric could be.

Many of the buildings in Calico were made of adobe, sun-dried brick, for lack of sufficient lumber. These had partly melted away, even in this almost rainless country, and have been reconstructed of concrete, roughened and colored in such a way as to resemble closely the original appearance. Every now and then we would spot a frame building in its original condition. No amount of skill could duplicate the beautiful weathering effect only time and the elements can give to exposed wood.

The main street was not called "Main" but "Wall Street." In the 80's there were five saloons, three restaurants, many stores and hotels in addition to the usual boarding-houses, assay offices and school. Cornish miners (as in many early camps) were there in numbers and many of these lived in caves in the hills. These were secure from wind and were no doubt much cooler than the town's man-made structures. Daytime temperatures around the Calico Hills in summer will often reach 110 degrees or more.

Top producing days for Calico Mine were in the 80's. The number of saloons, always an indication of the size and prosperity of the population, was listed at more than twenty at this period.

The town began to die in 1892 and became more feeble until 1929, when it lay down and quit breathing entirely.

LITTLE SCHOOLHOUSE is lovingly rebuilt with original design in mind. Hill behind shows all the colors of calico cloth.

SKILLFUL BLENDING OF OLD with pseudo-old is evident here. Original signs seldom survive, but if these are re-creations they have authentic flavor.

California

THE RIVER WAS FULL OF GOLD

Camp Seco, Calif.

Oregon City, California? No mistake. It was rough and tumble mining camp during early years of the great gold rush to the Mother Lode. Among the first outsiders reaching the strip coursing 150 miles along the lap of the High Sierra were Oregonians barely settled after crossing the plains to the Willamette Valley. Oregon so stimulated them they carried to many gold camps names like Oregon City, Oregon Creek, Oregon Hill and there were several Oregon Gulches, one bisecting a shallow valley not far from the Mokelumne River which was "full of gold."

The population of Oregon City quickly grew

VIEW, looks directly through ruins of store buildings adjoining Adams Express Co. Stones used in construction were undressed but some care was used in selecting flat surface for facing out. Roofs have long ago disappeared. Walls get wet in winter to permit growth of grasses on top edges and long, hot summers dry them to sere, yellow state.

more cosmopolitan, news of riches there attracting men from other areas. Mexicans from Sonora were very numerous along the gold-flecked trail they called Veta Madre. Sonorans soon outnumbered Oregonians and deploring a lack of water, they gave the place a new name, Campo Seco or dry camp.

By 1854 the town had three hotels, many saloons, a brewery and that year a disastrous fire which razed all wooden buildings. With placer gold still flowing and a shallow hard rock mine nearby, inhabitants felt justified in building new hotels, rebuilding saloons and refurbishing stone structures, one the office of the Adams Express Co.

But prosperity had only a year or so to go before it sagged. Placer gold was then exhausted and the quartz veins were pinching out. A few people moved away, a store closed and almost unnoticeably Campo Seco headed for ghostdom. Then somebody uncovered a deposit of copper nearby, a protruding piece of native, almost pure, copper.

The value of copper, always fluctuating, reached a high point in 1860. A newly organized group of financiers called Penn Copper Co. bought options on the property and soon had a big operation in full swing, gold almost forgotten. From then until about 1924 the fortunes of the dry diggings went up and down according to the price of copper.

In the early 1920s a group of eleven San Francisco Bay communities in need of water united to form the East Bay Utility Co., with the objective of placing a dam across the Mokelumne River to form a long reservoir above. Flood waters would cover many river bars that had yielded millions in

FRAME BUILDING, one of few in Campo Seco. Originally a saloon, some signs of old bar still evident inside, later a meat market, one old picture showing dim outline of steer's head on false front. Still later, contemporary with building of nearby Pardee Dam, enterprising merchant made oblong opening at near end, served drinks to construction workers, some soft by law, most spiked or neat "white mule" by demand.

BELOW BUTTE PEAK, high, conical mountains visible for miles around, is site of Butte City now represented by only solid structure built there. Basin, 1½ miles south of Jackson, was early discovered to be rich in gold, causing immediate growth of town built almost entirely of adobe and wood. One exception is this structure of Calaveras schist fieldstone with doors and windows of fired brick built by Xavier Benoist in 1854. Upper window spaces and ground level doors were fitted with iron shutters, familiar to Mother Lode visitors. After some years Benoist sold out to one Ginnochio whose name relic bears today. Store was built near old trail and when State 49 was put through it stood so close to edge passing cars almost brushed fenders. Then thieves stole heavy iron doors so conveniently close. State erected sturdy cyclone fence with several strands of barbed wire at top to protect historic building against further vandalism, an unsightly but effective barrier. Only other evidence of one time teeming town is cemetery above where bodies of many nameless miners lie.

gold and the corporation was forced to buy many dead claims at inflated prices set when rumors of the project reached the owners.

As work began hundreds of workmen poured into construction camps near old Campo Seco and suddenly a new enterprise sprang up—moonshining. After work laborers came in droves clamoring for something to drink with more authority than near beer. All right, said some Campo Secoans, we'll give it to 'em. They set up a still and shop in one of the old stone buildings, the illicit drink emporium never raided by prohibition agents and flourishing until the Pardee Dam was completed in 1930. Then, according to local legend, the operators of the traffic who had prudently continued to pay insurance premiums, set fire to the wooden interior of the stone building and faded out of history.

184

$40,000 NUGGET

Carson Hill, Calif.

They were fifteen feet down, four Americans and a Swiss, working their claim at Carson Hill in the Mother Lode country of California. Darkness was falling but the men kept on digging and shoveling and rubbing the dust out of their eyes. Suddenly one of them, generally thought to be Perkins, struck a rock. Failing in an attempt to heave it out of the hole he decided to look at it closer in better light. He could thank his lucky stars he did. It was a big gold nugget. Taken down to Stockton, weighed on the Adams Express Company scales, the chunk of gold made the newspapers all across the land, reports giving the weight as anywhere from 141 pounds to 214 pounds, 8 ounces, depending upon avoirdupois and troy weight plus enthusiasm. In time the true weight was established at 195 pounds.

Mr. Perkins came from Lexington, Kentucky, to the gold fields at the first word of discovery. After mining a few years he still had never owned more than $200 in gold dust at one time but he had joined with four others and still had hopes. The men panned all available gold from their creek at Carson Hill and were working up the lode from which the placer gold had apparently come. They were doing fairly well on that fateful November 29 day of 1854 and were reluctant to knock off but after finding the big rock it is to be assumed they did.

The record does not state how big an argument there was over ownership of the nugget but it was decided that since Perkins owned the biggest share of the claim he was the "principal owner." So he and a fellow miner started for New York with their prize. Neither got that far at that time. At some point along the journey a New Orleans man offered Perkins $40,000 for the nugget which he accepted and promptly dropped from history. The

DETAIL at entrance to wine cellar of James Romaggi house at Albany Flat, built 1852.

MONUMENT stands on bank of Stanislaus River at site of almost vanished Melones, first called Slumgullion, now camp ground operated by owners of nearby tavern. This operates in one of the few buildings remaining from days of ferry and gold camp. First miners, Mexicans from Sonora, claimed to have found nuggets like the seeds of "Melones."

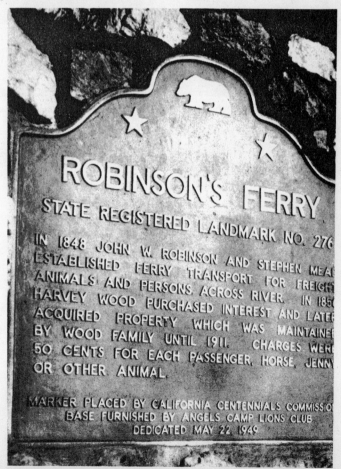

185

THIS BUILDING is one of best preserved and most elaborate in Mother Lode. Pictured in several early publications it is variously termed "Romaggi Fandango Hall" and "Romaggi Adobe." Originally, at least, it was erected as home for James Romaggi, an Italian preferring grapes to gold and setting out vines and fruit trees, nearly duplicating green slopes in homeland. Appellation "Romaggi Adobe" is baffling since walls are constructed of selected, coursed slabs of amphibolite schist. One old photo shows badly weathered roofs of boards, doubtless once covered with shakes or shingles. Nearby road led to Los Muertos, scene of several battles between Mexicans and Americans in fall of 1852.

record follows the mass of gold to New Orleans where it was deposited in the Bank of Louisiana. It was later sold, the new owner taking it to Paris and exhibiting it as the largest nugget ever taken out of California or the United States. Which perhaps it was.

There have been no huge nuggets of gold reported for a long time but during the last half of the 19th century big chunks were being found all over the world, hysterically announced in the press as being the largest wherever found, either by weight or value. The word "nugget" is thought to be derived from "ingot," defined as any lump of pure metal cast into a particular shape. While a natural chunk of metal, specifically gold, is termed a nugget, it need not be pure metal but could include any amount of the matrix from which it came. Those found in California usually included some quartz as in the case of the Carson Hill find. The famous Welcome nugget found some years later in Australia and roughly the same bulk as the California one, was all gold and therefore holds first place.

There were many other lucky finds on Carson Hill, a man named Hance taking out a 14 pound lump of gold lying at the top of the hill. Scattered around and on Carson Hill were the rich Morgan mine, the Reserve, South Carolina, Stanislaus and others totaling a fantastic yield of $2,800,000 in gold during the most productive year, 1850. Little wonder mining authorities term Carson Hill the "classic mining ground of California." Ironically the man who made the original find and for whom the hill was named shared in little of the wealth produced there.

James S. Carson was a sergeant in Col. Stevenson's New York Volunteers and when the regiment was disbanded at the end of the Mexican War he was stranded in Monterey, California, with many other soldiers. With the news of James Marshall's discovery of gold in the race of Sutter's Mill, Carson joined a company of ninety-two men, mostly ex-soldiers, going to the gold fields. In the party were some who would leave their names for posterity in the Sierra foothills. The Murphy brothers

headed northeast to found Murphy's Camp. George Angel left his mark on a camp later celebrated as the home of Mark Twain's Jumping Frog and Carson, called "Captain," staked his claim and settled down to panning the creek sands, in ten days recovering 180 ounces of gold to excite all members of the party.

They scattered to locate claims but Carson became ill with "rheumatism" or some affliction which incapacitated him. After many months in bed he went back to the creek but again was taken sick, this time even more seriously, and was removed to Stockton. Recovering long enough to be elected to the state legislature from Calaveras County, he was making plans to return to his claim when he was stricken with his final illness. While he lay in his bed millions of dollars' worth of gold were taken from his hill. He died at Stockton in near poverty in 1853.

ACTUAL TRACES of original buildings of Melones are hard to find. These disappearing stone ruins are secluded in grass, brush, few hundred feet from road. Photographed in very early morning light remains seem properly spectral.

CERRO GORDO, CALIFORNIA

The town's mineral wealth was first discovered in 1865 by Mexican prospectors, who applied the name, "Cerro Gordo." Literally translated, this means "Fat Hill."

For two years not much happened, then one of its discoverers showed a few chunks of silver ore to some mining men in Virginia City. That did it. Los Angeles, a small dying cattle town, received one of the first loads of bullion and revived suddenly.

The moving force to get things going at Cerro Gordo needed something more dynamic than the siesta-taking Mexican pioneers. Mortimer W. Belshaw provided the required spark. He had studied engineering and knew just how to do it. He took over the Union Mine which was producing the lead he needed for smelting. Machinery for smelters was hauled in and lifted over cliffs with an ingenious block and tackle system. A road was built and water piped in.

Ore was hauled to the bottom of the grade where a town named Keeler sprang up as a terminus. This was located on the shore of a large lake reflecting the highest part of the Sierra. Owens Lake is gone now, but the steamboats, *Bessie Brady* and *Molly Stevens*, made regular trips across it in those days. The terminal on the far shore, at the very foot of the Sierra, was Cartago. Next the precious stuff went to San Pedro. All this cost more than $50.00 a ton, so development of smelters on the spot was well worth while.

Cerro Gordo had more than its share of violence. For a time there were almost weekly shootings. The daily six-horse stage was frequently held up. So were the wagons hauling Belshaw's "Long Loaves," 85-pound slabs of precious metal from the local smelters intended for the U.S. Mint.

ALMOST ALL THAT IS left of Cerro Gordo is shown here. At extreme left, ruins of upper terminus of tram house, next (in back) is "Waterfall, Gilded House of Pleasure," at right of road (in repair) was residence of big wheel, M. W. Belshaw. Right, in front, is American House Hotel, lower center is livery stable. Above all tower tailings dumps of main shaft, mine head buildings are concealed behind them.

In later years a tram was built from a huge terminal close to the mine down the precipitous mountainside, leaping from crag to crag and alighting at Keeler. On this web of steel rolled the ore buckets, eliminating the mule teams, since supplies came up easily in the emptied buckets, powered by the down-going ones. Machinery was needed, though not for power but to hold back and control the flow down the cliffs.

In 1959 the tram house and machinery were taken down, to be used in new mining operations near Candelaria, Nevada. Some towers and cables, complete with a bucket or two, have been left.

ANCIENT MULE COLLARS hang in groups on pegs in livery stable, now partly open to the sky.

"AMERICAN HOUSE" STANDS nearly 5,000 feet above now-dry Owens Lake. Sierra rises on other side. Hotel did not have private bath in every room, but even so, ran up monthly water bill of $300. Commodity had to be hauled up by mule teams from artesian well near Owens Lake. Guests were admonished to be "sparing with the water."

CHINESE CAMP, CALIFORNIA

It was a fantastic battle—a Pigtail Waterloo. Nine hundred members of the Yan-Wo Tong were pitted against twelve hundred of the Sam Yaps and it was fought with farm tools and venom. And when the air was cleared of yells, the sounds of cymbals and firecracker smoke, the marshals hauled four men to the morgue, two hundred and fifty to the little adobe jails.

The big Tong melee took place in the Mother Lode country before the Civil War. In the preponderantly Chinese population of the camp were several Tong factions, always ready to quarrel with each other. Two of the groups were composed of miners working claims along the Stanislaus River at Two Mile Bar. One claim was held by Celestials belonging to twelve members of the Sam Yap, be-low it another operated by six brothers of Yan Wo.

A large boulder was dislodged on the upper level and rolled down into the camp below, hurting no one but sparking an argument. The only way to settle it, the powers decided, was by formal battle. And this was not a thing to be undertaken lightly. It required thought and judgment, however miscast. Several American blacksmiths of the town were called upon to make the proper weapons for opposing factions to use with dignity and honor, and into the forges went hundreds of hoes, rakes and whatever could be snatched up from the creek bed and farms.

On Sept. 26, 1856 the Yan Wo horde, mostly from Chinese Camp, clashed on the rocky flat with the defending host of Sam Yaps, hailing generally from

ST. FRANCIS XAVIER CATHOLIC CHURCH built in 1855 by popular subscription of funds and labor, was first regular house of worship in Chinese Camp. Even after church was established with Henry Aleric as first Pastor, miners worked at claims as usual on Sundays and the faithful attended service, piling shovels, pans and outer clothing outside door. Structure originally had shingled roof with belfry and small steeple surmounted by cross. By 1949 it had deteriorated badly and steeple was removed, leaking roof covered with sheet iron and several coats of paint. Cross was then replaced at apex of roof.

Pine in background is of comparatively rare species — *Pinus Sabiniana*. Digger Pine is fairly common on lower slopes of California foothills, has dropping grayish needles, uniquely branched trunk, is somewhat tender.

the nearby camp of Crimea House. As the lines drew close, several contraband firearms were found in both groups. No Chinese were supposed to have them, the law said, but in this case the firing was only spasmodic and did little harm. The fighting consisted mainly of noisy clatter, high-pitched yelling and beating of gongs. Since no important event could take place among Chinese without firecrackers, the smoke and popping of these was added to the general confusion.

Just about the time the going was hot and heavy, four American law officers rode in and stopped the proceedings, arresting a small mob of sweating contestants. Four Tong men lay on the ground and did not move, dead of stab wounds, and four others more or less seriously slashed. The Tong War of Chinese Camp had passed into history.

How so many Chinese came to be together at these diggings is not entirely clear. The several versions are no doubt partly true and each episode contributed to the total of some five thousand. One legend has a group of Englishmen arriving in 1849 to make their fortunes in the undeniably rich placer gravels along the Stanislaus. They discovered however that this would take considerable physical labor and to avoid this they made "raids" on several

OLD STORE has been converted to post office with gabbro cobblestones set in mortar and faced with brick. Outside lock boxes are for convenience of few remaining residents but most patrons go inside to pass time of day with postmaster. Plaque on corner of building honors Eddie Webb, born 1880 in Snelling, California, who was "last of the old-time stage drivers." He hauled freight, passengers and mail from Chinese Camp to Coulterville and Groveland. From 1898 to 1902 he drove the first stage over the new Shawmutt Road.

WHEREVER CHINESE MIN-
ERS LIVED they planted *ail-
anthus* — "Tree of Heaven."
Trees are very self-sufficient,
have persisted and multiplied until they appear native. Photographer made record of Mother
Lode buildings in early spring
before appearance of foliage
which obscures everything behind it.

neighboring mining camps, offering the Chinese
workers more money than they had been getting.
Altogether they lured away several hundred workers to operate the long toms—enlarged and more
elaborate than the rockers in general use after the
first simple pan workings.

Then it was said there was the ship's captain who
deserted his vessel in San Francisco and headed for
the diggings, bringing the entire Chinese crew with
him to do the pick and shovel work. Some say the
two gangs worked toward each other and when
they met, formed and named the town. If this is to
be believed, the yellow men must have been members of the same Tong.

In any event the usual evidences of the early day
gold camp sprang up—stores, banks, livery stables,
honky tonks and brothels. There were enough
whites and Mexicans intermixed with the Orientals
to erect a fine Catholic church, as well as hotel,
Masonic and Sons of Temperance lodges and Wells
Fargo Express office. An organization was formed
to bring water to the mines, solving the problem
by building an elaborate flume from Wood's Creek.

Today most of the buildings and all the Chinese
are gone but plenty of relics remain to give the
visitor a picture of what life was like in those hectic
days of the gold rush.

COLOMA, CALIFORNIA

In any tale of the California gold rush and particularly of Coloma where it all began, Johan Sutter's name looms large even though his part in the discovery was inadvertent and his actions antagonistic. He must have known his troubles were back to dog him when his foreman James Marshall found those fateful flakes of gold in the mill race.

Sutter had trouble in his native Burgdorf, Switzerland, where he was a merchant. Debts and women disrupted his life and he deserted his family, heading for America and landing in Santa Fe, New Mexico. In 1834 he heard glowing reports of wealth to be made in the fertile acres of the pastoral Sacramento Valley.

His course there was roundabout, by way of Fort Vancouver, thence by sailing vessel to the Hawaiian Islands and from there to San Francisco. His record stalled him in that booming city but Monterey gave him a better welcome.

By exercising some imagination he became "Captain Sutter" and was granted a tract of land on the Sacramento River for colonization purposes. An entry in his diary of August 13, 1839 reads: "Today with the help of my ten Kanakas and three white men I founded a colony called New Helvetia." As soon as an adobe fort was built the colony developed rapidly, soon having a bakery, blanket factory, kitchen and dining room for the help and luxurious quarters for the master.

During the war with Mexico Sutter managed to be a friend to each side and when it ended in 1847

and formal transfer of the territory to the United States was consummated by the signing of the Treaty Guadalupe Hidalgo in February, 1848, Sutter's land was left unaffected. He could concentrate on the affairs of his colony which gave the farm the most productive period in its existence.

Six years before, in 1842, Mexicans had found gold in the sands of dry Placerita Canyon near Los Angeles, the first known discovery in California. They "dry panned" the gold-bearing dirt by filling tightly woven baskets and tossing the heavy contents upward in the breezes, deftly catching gold and gravel which were then separated by hand. All this human labor made little impression on history and started no major rush.

Neither did an incident at the mouth of a small stream emptying into the South Fork of the Yuba River. Joseph Aram and wife were members of a party of immigrants who had left New York for San Francisco. Now nearly at their goal, Mrs. Aram went to the creek to do her laundry. The water was too shallow so she scooped out a hole in the bottom and uncovered a small nugget. No one was greatly excited although after the Coloma news, a few staked out claims.

Toward the end of August, 1847, Sutter and James Marshall formed a partnership to build a sawmill at a place called Cullooma by the Indians. It was to supply lumber for Sutter's Fort started about Christmas, 1847, and after seeing it underway, Marshall went to the Fort to oversee the fabrication of mill

193

EARLY APRIL OF 1851 SAW hotly contested race for honor of El Dorado County Seat between Coloma and Placerville, Coloma winning by act of Legislature April 25th. Until this time Coloma had struggled along with log jail from which prisoners made easy escape. New status demanded more secure hoosegow; $16,000 was set aside for construction, stone jail was built within year. In '57 Coloma was forced to relinquish position of County Seat to more flourishing Placerville, expensive and "escape proof" Coloma jail continued to serve El Dorado County until '62. It was then sold to its former jailer, John Tensher, for building material. Partially wrecked structure still offers imposing and picturesque ruin.

irons, leaving instructions for a ditch to be dug to carry water for the race. On his return he found the job being bungled by inept workers trying to dig the waterway from the upper end instead of the lower, the ditch filling with water as they progressed.

Marshall employed a handyman named Wimmer whose wife was an energetic woman doing much work around the property as well as her household chores. She was later to write: "They had been working on the mill race, dam and mill about six months when one morning about the last days of December, or about the first week of January, 1848, after an absence of several days at the Fort, Marshall took Wimmer down to see what had been done while he was away. The water was entirely shut off and as they walked along talking about the work, just ahead of them on a rough, muddy little rock, lay something bright like

gold. They both saw it but Marshall was first to stoop and pick it up." Doubtful that it was gold, he gave it to the Wimmers' little boy and told him to have his mother throw it in her soap kettle. Later the nugget was retrieved from the kettle untarnished by the "saleratus water" and all had to admit it was really gold.

The fat was now in the fire and Sutter was well aware the event would mean the ruin of his dream of empire. Without much hope his words would have any weight, he asked Marshall to keep the business quiet. Instead, his partner went to Sacramento to display the nugget and was laughed at as a crackpot trying to pass off a chunk of pyrites as gold. Had everyone laughed, the rush might have been delayed, although it was not likely all the gold later found could lie undetected forever. The believing one was

ALEXANDER BAYLEY TOOK UP CLAIM at a site near Coloma, erected two-story homestead with attic and large fireplace at end. Soon rumors were flying railroad would build through then booming Coloma and would establish station near Bayley home. Acting on this hot tip, Bayley spent $20,000 on elaborate hotel, shown here. Railroad was never built, hotel called "Bayley House" and now privately occupied by owners of ranch on which it stands, is only large structure for miles around.

Sam Brannan, a San Francisco publisher on a business trip to Sacramento. Brannan looked at the nugget through eyes trained to minerals and publicity values. He went home, spread the news to the world, and in a year or two the world came to the Sierra and reaped its harvest of wealth with neither Brannan or Marshall getting any of it.

Thousands of wildly shoving men flocked to Coloma and soon were spreading up and down the length of the Sierra Piedmont. On their ruthless way the goldseekers overran the Sutter domain, trampling underfoot all the man's vision of grandeur. Even his Kanakas and Indian help rushed to the hills, leaving New Helvetia to decay.

Forced to join the rabble, Sutter gathered up his pitiful remnant of supporters and moved to a stream in the area in an effort to share in the new wealth. Establishing a settlement called Sutter's Creek, he encountered trouble with the American way of life,

was run out of the diggings for what the Yankees called his system of "slavery."

Back in Coloma, Marshall was also having a bad time. The fact that he was not an employee but a partner of Sutter's gave him the right to claim the ground as his by mineral discovery. It also explained why Sutter went to diggings other than Coloma. The man who should have been revered as the discoverer of wealth that would change the course of history was instead hated and despised because he was forced to post armed guards to keep away swarms of prospectors who disregarded his claims. When he appealed to the courts, friends of the trespassers filled the jury box and even his attorneys turned against him in the hope of getting shares of his claims if he lost the suits.

During the next ten years Marshall was an outcast, spied upon, cheated, abused to the point he gave up mining his own property. He tried to make a

THIS WAS HOME OF JAMES MARSHALL at time of his discovery. It stands on rise directly above Coloma, across road from old Catholic Church. Latter is long abandoned, given over entirely to swarm of bees which is established in walls directly over entrance. Photographer was anxious to obtain record of church interior, nearly intact, was unwilling to climb in through window, even more reluctant to penetrate angrily buzzing bees.

living lecturing throughout the west but this effort to justify his position failed too. Twenty years after the discovery, he returned to the site to find things completely changed. Huge combines of moneyed interests had squeezed most small claims from the original settlers, the law courts upholding the consolidation in many cases. Marshall was left out entirely together with many others who had done the spade work.

In 1872 a sympathetic reporter for a San Francisco newspaper took up the cudgel for James Marshall and wrote a series of articles which so changed the mind of the fickle public the legislature was forced to appropriate for Marshall a sum of $200 a month for two years. By the next session public sentiment had cooled and relief funds were cut in half. On August 10, 1885 James Marshall died a broken pauper, was buried on a hill above and within sight of his discovery location.

DELIVERY WAGON OF "People's Store" is well preserved from early days of Coloma.

196

OLD PHOTO FROM California State Library shows Sutter's mill. Figure in foreground is thought to be that of James Marshall.

BITTER DISCOVERER OF GOLD in Coloma, James Marshall, pushed out of rights to mine own claims and tiring of doing odd jobs for living, went to nearby Kelsey, established new mine, the Gray Eagle. In order to provide funds for pushing tunnel, he started blacksmith shop, doing good work but made little profit. Here he died in abject poverty on August 10, 1885. Body was taken to site on hill above old home at Coloma. In 1890 this monument was erected over his grave by Native Sons of the Golden West. Marshall's figure points finger to spot of discovery so momentous to his state and world, but bitterly disappointing to finder.

ACTUAL SAWMILL BUILT by partners Johan August Sutter and James W. Marshall had long disappeared when period of exceptionally low water in American River revealed bits of timbers sticking out of gravel. Investigation showed enough remains to exactly pinpoint location and even give some idea of ground plan and construction. Other artifacts included axes, bolts and implements, now all carefully sheltered and displayed in museum in State Park at Coloma. Site of mill was permanently marked with monument.

COLUMBIA, CALIFORNIA

John Huron Smith decided he needed one more drink to top off his monumental glow. With bad luck he picked a bar owned by the John Barclays of unsavory reputation. Martha Barclay was alone at the bar and refused Smith his drink. In a violent argument Smith gave Martha a hard shove just as Barclay entered. Drawing his pistol, he killed the belligerent Smith.

The whole matter might have ended there as justifiable had the Barclays not been in constant trouble with the authorities. A friend of Smith's, State Senator J. W. Coffroth, took up the affair and incited the people of Columbia to form a mob and take matters into their own hands. They broke into the jail where Barclay was being held and in the dead of night rushed him to the high flume that carried water to the town. A rope was thrown over the timbers, one end knotted around the prisoner's neck. He was jerked off the ground and one man held up a flaming pine torch to see how the victim was making out. Barclay was holding the rope above his head in a desperate grip, his executioners having neglected to tie his hands. It didn't take long for one of the lynchers to beat the hands loose with the butt of a pistol—and Martha was a widow. The early days of Columbia in the Mother Lode were highlighted with stirring episodes like this.

The glitter of rich gold in the gulch at the foot of Columbia's Main Street was exposed by accident. On March 27, 1850, Dr. Thaddeus Hildreath,

his brother George and several other prospectors, reached this point at nightfall and camped under a large tree, with every intention of moving on in the morning. During the night there was a torrential rainstorm which soaked every blanket. The morning was warm and sunny, the blankets spread out to dry and to pass the time the men took their prospecting tools to the gulch to the foot of what was later called Kennebec Hill. Color of such brilliance showed up in the gravels every man in addition to John Walker, who had made the first find, stayed on. In the next two days the men took out thirty pounds of gold worth $4,680.

The resultant rush to "Hildreth's Diggings," later named Columbia, surpassed almost all others in history. Bursting from a population of nothing to a roaring camp of 5,000 gold-starved souls took

OLD WELLS FARGO EXPRESS COMPANY building, best known of remaining structures in Columbia, architectural showpiece of the Southern Mines. Original office was established in American Hotel lobby. When hotel burned it was moved to Fallon House with William Daeger as express agent. Present structure was erected by Daeger in 1857, with grand opening early in '58, builder continuing as agent until '72.

Brick sidewalks laid diamond-fashion was characteristic of times, have escaped fate of similar ones later covered with cement. Lavish use of bricks in Columbia indicates excellent quality of lateriric clays in locality. Two brickyards operated during boom, were situated on old Dambach Ranch in Matelot Gulch, two miles north of Columbia. Marble-like limestone formations laid bare by sluicing were not utilized as building material although marble quarry here shipped cut stones to San Francisco as early as '54. Delicate, lacy wrought iron balcony grilles were shipped around Horn to San Francisco, hauled to Columbia by mule freight.

only a month. Obviously enough permanent buildings to house this host could not be built so quickly and miners slept under every conceivable kind of shelter—or none at all. April is a mild month in the Mother Lode country and many a miner threw a blanket on the ground when the day's digging was done and collapsed in weariness. He slept in his sweat-soaked clothes and worked in them the next day. When even he could no longer stand the aroma of "ripeness", he would put on his other shirt and hang the first one on a branch to freshen. If it was perchance sprinkled with rain, so much the better. If not, he wore it again when the relief shirt became unbearable.

A lady reporter from San Francisco was said to be interviewing the miners about their lives and habits, asking one bearded man digging in the gravel how he did his laundry. Wiping his brow with his sleeve, he told her: "Lady—we don't use much starch."

The hundreds of flimsy frame structures erected were soon destroyed by fire. Brick buildings replaced them but in the next decade many of these were doomed by the discovery that the ground beneath them held a wealth of gold and the metal could be sluiced out. The first building to go was the first put up and the bricks were sold in other camps. By the time the '60s were over half the buildings in town had been demolished and the materials sold in Sonora and Copperopolis. One stately structure was spared, digging ending at the yard of St. Anne's Church.

Sluicing became such a mania owing to the immense pay-off the entire area around the town was soon a boneyard of bare limestone rocks which stand today as mute reminders of the period. Other towns were also washing soil down the creeks until the valleys were choked with silt and farms covered by mud when the water was high. The mass of soil and debris descending from the mountain camps became such a problem that the State Legislature passed laws banning all such sluicing.

During the boom days prices of commodities reached heights undreamed of in California. Sugar brought $3 a pound, molasses $50 a barrel, flour $1.50 a pound and onions $1, sardines and lobsters $4 a can, candles 50c each and the essential miners' knives $30.

TUOLUMNE ENGINE HOUSE. Columbia h a d history of bad fires, worst on July 10, 1854 and in August '57. After latter committee was authorized to purchase fire engine. Arriving in San Francisco, delegation looked at "sample"—hand pumper made for King of Sandwich Islands (now Hawaii). Rig was named Papeete, gaily decorated with paintings of back-bar type damsels and ready to ship. Enamored citizens of Columbia made successful dicker and rig still stands in Columbia fire house with its hoses of cowhide sections riveted together.

Printing office upstairs published two newspapers, *Columbia Gazette* and *Miner's Advertiser*. Bill Steinfeller's Saloon did business on ground floor. At extreme right was "Doc Parson's" drug store, later notorious Pay Ore Saloon.

About 1858 a novel system of furnishing illuminating gas to the town was completed. Large kilns were constructed to roast pitchy pine from the high mountains, the gas carried to houses through wooden pipes. One difficulty after another beset the new company, pipes leaking, the cutting of wood for burning becoming prohibitive in cost. The gas system lasted only a few months and Columbia was back to kerosene lamps, these serving until the advent of electricity at the turn of the century.

The first public high school system began in rented quarters in '54 and six years later moved into its own two-story brick school house. Still standing, the building is one of the oldest schoolhouses in California, classes being held there until 1937.

During Columbia's big, booming years the streets were jammed with traffic. Stage coaches ran on daily schedules. Freight lines operated from Stockton, bringing all sorts of provisions and supplies. The usual gambling rooms, saloons and dance halls were plentiful and houses on the back streets offered their fancy women. An arena was built for a special type of exhibition, fights between bears and bulls.

The contests were advertised as battles between "Wild Bulls from Spain and Savage Grizzlies from the Remote Mountains of California." Often as not the bull was a doltish reject from the Sacramento slaughterhouse and the bear some mangy specimen cornered in the foothills. Usually both animals were interested only in escaping to the free hills and the miners would demand their money back. And even when the bear was gored into a shapeless mass, the miners would still insist on a refund. Horace Greeley, writing about these battles in the New York Tribune is said to have started the use of the terms "bull" and "bear" in relation to the fluctuations of the stock market.

Columbia was needing more and more water for mining as well as domestic use and to meet the demand the Tuolumne Water Company was organized in 1851. It constructed a vast network of reservoirs, ditches and flumes many miles in length. The miners complained the Company was charging excessive rates and needed some competition, and so organized the Stanislaus River Water Company in '54. It's completed aqueduct wound 60 miles through the mountains to Columbia. The project cost over a million dollars and by the time it was finished so were the lush days of Columbia. Surface gold had been virtually exhausted and expensive hardrock mining was under-

COLUMBIA'S LITTLE JAIL was stoutly constructed, had two cells each with opening through which meals were passed to prisoners.

taken reluctantly. The population declined and by 1860 the Tuolumne Company bought out the miners' water works for $125,000.

During its heyday, Columbia had a large Chinatown. This was natural in any West Coast mining town but surprising enough, this one had Italians, French and Irish sections as well as ones called Negro Hill, French Flat, Texas Flat and a neighborhood of Chileans. Most of these sectors were filled with flimsy wooden shacks and as the town began to fade, so did the foreign "ghettos." The same fate befell a double line of cabins extending the whole distance, four miles, to the slightly older town of Sonora. Hardly a sign is left of these shelters. The once sprawling metropolis gradually shrank to its solid nucleus of brick.

But it did not die completely. After the gold rush was over the more substantial buildings did not fall into complete decay nor were they "prettied up" or covered with garish new fronts, as in the case of many of the better preserved towns founded by the Argonauts.

"Recognizing the opportunity to preserve and interpret for future generations a typical Gold Rush town, the state legislature enacted legislation creating Columbia Historic State Park," says a brochure on this Park, "In addition to preserving the remaining historical structures in the main business section of the town, lands are in the process of being acquired in the surrounding blocks in conformity with a master plan approved by the State Park Commission on Sept. 17, 1948, thus assuring the preservation of outstanding historic sites and providing for an adequate setting for this ' Gem of the Southern Mines.' " Due to this studied program there are no modern signs or neon lights and the buildings, while preserved, do not have a stark, "rehabilitated" look, showing instead the effect of a mellowing with age.

EARLY MORNING LIGHT reaches under ornate balcony of hostelry once known affectionately as "What Cheer House," more formally as Morgan's Hotel and later City Hotel. First building on site was frame structure, bought by George Morgan early in July, '54 and remodeled for saloon and was burned to ground ten days later. In '56 he built the first unit of two-story Ale House and Billiard Saloon. this entirely destroyed by fire in '57. Present brick building contained lodgings, theater, bar and Music Hall upstairs, was still operating as City Hotel until 1930s.

MORE BULLETS FOR THE NORTH

Copperopolis, Calif.

The ledge of rock had a greenish-rust color but it sure didn't look to Hiram Hughes like there was metal in it. They said gold was where you found it and gold or silver was what he was looking for and, well, was there any left around here? It didn't seem so after all the digging around he'd done. Now that rusty looking rock—he sure would look like a danged fool taking some of that into an assay office. But what if he did? Only a gimlet-eyed metallurgist and a few Mexican loafers would know. Where's that chipping hammer . . . ?

Hiram Hughes was a Johnny-come-lately to the gold country, this Calaveras area on the Sierra's western slope, and he came here believing he just might find some of the yellow stuff overlooked by the others ahead of him. By 1858 most good or promising gold deposits had been located but Hughes while tardy was also persistent. After combing the Calaveras hills he worked north along the Mother Lode and into the Northern Mines. The next year found him in the Washoe silver region but he could find no trace of that white metal either.

So when he returned to Quail Hill where he spotted the greenish-rust colored rock, Hughes was about ready to quit looking for anything but a bottle of whiskey to help him forget all the hard work. But before he stopped in a saloon he took the chunk of rock to the nearest assay office. The report made him want to holler clear back to Kansas. The sample was nearly a third copper and worth $120 to the ton.

Just about this time another prospector, Thomas McCarty, made a similar discovery in the same area. He took as partners W. K. Reed, Dr. Blatchy and Thomas Hardy. The year was 1860, the country full of rumors that a civil war was about to explode and McCarty's discovery was named the Union Mine. In a few months the Keystone, Empire and Napoleon were added to the complex and a town called Copperopolis was growing up around it.

In 1863 W. K. Reed built a toll road, usually referred to as Reed's Pike, a rough trail over which ox teams hauled $1,600,000 in copper ore the first year. Although it had to go all the way to Wales to be smelted, the finished metal provided most of the copper needs of the Union Army during the war. And this gave Copperopolis, with a population of 10,000 a boom bigger than that in any of the gold camps nearby. When Reed sold out his interest in the Union, now the largest producing copper mine in the country, he got $650,000 for it. Shares in the mine, if sold by the foot, brought $200 for that much ground. During this period copper was worth an all time high of 55c a pound. Six mines were going full tilt and a railroad was being brought in from Stockton.

At the end of the war copper dropped to 19c and mines closed or curtailed operation. The Stockton-Copperopolis Railroad came to an ignominious end at Milton, about two-thirds of the way in and the place familiarly termed "Copper" was on the way out. In 1902 the Union reopened with a new smelter and 500-ton flotation mill. It produced varying quantities of copper with surges through the two world wars, then again closed. Since 1861 the mines produced 72 million pounds worth something over $12 million.

One hundred years after the big copper discoveries another product, asbestos, was located not far away. In 1960 Jefferson-Lake Sulphur Co. of Houston, Texas, paid $4,652,000 for a 500-acre tract on which to build a huge asbestos operation. This tremendous enterprise is not close enough to Copperopolis to mar the beauty and charm of the old copper camp.

LARGE STONE CORRAL near Copperopolis is one of several in area, this one of best preserved. Most were built by Chinese laborers during mining heyday.

MARBLE STONE suggests question instead of identifying long-forgotten miner who rests here. Likely it is simply-marked foot-stone, strayed from more completely identifying head-stone.

SOLID BRICK BUILDING served as Union Mine warehouse in Civil War days. Small, frame, sheet-metal-covered structure was successively store, saloon, laundry, etc.

5 Mo. and 24 days.

Stop traveler and cast an e
As you are now. so once was
As I am now so you must be
Therefore prepare to follow me.
Prepare for death make no delay
I in my bloom was snatched awa
When death did call me to depar
I left my friends with acheing hear

CLASSIC EXAMPLE of "tombstone poetry" carved on marker in Copperopolis cemetery. Burial here was distinctly segregated into four sections—Masonic, I.O.O.F., Catholic and Protestant—separated by 4-foot stone walls.

BUSIEST SECTION of old Copperopolis during Civil War. Left was company warehouse, center building under old oak tree Copper Consolidated Mining Co. offices, right, one of most historic structures in California. Copper produced here was important to Union cause, regiment established to protect mines from possible Confederate sabotage. Soldiers used building as armory for entire period. When news of Pres. Lincoln's assassination reached town "Union Blues" assembled here and formed column on street in foreground, marching north several blocks to Congregational Church for services in honor of martyred war leader. In earlier gold camp of Columbia several brick buildings were torn down to expose rich ground for sluicing. Some salvaged bricks were used to construct this armory. Huge iron doors are considered largest in Mother Lode country.

COULTERVILLE, CALIFORNIA

In spite of the hordes of Chinese and Mexicans in the town, the name Coulterville prevailed. It was originally called Banderita and there are two differing versions explaining the use of the name which signifies "little flag" or "bandana" in Spanish.

When the first whites, who of necessity spoke practical Spanish, arrived in the area they found a goodly number of Mexicans already hard at work. Most of the laborers were wearing small bandanas. In another story when George Coulter left his trading post on the Merced River in 1850 and set up shop on Maxwell Creek, site of the fabulous new "diggin's," he hoisted the only avail-able American flag—a small one—over his tent. The Mexicans took it for the familiar square of colored neck cloth and named the camp Banderita.

The name was of short duration. Coulter's activities were so numerous and varied that his name seemed logical for the town and Coulterville it became. The original Mexican-style plaza, surrounded by nondescript brush "ramadas" and adobes, was maintained but soon outlined with substantial stone and permanent adobes. The influx of more than a thousand Chinese was responsible for many of the latter, this frugal race choosing adobe and rammed earth as being the most economical.

SUBSTANTIAL BUILDING is one of those replacing brush *ramadas* of earlier Mexican occupation. Completed in 1851 it was the second stone and adobe building in Coulterville and among the first in Mother Lode. Built for the Gazolla Store, it was subsequently used as saloon, fandango hall, restaurant and hotel. Ancient umbrella trees, recently beheaded, shade sidewalk.

The first of the pigtails had appeared as early as 1850, establishing a little settlement at the north edge of town. There were the usual twisted streets and opium dives coupled with the inevitable joss house and public bake ovens. These last were built of brick and mortar or mud and were centers for gossip and scandalizing when housewives gathered to do their baking.

Along with the Chinese and half as many Mexicans, there were three thousand American miners and their hangers-on to swell the population of the wildly booming gold camp. The Americans left the placer operations to the foreigners and took to the immediate hillsides to establish the fabulously rich hard rock mines, notably the Mary Harrison. This mine was discovered around 1867 and operated more or less continuously until closed permanently in 1903, after being worked to a depth of 1200 feet by shaft and winch.

The whole area is rich in fine rock, mineral specimens and outcropping, and produces Mari-posite, named for the county. The technical name for the blue-green banded material is chrome mica and it is available everywhere locally. Collectors find white quartz and carbonate minerals such as dolomite, ankerite and calcite. The gold bearing ore consisted of iron pyrites, usually somewhat oxidized.

One completely unorthodox "gold rush" assumed a comic opera aspect, taking place in the middle of the town at the turn of the century. Fire in 1899 destroyed many of the structures. One of the gutted stone buildings was demolished and the rubble shoveled into holes and ruts of the muddy street. A substantial cache of gold, concealed in the wrecked building, was this way buried in the street undetected but the first heavy rain exposed a number of gold coins and nuggets. Almost the entire population turned out to flail the street with shovels and any tool available, leaving it a shambles.

TINY STEAM LOCOMOTIVE was used to haul ore from Mary Harrison mine. Stretch of track was four miles in length, famous as the "World's crookedest railroad." Branches at left are part of Coulterville's "Hang Tree." Dawn of March 16, 1856 saw body of Leon Ruiz dangling from limb. Ruiz was thus punished for slaying of two Chinese miners at Bear Valley and robbing their sluice of gold dust and nuggets worth six hundred dollars. Old oak saw long series of lynchings and "lawful executions."

GHOSTS CROWD AROUND DEATH VALLEY

DARWIN, CALIFORNIA

A group of emaciated, weary men had negotiated fearful stretches of desert and mountains and were camped in the Argus Range. They were hungry and nearly exhausted. The last straw was the discovery that the sight was missing from the only serviceable gun and the killing of any game seemed impossible. An Indian guide, a native to the region, said he could fix the gun, took the weapon and disappeared into the hills. Before long he returned with it. The gun had a new sight of pure silver!

At this point, the main object was to reach the haven of the San Joaquin valley, but the thought of the native silver from which that gun sight had been made stayed with some of the group.

Years later, one Darwin French headed an expedition into the Argus Mountains to search out the lost "Gun Sight Mine." It was never found, but the party did locate mineral deposits worth investigating, and a camp was set up to start mining operations. While Darwin French was the exploring type, not a miner, and soon departed, the embryo town took the name of Darwin and as such developed into a lusty young giant with all the trappings, the saloons, red light houses and roisterous goings-on characteristic of those days.

FIRST SCHOOL IN Darwin was built with funds raised by "passing the hat."

DOWNIEVILLE, CALIFORNIA

Juanita was a good-looking Mexican girl who entertained young miners in her little Downieville cabin . . . until one of her guests pleased her so much she invited him to move in. He jumped at the chance.

A young Australian, Jack Cannon, was not aware of these developments. Juanita had shown him hospitality on several occasions and one morning he was reeling down the street, partly supported by half-drunken companions and partly by thoughts of Juanita's charms. At the door of her cabin he told his friends to go on, that he was going to see a man about a kangaroo.

The others knew about the newly established love nest and tried to argue Jack out of his idea but he pushed open the door and went in. Instead of welcoming him with a loving embrace, Juanita slipped a knife between his ribs. Another version of the legend has Jack opening the door but heeding the advice of his comrades after seeing Juanita had a man, then returning at a later hour to apologize and then getting the knife.

In any event, the result was death for Jack Cannon and the calaboose for the beautious Juanita. The end of the story might have been the funeral but racial prejudice reared its ugly head. Mexicans in Downieville and all California mining camps were barely tolerated. Little excuse was needed to make it rough for them. Forgotten or ignored was the fact of sex and when Juanita was found guilty of murder the same day it happened, she was promptly strung up to a beam of the bridge over the Yuba.

This was mining camp justice but California and the country as a whole reacted with revulsion. Publicity was so unfavorable that lynching even in the California camps became unfashionable for a time.

The first man to pan the water of the Yuba at the forks was Frank Anderson in September, 1949, but he had little success. A few months later there arrived a motley crew headed by one William Downey, a Scotsman. His retinue consisted of ten Negro sailors, an Indian, an Irish boy named Michael Deverney and a Kanaka called Jim Crow.

The group erected several little log cabins above the point where the North Fork of the Yuba joins the main stream. Although snow soon fell and a skin of ice formed on the quiet pools, persistent panning yielded considerable gold. Snow was brushed away from extruding quartz veins, the crevices yielding as much as $200 a day. Most surprising reward came when Jim Crow cooked a fourteen-pound salmon caught in the river. When the eaters got to the bottom of the kettle they found a sizable flake of gold.

Inevitably, a stampede converged at The Forks which was soon renamed Downieville for the leader, now respected and endowed with a courtesy title of "Major." Claims and men spread up and down both streams and by 1851 the camp had a population of 5,000.

Not all of these were miners, one authority claiming "there was only one producer to eight leeches." But the bars were long and shiny with roulette wheels spinning all night. Streets seethed with pack trains of mules, burros and freight wagons. There was no way to haul supplies and prices of commodities proved it—$4 a pound for sugar and boots $100 a pair.

When religion came to Downieville the town had no other edifice for church purposes than the Downieville Amphitheater, located on what came to be Piety

CATHOLIC CHURCH OF IMMACULATE CONCEPTION clings to steep canyon-side, seems to be all steeple, chapel is tiny by comparison. Originally built in 1852, first structure was destroyed by fire 1858. This edifice was erected on site shortly after; Fr. Dalton was first Pastor.

Flat. The intrepid preacher, first to enter the roistering camp and deliver a sermon, was Rev. William C. Pond.

Surprisingly, the miners welcomed Pond and his preaching with an enthusiasm so great funds were provided for a church. It was built in a few months but the week before dedication was scheduled, the building burned to the ground. Thoroughly discouraged and dejected, the minister opened the door of his cabin to a miner with outstreached hand who said he had walked four miles into town. "Here's a hundred dollars, Mr. Pond," he said, "to start a new church." Contributions came thick and fast and in a short time a new fireproof structure of brick and stone was ready for use.

Stories of fantastic finds of gold in and around town would make it appear more churches could have been built in record time. Weirdest is an unverified tale that on August 21, 1856, James Finney found close to town a nugget weighing 427 pounds, Troy. Even allowing for the fact that most California "nuggets" had considerable quartz matrix adhering to them, this one was worth over $90,000. It was sold to bankers Decker and Jewett and sent to the Philadelphia mint where it was displayed for several years. This would be the largest nugget found in California, the the second largest in the world.

In 1858 John Dodge, who was working the forks of the Yuba between '50 and '53, told of an experience plausible enough in view of the highwayman menace. He, said he, Bill Haskins and an unidentified Dutchman were working an abandoned claim on the middle Yuba. Digging in the bank he came to a chunk of pure gold, too large to pick up after being wedged out. Being "very excited" and fearing discovery, the men posted the Dutchman as a guard and went to work on the chunk. On complete exposure it showed some attached quartz, "not over five pounds." This was chipped off, the nugget dragged into the cabin and shoved under the bed.

The men stayed away from Downieville that night and the next day, Sunday, trying to figure out some way of weighing their find, their gold scale being capable of handling only a pound and a half. A novel scheme was concocted, weighing pieces of rock until they had enough to balance the chunk of gold, and it proved to weigh 227 pounds. Any idea of taking it to the express office was ruled out as causing too much excitement and putting the owners' lives in jeopardy. The men spent Sunday working halfheartedly as the nugget held their main attention and a decision was finally made as to disposing of it. Dodge went to town late Monday, bought a cold chisel and the men spent all that night cutting and dividing the big lump. "It seemed like vandalism," he said.

DOWNIEVILLE IS SITUATED in bottom of narrow ravine where North Fork of Yuba enters larger stream. Main street parallel to Yuba is only one somewhat level, others like this one rise steeply by means of switchbacks and terraces of dry-laid schist rocks. Near site of National Theatre was location where trial was held for miner who had stolen pair of boots. Man was convicted, promised release if he returned boots to owner, set up drinks for crowd. Prisoner was glad to comply, was so generous with drinks that judge, jury and witnesses were soon celebrating uproariously. In resultant drunken brawl, culprit re-stole boots, slipped unobstrusively out of town.

When the job was finished they caved down the workings, had a brief nap, cooked breakfast, wrapped the gold in their blankets and boarded the stage for San Francisco. The stage passed Goodyear Hill and Nigger Tent, rendezvous of road agents, without incident and after arriving in the Bay City, they caught a ship for Panama and New York where they sold the gold for cash, about $50,000. The find was made in '53 and in '58, when John Dodge told the story, he was working as a teamster in the Australian gold fields, but "had a good time while it lasted."

A claim on the North Fork of the Yuba was called Sailor's Diggings, being manned by English sailors in '51. The seamen were said to have found many nuggets from a top size of 31 pounds down. When they had enough, they headed back to England with two large canvas sacks of gold.

On a fine Sunday morning of June, 1856, Major Downey went for one of his habitual walks, this time to the top of a hill on slate Creek to look over the country. While enjoying the view, he scuffed his toe on the ground and unearthed a chunk of quartz about the size of a man's hand. He loosened it and let it roll down the slope. Some time later one of the numerous Chilean miners went up the same hill hunting quail. He shot one, the dying bird fluttering into the hole left by Downey's rock. On picking up the quail the Chilean noticed a glint. Half buried was a piece of gold and quartz which, when cleaned by the assayer in town, yielded nearly a pound of pure gold, about $200 worth. The hill was soon covered with claims and more than fifty miners made fortunes there. Far more wealth was almost discovered by Major Downey than he ever found in his claims. Disgusted, he left shortly for the Cariboo fields in British Columbia.

A middle-aged lady in pinched circumstances came to Downieville to start a boardinghouse on a shoestring. A brother there set her up a tent house with board sides but no floor over the dirt. She got a stove, a long table, some chairs and thirty boarders at $12 a week. She was raking and sweeping the "floor" one day when she noticed what seemed like a piece of gold. The chunk she picked up was exactly that and it wasn't the only one. She rushed to tell her brother who helped her move out the furniture and start panning the floor. Before the day was over they had $500 and when the boarders arrived they were told to eat elsewhere. A month later she returned to the east and told the folks her boardinghouse venture had been very successful.

After two summers of working the gravel beds at the edge of the Yuba between Downieville and Goodyear's Bar, the pickings were getting somewhat thin. The miners, confident the middle of the stream bed would yield plenty, contrived to build a flume. It was built in the spring and successfully dried up the stream by diverting the flow, but the first high water from melting snow took out the entire project and it was never tried again.

Hardly anyone was willing to admit the real glory of Downieville was fading but two events in 1865 made the fact hard and clear. Pond's church was closed for lack of a congregation—and the Chinamen came. Mr. Pond went sadly to another call in Petaluma and the church structure was sold. The Sons of the Flowery Kingdom were not tolerated except in menial capacities, such as washing dirty clothes for the miners, as long as gold was plentiful in the creeks. But as the supply grew scant they were permitted to glean the white man's leavings.

The pattern was repeated over and over in the mining camps of the west but in Downieville the Chinese put a different twist to it. They saw how the miners had tried to divert the Yuba by flume so the hardworking Orientals patiently and tirelessly carried large rocks from the edges of the stream to make a new channel. When the exposed gravels were worked out, other parts of the river were opened up likewise. The moved rocks were stacked in piles and many of these cairn-like humps remain today.

DOWNIEVILLE'S MAIN STREET remains much as it was, despite frequent fires and floods. Structure in center is original Craycroft Building, in basement was famous 75-foot bar. At intersection, road turns right one block to bridge crossing Yuba. From beam of original bridge dangled body of Juanita, only woman hanged in California.

EL DORADO and SHINGLE SPRINGS, CALIFORNIA

Mud Springs—a name to conjure with but not to mention to your mother. Yet that was the camp's name. The first seekers of gold there gathered around the water supply in such numbers they trampled the ground into a quagmire—and the camp had a name—Mud Springs.

In addition to attracting an increasing number of Argonauts, Mud Springs was an important stop on the old Carson Emigrant Trail and it soon became a crossroads station for freight and stage lines. At the height of the gold rush the population mounted to several thousands, the town complete with "full quota of saloons, hotels, and a gold production that gave its citizens just cause for pride." It was during this period the town was incorporated and this same civic pride caused a change in the name to El Dorado.

Picturesque place names are also in evidence at some of the neighboring camps which sprang up during the gold rush and have since disappeared —Loafer's Hollow, Deadman's Hollow, Dry Creek, Missouri Flat, Empire Ravine and Shingle Springs.

Though rich while they lasted, the original placer deposits were quickly exhausted. Then the lode mines came into being and for a time there was a continuous line of quartz mills extending south to the crossing on the Consumnes River, the spot then called Saratoga and later Huse Bridge. The stamp mills were of varying capacities, the one at Logtown, a mile or two from El Dorado, having eight stamps.

A good many of the more important buildings were erected on ground later found to be rich in gold and the miners waited impatiently for them to be considered outmoded or "menaces to health and safety," so they could wreck them and mine the sites. Ten thousand dollars in gold was said to have been extracted from the soil where the dance hall stood.

El Dorado's near neighbor, Shingle Springs, gained its cognomen from its shingle mill and a fine spring of very cold water. The Shingle Spring House was built in 1850 of lumber brought around the Horn and had an apparent knack of spawning brawls in the lustier days.

Mining there began that same year, the surrounding gulches filled with cabins, most of them hastily thrown together. For the first few years the miners were forced to get their supplies from Buckeye Flat (named by men homesick for their native Ohio) but by '57 a store was established at the camp. This was a commentary on the slow development of Shingle Springs and of its rather small gold deposits. Most of the gold camps grew so rapidly stores and supply houses sprang up within a few days or weeks of the first strikes.

Prosperity did suddenly smile on Shingle Springs but from an entirely different direction. In '65 the Sacramento Valley Railroad extended its line from the camp to Latrobe. For two years Shingle Springs enjoyed a top place in the ranks of gold towns and then fell flat. The Central Pacific Railroad from Sacramento via Auburn diverted the overland traffic from the Placerville Road and Shingle Springs reverted to the status of a village.

WELLS FARGO BUILDING — most impressive and unaltered remnant in El Dorado — Shingles Springs district. Also housed Phelps Store. Constructed of semi-dressed native stone, it is impressive with deep-set, arched doors in upper and lower stories. Structure once boasted elaborate balcony. Peaked roof, common in gold country, is intact where disappeared from most other buildings. Even brick chimney remains sound.

211

FIDDLETOWN, CALIFORNIA

The year of first discoveries of gold in the Sierra foothills was drawing to a close when a party of prospectors found rich deposits in the gravel of a creek entering the Consumnes River. So absorbed were they in sloshing out a few dollars to the pan no one noticed darkening skies until the first downpour of the winter season forced them to seek cover. Only then did they think of building makeshift shelter.

The winter was a wet one, continued rains forcing the men from Missouri who made up the bulk of the settlers to stay in their flimsy houses. Most of them had played the fiddle for dances "back home" and they now spent most of their time scraping out "Turkey In The Straw" and other nostalgic melodies. It was "moughty blamed natural" to name the town—Fiddletown.

This was as wild a camp as any in the Mother Lode. Eighty-two-year-old Thomas Davis who lived in Fiddletown many years is quoted by the San Francisco Examiner as saying: "There was plenty of activity and violence. I always remember mother's description of a Saturday night when the miners had come to town after a horse race. One man was leaning against the pillar of the hotel porch when an enemy knifed him. He clutched the pillar, spinning around several times before he hit the ground, dead." Another incident is related by N. B. Randall who runs the museum housed in Schallhorn's Wagon Shop: "The storekeeper shipped millions in gold out of town. He knew robbers were after him and barricaded his store. But one afternoon when he came back from a trip he found the men inside it. They killed him with a hatchet."

While all this was going on many other camps were springing up in the area fringing on the Consumnes, most of them with names reflecting the circumstances of their founding—French Flat, Drytown, Loafer Flat, Suckertown, American Hill, Arkansas Hill, Yankee Hill, Plymouth.

Fiddletown itself flourished. Although the placers petered out, hydraulic mining came in and paid huge dividends. Buildings were going up all along the main street, much more substantial than the jerry-built structures of the first winter. A deposit of rhyolite tuff had been discovered close by, and since this material is easily worked when first uncovered, hardening on exposure, it was used extensively. Other buildings used bricks made of clay found nearby and fired in a local kiln. Others went up with schist blocks accurately

RAMMED EARTH ADOBE OFFICE of Dr. Yee near center of Fiddletown's Chinatown. Genial Oriental escaped ostracism suffered by most of race in gold rush days, his sunny smile and expert dispensing of herbs winning hearts of miners. Original roof of shingles was replaced by sheet metal which served in its mundane way to protect venerable structure from usual fate of adobes, melting away when roof deteriorated. Present tenant, Yow Fong Chow, is sole remaining representative of 2,000 Chinese once living in Fiddletown, popularly known as Jimmy. Note original iron shutters at windows, typical of period but not always used on adobe buildings.

cut and fitted. And elegant marble, quarried locally, was given such utilitarian use as lining the basement of Henry Schroeder's Brewery.

Allen A. Woolfolk, old timer in the place, tells of some early structures, most of them now gone. There was a dance hall built by a Mr. Eaurow, two blacksmith shops—Pigeon's and McClary's. Four hotels took care of the transient and some of the permanent residents—the N. S., St. Charles, Flag and the ostentatious Charlesville. Charles Hikinson ran a large livery stable which was destroyed by fire as were most of the frame buildings in this and other towns. The Farnham's lumber yard and their lumber-built home were spared those holocausts and the house stands today. It is owned by George Pacini, an Italian grape grower. This fruit has figured in the history of the town from the beginning of the hydraulic period. The winery in those days was run by Peter Smith and Sons who had their own vineyard. Fiddletown's Chinese population was as high as 2,000 with the usual assortment of stores, medicine shops, joss houses and opium dens.

Two judges held jurisdiction over the community, as colorful as any magistrates in the gold rush country. On one occasion, it is related, Judge Yates listened to a long-drawn-out case in which one of the witnesses was displaying a complete and obvious disregard of the truth. His patience at last giving way, he brought his gavel down hard and thundered: "This court is adjourned!" He allowed the contrasting silence for a moment and then blasted: "This man is a damn liar!" After another pause he lowered his voice dramatically. "I declare this court in session."

The other jurist, Judge Purinton, made frequent trips to San Francisco and Sacramento and became increasingly annoyed at the titters when he wrote "Fiddletown" after his name on hotel registers. When his indignation reached its limit, he pulled some legal strings and had the town's name changed to the more dignified one of Oleta.

The town accepted this gesture to propriety for a few years then the more fitting Fiddletown was restored. The place now drowses in a pleasant bower of grape vineyards, prune and walnut orchards, green pastures where stock grazes. The old wild days are long gone and the camp is bypassed by most tourists. Some of the few remaining residents would like to see more of them stop, the rest wish to retain the peace and quiet which now hangs over Fiddletown like a golden haze on a summer day.

HOME OF MRS. L. E. FRINCHABOY who supplied photographer with much of Fiddletown facts. Beautiful example of frame architecture of the period house was finished 100 years ago, built by young Mr. Chestnut as a home for his intended bride, Patience Neff. Couple moved in later that year. Mrs. Frinchaboy, her husband and three sons (who served in both World Wars) moved into house in 1939. House contains many interesting reilcs such as fireplace of local marble. Famed violinist David Rubinoff, long honorary "Mayor" of Fiddletown, frequently visits old camp with family, staying overnight as guests of Mrs. Frinchaboy.

SCHALLHORN BLACKSMITH AND WAGON SHOP was erected in 1870 of rectangular blocks, 12x18x20, of Valley Springs rhyolite tuff. Source of material is one and a half miles out of town. Builder Chris Schallhorn sawed most of blocks himself, built sturdy wagons in shop for many years. Building now serves as part-time museum, proprietor Randall "closing shop" when mood dictates.

FRENCH GULCH near Whiskeytown once boasted street lined solidly with false front buildings. The few remaining are defaced by posters in front, show atmosphere and age in rear. At left is stone structure serving as bank, other was store with living quarters on upper story. Backyard fence is smothered with ancient grapevines, leafless here in March. First discoveries were made and mining done by Frenchmen in 1849. Later main workings were operated by Washington Quartz Mining Company. When rich veins were discovered in 1852, Shasta **Courier** reported: "Such rich diggings have been struck that miners are tearing down their houses to pursue the leads which run under them."

GARLOCK, CALIFORNIA

The six mills in Garlock separated the gold from the ore hauled down from Randsburg and needed the water in the local wells. So did most of the few hundred souls in the camp. But there were those who scorned water like the plague and kept Cheney's Thirst Emporium in business . . . like "Lily of the Valley" who ran a one man hoisting operation at the bar, then roamed Garlock's street, crooning: "Oh, she's the lily of the valley, the bright and morning star".

A few desiccated cabins stood at the edge of the barren El Paso Range and the people who lived there paid $1 for a 52 gallon barrel of water. It would last the average family a week, with restraint on such things as laundering and dishwashing. Then some enterprising individual came to the cabins and dug a well. He was ridiculed . . . "Why anybody would know there isn't any underground water in an area where the annual rainfall is nothing minus." The digger was deaf to all this and found the water table at a depth of only 28 to 30 feet. He may have become a patron saint of the area which soon became a regular stopping place for prospectors and their wagons. And its name became Cow Wells.

Pioneer Robert Kelly wrote: "Plentiful water was necessary for the stock in the corrals. The large water tank was kept full by pumping with a large rotary contraption, pulled in a circular motion by a large, lazy black mule which needed constant prodding or he would go to sleep in his tracks. With sufficient urging he would stay on his job and pump a sufficient amount of water within a reasonable time to take care of the next day's needs. Then old Mule was turned back to his corral until his services were needed the next day . . . the tank also served for refrigeration in summer time, where my mother kept the butter, milk and other food."

These simple days came to an end with the need to mill the ores from the Rand mines. The poverty-plagued, discoverer-owners on Rand Mountain were determined to keep the mine "in the family" but even though the ores were extremely rich, it cost too much to ship it away for milling and it was out of the question to mill it on the spot as they had no water. Now with water at Cow Wells, a mill could be built there and ore hauled to it by wagon.

Eugene Garlock, always referred to as Gene, built the first — the Garlock Pioneer Mill — and the enlarged cluster of cabins took his name. A load of ore was driven down the grade from the Yellow Aster, at first called the Rand mine, and Dr. Bur-

cham, the physician-wife of one of the partners. came with it to see that none of the ore was carried off — as it often was when shipments were piled around the mills, this taking of specimens termed a polite form of high-grading. The brick of gold resulting from the first milling was worth $800 and to Dr. Burcham fell the task of personally taking it to Mojave, as there was yet no Wells Fargo. She was nervous about bandits but did the best she could to conceal the brick under her skirt.

When the little Garlock Pioneer Mill proved inadequate to handle the increasing amounts of ore, five more were built — the McKernan, Kelley, Smith, Henry and Visalia. Gold was extracted by simple amalgamation, the ore not being refractory, and the power came from steam. Fuel was the big problem in this desert-type country. Brushy, twiggy, fast-burning branches had to do and it was fed to the fires with hay forks.

All ore was hauled by heavy wagons with broad iron tires to stay on top of the sand. The grade down from the Rand was steep with plenty of rough spots in the lower flats and deep washes. The wagons had to be eased down, then pulled by sheer horse or mule power.

The mule skinner's vocabulary is legendary, most drivers working a long string of vitriolic words to a high pitch of profanity as they lashed savagely with the whip. Little Joe did not believe in that kind of brutal treatment. When his team arrived at a bad gully, says Old Jim McGinn, who knew Little Joe in Garlock's good years from 1896 to 1899, he would walk around to the near lead animal, place his mouth close to the ear, whispering words of affection and encouragement. And he made the rounds, whispering in all the animals' ears. Then he got back in the driver's seat, picked up the lines and it never failed. At the signal the animals surged against their collars and took the load right out of the gully.

There were few buildings in Garlock but they made a break in the arid expanse. There was the Doty Hotel, a board and batten, two story structure. Another hotel was the Lilard, where the three daughters of the owner waited on table and later in the evening played the piano and sang for guests. Instead of tagging the girls with the usual "Faith, Hope and Charity", these were called "Tom, Dick and Harry".

The stable, or Big Barn, where horses on the Mojave-Randsburg run changed, was quite impos-

WEATHERED BUILDINGS—all that is left of once busy Garlock. At left is blacksmith shop, complete with forge; at right, livery stable — one end entirely closed for grain storage, rest of building open to weather on one side. Mountains in background are El Pasos, centered by El Paso Peak, 4,500 feet. Comparatively low range runs in east-west direction, is separated at western end from Kiavahs by Red Rock Canyon, scene of many early gold discoveries. Kiavahs, also a low range short distance north, ends at foothills of giant Sierra Nevada.

ing as were the McGinn Grocery, Lew Porter Store and the two saloons — Miller-Montgomery Bar and Cheney's Thirst Emporium. The first "postmaster" was Ida Kelly, wife of Kern County Constable John Kelly. Long after the demise of Garlock he would discover — by proxy — the famous Big Silver mine near Randsburg.

Garlock was fortunate to have a doctor all through its heyday — W. H. Wright. With his wife and three small children, Dr. Wright arrived by train and stage in 1896. One of the children, Sher-

man L. Wright now of Oakland, recalls those days: "The house which father constructed consisted of two rooms with lean-to at the rear. It was made of 1 x 12 inch boards nailed upright to a 2 x 4 framework. The total floor space was about 400 square feet. The front room was used as drug store, doctor's office, dental office and for general assembly of many miners. Later, about 1899 or 1900, half of this room was partitioned off for a post office which was operated until 1903 when it was abandoned for lack of business. The other room and

WELL PRESERVED REMAINS of arrastra include wooden parts, unrotted in dry desert air. Crude contraption crushed ore from mines of Randsburg before mills were built there. Ore, dumped unguarded around grinder, presented irresistable temptation to high-graders who claimed they were only selecting specimens. At first practice was condoned by mill owners but when samplers took to carrying off sacks full of jewelry rock, guard was posted.

lean-to were used for living quarters, kitchen, laundry etc., quite a common arrangement in those days.

"Aside from carrying on a general practice of medicine, my father practiced some dentistry consisting mainly of extracting and giving relief to aching teeth. I do not know that he did fillings or other repairs. In his spare time father was also a miner, preacher on Sundays and at funerals, Fourth of July orator, school board member, surveyor and self-constituted authority on anything. . . ."

The three children attended Garlock's little school. Desks were hand made, four feet wide, accommodating two pupils each. Girls were grouped on one side of the room, boys on the other. A wood-burning, cast iron stove stood in the center, gal-

vanized water pail and tin dipper near the front door. At the far end was a platform, teacher's desk and blackboard. The school doubled as church and meeting place for the Garlock Literary Society which was considered an "uplifting influence" to the town morals and a means of recognizing local talent at entertainments.

In the winter of 1897-98, a shadow fell on Garlock. A 28-mile railroad spur was completed to Johannesburg, connecting the Randsburg complex with the Atchison, Topeka and Santa Fe at Kramer. The line ran within a mile of the Yellow Aster and the mine could now ship ore to Barstow for more efficient milling. For a time some poor grade ore was still ground at Garlock, then a screw-pipe water line was laid from the springs at Goler to Randsburg, making possible the construction of a 30-stamp mill right at the mines. When this was followed by a huge 100-stamp mill, the death knell of Garlock was sounded. The little school house, crowded to capacity during boom years, had only the three Wright children in 1902 and 1903.

"We remained at Garlock until 1903." says Sherman Wright, "by which time the population had dwindled to our family and a Mexican, Juan Barsarto, who took in washing. We abandoned our house and asked Juan to drive us in our four wheeler wagon to Mojave. We gave Juan the horse and wagon and took the train for Oakland. . ."

Garlock became a true ghost and except for an occasional tenancy by some wandering prospector, it remained completely deserted until 1911. In that year the Southern Pacific constructed a rail connection from Mojave to Keeler and crews camped in Garlock's weathered buildings. As rails extended they moved on and the little town was again empty.

Then in the early 1920s came a new resurgence. A salt company started mining the saline deposits of nearby Kane Lake. Mine owner and capitalist J. D. Voss and associates made a determined attempt to develop the old Apache mine in nearby Iron Canyon, and a new mining project took form at Mesquite Springs. There was a general occupancy of houses in Garlock, the need for a post office again, a new store was started by John Norton and a boarding house by Sarah "Granny" Slocum.

But ghosts would have the town. The salt project failed and the crew moved away. The men at the Apache mine folded their tents. No one asked for mail and the post office closed on June 30, 1926 — but who can say it was for the last time?

CENTRAL GEARS in museum-piece arrastra shows simple machinery. Turned by another gear operated by steam engine, central rod revolved, turning horizontal beams. Each of these was fastened to granite block, several shown here. These were dragged over ore thrown into pit, crushing it for gold extraction by amalgamation. Crude process wasted much gold, recovered later by mills in further processing by cyanide method, mine owners not sharing in salvage.

GOLD CAMP AND TROPICO MINE, CALIF.

Potter's clay, that humble substance used to make the feet of idols and sewer pipe, had a special meaning for Ezra Hamilton. It not only solved a problem for his Los Angeles Pottery Co. but led to lush living for himself, his goldfish and silkworms.

The need for drain tile in the Los Angeles area was acute around 1878 when booming expansion was eliminating the privy and bringing the plumbing inside, The pottery concern was able to make the tile but it needed better quality clay than the local soil produced. So Ezra Hamilton jumped at the chance to buy a carload of fine clay from the sample submitted by Dr. L. A. Crandall.

This clay was red, conspicuous in the formations of sandstone, volcanic tuffs, dacite and rhyolite in the hills bordering the north side of Antelope Valley, about five miles from the town of Rosamond, which was some fifty miles from Los Angeles. Dr. Crandall had been looking for gold here and thought the clay might have some value.

It did and was soon being dug out of Crandall's hill in huge quantities and shipped to the Los Angeles tile plant. Hamilton balked at the large shipping costs and in 1882 bought the property from the doctor, at the same time taking out two additional mineral claims, labeling these Pottery 2 and 3.

As Los Angeles boomed so did the tile works but in the early '90s both slowed down. Enterprising Ezra took to panning out some of the clay in his desert hill and found some bright yellow particles that turned out to be gold.

Now more excited than he was over the original clay sample, he and his son Truman set out for Rosamond as a team. At the clay pits they searched diligently on the north side of the hill, washing pan after pan, always finding a few specs of gold. Then in a gully they found several nuggets and then came a pan in which almost all the dregs were pure gold. Ezra said later: "I looked at that gold. It was rough and lay among broken stones, not gravel. I says to myself, it's a native of this place." In 1896, after more searching for the lead from which the float came, he located it in one of the most exposed spots near the ridge of the hill. An assay showed samples around $35 per ton.

Hamilton returned to Los Angeles, quietly closed out his interests, and returning to the Joshua trees in the desert, set about staking claims. Father and son became acquainted with a colored man who had a ranch south of the hill, one Charles Graves. They became close friends and Graves accepted Hamilton's invitation to stake out any claim he might fancy on the eastern quarter of the hill. "We've got plenty," Ezra said, "and we think you would make a good neighbor." Graves, who had left his Kentucky home in 1882, staked out two claims of the usual size near his ranch, 600 by 1500 feet, naming them Home No. 1 and Home No. 2.

With two other sons, Lester and Fred, joining Truman, Ezra Hamilton devoted his entire energies to the prospective mine. The first ore removed from the hard outcropping was that which showed the good assay at the start and the first payment check was for $4,600, spent for further ore removal and a little two-stamp mill, erected at what would be the Lida tunnel. It was powered by a small steam engine and to fire it the surrounding desert was

stripped of sagebrush, Joshua trees and ocotillo stems, the fuel flaring up and dying down like paper. When it was gone the Hamiltons had to import solid wood from the Sierra, hauling it across the Mojave Desert by wagon.

In two years it was clear they had more claims than they could work so they sold one for $100,000. After the Los Angeles TIMES printed a feature story on the big sale, Dec. .12, 1900, prospectors, promoters and legitimate investors flocked to the scene to make hay while Hamilton's sun shone. And instead of the Hamilton's vein pinching out at a shallow depth, it improved as the mine deepened. They bought the old stage station site at Willow Springs where there was a generous supply of water and erected a new five-stamp mill there.

The fame of the Hamilton mine reached St. Louis, for the World Exposition there asked Ezra Hamilton for an exhibit and he sent one to make all eyes pop. Some of the ore specimens had solid gold sticking out of the quartz matrix and would assay at about $90,000 to the ton. The three Hamilton boys went to the fair on funds derived from a ton of ore each from the stope of the Lida — $5,000 for each son.

Hamilton now had time and money to carry out some of the plans for Willow Springs, the first a health resort for those suffering from lung trouble. To the buildings he added a large goldfish pond with landscaping — an oasis contrasting markedly with the uncompromising desert. And the grapevines did so well additional plantings were made to support a small winery. Also planted were mulberry trees, the leaves of which would feed his hungry silkworms.

The next few years saw many changes on the hill. Charles Graves leased his claims to the Hoyt Brothers Company and they in turn sold all rights to the Big Three Mining and Milling Co. which combine then bought several of Hamilton's claims. A J. B. Freeman was president of a firm that "perfected" a new dry wash system which would have saved hard-to-get water had it been more successful. The mill, erected in 1904 to extract gold from the Big Three holdings, operated at a loss for several years and at length the discouraged mine owners allowed the mine workings to stagnate. By this time Hamilton had sold the rest of his holding and things on the hill were very quiet.

In 1907 the mine complex received a temporary shot in the arm, mainly in the form of promotion by J. M. Overshier, president of the Tiger Head Min-

SIMULATED MINING CAMP CEMETERY, another exhibit at Gold Camp, typical of many found in desert mountains around Tropico.

EZRA HAMILTON makes spectacular discovery of gold on crest of Tropico Hill in 1896. (Photo courtesy Goldcamp Museum, Burton's Tropico Mine Tours).

ing Co. He made some pretense of opening the mines while active with stock selling, then quietly decamped.

After the Antelope Mining Co. took a one year lease in 1909 with no results, another company took over. Some of the stockholders came from a small community called Tropico, near the present Forest Lawn Memorial Park at Glendale, and they named their group the Tropico Mining and Milling Co. President V. V. Cochrane, with leading stockholders B. Gross and O. S. Richardson, were successful in consolidating the many past ownerships and in having them patented. The Tropico Company was successful also in finding paying values and operating the mines until 1934 with a one year break in 1923. A J. F. White held the lease for that period.

When the Antelope Valley was being opened up by real estate promotions in 1900, one flamboyant advertisement in FIELD AND STREAM lured at least one family, the Burtons with four sons, one twelve-year-old Clifford. The family settled on a ranch in the valley not far from the present Mira Loma, now site of the county prison.

Young Clifford worked on the ranch with the others but at eighteen took off for the rocky desert hills with a friend, Mel Sanford. The two made a good strike near Ballarat in the Death Valley area and sold it for $4,500 to a well known mining figure, "January" Jones. Clifford used his share to study geology, mining techniques and refining methods, attended a mining and assay school in Los Angeles, returning to Antelope Valley and a job at the Tropico mine in 1912.

Burton was able to suggest methods to improve milling that eliminated many of the worst difficulties and in 1914, as mine superintendent, he sent for his favorite brother Cecil. The Tropico then humped in production, operating profitably until 1917 when the war forced a near closure.

Returning from the service in 1920, the Burton brothers again went to work for Tropico but rising costs and decreasing ore values made the going hard. Many stockholders sold out to the Burtons who eventually had a controlling interest. In the early '30s a number of farmers turned miners began finding small amounts of good ore in the hills and trucked it to the Burton mill for "custom" refining. Then came President Roosevelt's edict raising the price of gold from the prevailing price of $20.07 per ounce to $35. The Burton Tropico mine was on the way to another bonanza.

Clifford Burton was able to see the best gold values would increase in a westerly direction and accordingly stopped all other extensions, opening up new tunnels from several lower levels, proving there was more gold here than even during Ezra Hamilton's heyday. More and more mines in the hills, as far away as Death Valley and Twentynine Palms, were sending in custom jobs until the Burtons were forced to expand their mill facilities to handle ore from four hundred mines.

They also established a "trading post" on the Tropico premises, outfitting and grubstaking prospectors, selling equipment and supplies to established miners. The Tropico mine in 1942 was extending its operations to the Ruth mine near Trona, California, and the Fortuna near Yuma, Arizona,

HILLS AND GULCHES around Tropico mine are included in "Rosamond formation", offer everything from clay to gold. Here on northeast slope of what would be called Tropico Hill, Dr. L. A. Crandall found samples of good quality clay. Discovery of material and timely acceptance by Ezra Hamilton for his Los Angeles pottery works diverted further prospecting for gold until after business recession slowed tile production. Hamilton gophered entire hill, evidence shown here in small dumps scattered over hill. Large excavation in foreground shows enormous amounts of clay were removed and shipped to Los Angeles.

when the whole operation ground to a halt with the government curtailing gold production with order L.208.

Keeping the mines in shape through the second World War was a hard struggle but the glad day did come when the Tropico was allowed to reopen. But now costs had risen to new peaks, machinery had deteriorated, some needing expensive replacement. Miners' wages had risen to a level never before heard of and everything was inflated except the value of the end product, gold being frozen at the price that had seemed so high in pre-war days—$35.

Cecil Burton died in 1947 and Clifford attempted to carry on but was felled by a fatal heart attack two years later. His son, Clifford G. took over, making a gallant struggle to regain the Tropico's former glories but the case was hopeless and in 1956 the Tropico closed down again. This time the pumps were withdrawn and the water level started to rise. Probabilities indicate it will eventually reach to between the 300 and 400 foot levels, flooding all workings below that depth.

The property stood idle until January 1958

when a group composed of Mr. and Mrs. Glen A. Settle, Mr. and Mrs. George F. McNamee and Eric Burton obtained a lease from the Burton Company with the intention of preserving the mine property, keeping it intact and establishing a museum site to bring back the glamorous aspects of early gold mining days. Earlier Glen Settle married Dorene, daughter of Clifford G. Burton, and became assistant manager. The couple has furnished much material for this story of Tropico and the group has moved in many old structures from almost inaccessible old mining camps in nearby desert and mountains. Included are a mine boarding house, railroad section house, freight depot, post office, mine superintendent's home and first school house built in Palmdale. They are grouped along a "Main Street" to create the illusion of a genuine mining camp.

The Tropico Gold Camp is closed to visitors in summer due to extreme desert heat but there are weekend mine tours the year around as the underground levels are always cool. The old mine is intact, almost ready for reactivation should gold values rise to practical levels.

GRASS VALLEY, CALIFORNIA

When Lola Montez, the fiery and exotic dancer in the Latin manner, bought a house in Grass Valley and settled down there, the forthright women of the town could be expected to throw up their hands in alarm. Instead they respected her, not because they saw she was going to keep hands off their errant husbands, but because she worked diligently in her garden. It was not a gesture. She liked gardening and was good at it, transplanting such difficult subjects as the native cacti. And too, she was aware even dirty, old, digging clothes looked good on her.

A remote, back-country mining camp was not Lola's native habitat. Her beauty was far more outstanding than any extraordinary talent as a dancer,

yet her time was not booked solid and when she was out of audiences she retired to Grass Valley to think about new dance routines and possible engagements.

Born Eliza Gilbert in Ireland, she eloped with an army officer at fifteen and after quickly shedding him, picked up some rudiments of dancing and walked onto a London stage as a professional—the Famed Spanish Dancer, Lola Montez. Her undeniable beauty brought her to the attention of Ludwig of Bavaria, that monarch being between mistresses. She was said to have caused a revolution in that country, fled back to England and married again. This caused her some embarassment because she neglected to end her first marriage legally, but it enhanced her stage career. She was more popular and earned more money at this period than before or later.

Lola decided on a United States tour. The *New York Times* gave her so many press notices she had a public reception in her hotel suite. Joseph Henry Jackson, said of her: "There was an aura of delicious scandal about her. She was graceful and she was beautiful and that was enough." It was enough to carry her across the country, though with diminishing returns. From San Francisco she drifted to the gold camps, winding up in Grass Valley to lick her wounds and plant flowers.

The dancer liked pets, had in her collection a small bear, several parrots and monkeys. She was slightly bitten by one of her bears which inspired this verse by Alonzo Delano:

When Lola came to feed her bear
    With comfits sweet and sugar rare,
Bruin ran out in haste to meet her,
    Seized her hand because 'twas sweeter.

Legends about her concern an editor who wrote a derogatory story and received a visit from the dancer. She carried a whip with which she taught him a lesson on how to treat a lady. Another is about a preacher who let slip some slighting remark about her in a Sunday sermon. Next evening she knocked on his door, very briefly dressed in costume for her famous Spider Dance. While the "unfortunate" minister watched, she performed the dance on his doorstep.

The most important impression Lola made in Grass Valley was on a little girl who lived with her mother a few houses away—a girl named Lotta Crabtree. She was a constant guest at Lola's and it was natural enough the performer should teach songs and dances to the talented child.

When the exotic Montez left Grass Valley to re-

SECTION OF GIGANTIC CORE removed from ever-deepening shaft of hard rock mine in Grass Valley during town's golden age of mining. Shaft was bored by machine directed by operator who rode in cage directly over cutting equipment. When section of core was cut, operator and machine were lifted from shaft, section loosened by driving wooden wedges around circumference. Hoist was then lowered, attached to core which was lifted out. Repeated drilling and removal of rock sections sank shaft deep into bowels of earth. This sort of mining with expensive equipment spelled doom for earlier miners with their simple pans and rockers.

turn to the stage with an engagement in Australia, the residents sincerely missed her. But she returned, the tour a failure, staying only long enough to sell the house, then departing on a lecture circuit. This too was an abbreviated affair and things went from bad to worse. Broke in New York, Lola Montez died five years after leaving the mining town.

In Grass Valley little Lotta Crabtree was growing up the way the flamboyant dancer would have her. The mother, Mary Ann Crabtree, encouraged the dancing and taught her all she could. They started a tour of the mining camps beginning with Rabbit Creek where the bearded miners went wild over the lovely black-eyed child, throwing nuggets at her feet. Success in another camp was punctuated by gunshots, Lotta and her mother lying on the floor while bullets whistled through the walls as a pair of drunken miners shot it out in the street. All this was left far behind as the "darling of the mining camps" went on to

world fame. She lived to be nearly eighty, leaving a fortune of $4 million to charity.

Grass Valley received its name when a party of weary emigrants arrived there in 1849 after a hard journey across country and the Truckee Pass Trail. They allowed their bony nags and cattle to eat their fill on luxurious, waving grass on the well-watered spot. There were white men there earlier but they did not stay, Claude Chana and his party of French emigrants who passed through in 1846.

Late in the summer of '49 a party of prospectors, originally from Oregon, wandered northward from the El Dorado diggings. They searched along the streams and found enough to hold them until cold weather set in, then left for the lowlands. That same fall another party headed by a Dr. Saunders had taken the precaution to build a cabin on Badger Hill near what was to be the site of Grass Valley.

Another party settled in Boston Ravine a short

THIS HOUSE ON MILL STREET in Grass Valley was home to famed exotic dancer, Lola Montez. While licking her wounds caused by recent cool reception of her performances in San Francisco, Lola was a warm hostess to all sorts of theatrical and literary people. Here gathered such lights as Ole Bull, Stephen Masset, and two nephews of Victor Hugo, along with many others less known but equally thirsty guests. Liberal potations encouraged wild applause for Lola's performances in her parlor. New husband dancer had brought to Grass Valley was less enthusiastic, bitter quarrels followed soirees. Lola washed mate out of hair by going to San Francisco for divorce. On return to Grass Valley, parties were resumed on even less inhibited level.

IN BACKYARD OF LOLA MON-
TEZ residence is picturesque
shed topped by dove cote. Little
structure sheltered dancer's men-
age of pets including young grizzly and brown bears. Other
members included parrots and a
monkey or two kept in the house.
Animal pets were less in Lola's
affections after divorce gave her
greater freedom to fondle succession of young male guests. While
photos of Montez home were
being taken, crew was laying new
pipeline in street. One crash-
helmeted worker sauntered over
and inquired of photographer,
"Say, who the hell was Lola
Montez, anyway?"

distance away, the gulch also becoming part of the town. The first Christian burial in Nevada County took place in Boston Ravine. Services were held by Rev. Cummings for an emigrant who had made it this far only to die almost within sight of his hoped-for destination. A dozen smaller camps sprang up nearby, some with names of wonder—Red Dog, Gouge Eye, Little York, Quaker Hill, Walloupa, Sailor Flat and You Bet.

Some of the rich placers in the district were Humbug Flats (first considered a failure), Pike Valley, Grass Valley Slide, Thode Island, Lola Montez and Kate Hardy. Hard rock mining was the mainstay

and the reason Grass Valley lived so much longer than camps having only placer beds. The discovery of a rich lead on Gold Hill in 1850 by George Knight gave impetus to a vast network of later discoveries and many crude mills to crush and reduce ore.

Millions of tons of tailings surrounding hundreds of old shaft heads and mills attest to the huge activity continuing eighty years with a total production of gold amounting to more than $80 million. Under the complex of once-active mining buildings is a vast labyrinth of tunnels and shafts. One vein extends almost two miles and one tunnel drops to 7,000 feet, the bottom 1,500 feet below sea level.

226

HORNITOS, CALIFORNIA

The origin of Hornitos is clouded in doubt. While the gold rush had a violent impact on the sleepy little village it was not the cause of its birth as in the case of most of the towns along the Mother Lode. The Mexican settlement was many years pre-gold rush, built around a central plaza in approved Spanish style, the adobe buildings low and sprawling. A main street ran beside the plaza and formed one side of the square. In the evenings the strumming of guitars issued from the doorways and gay, though decorous, dances were in sway almost every night—*bailles* that included

Las Chapanecas, Fandangos and all the rest. Daytimes saw the Mexican sports—bull fights, bull and bear contests and long-legged fighting cocks pitted against each other. Saints days and fiestas were observed, mass celebrated in the small adobe church.

TUNNEL ONCE RAN UNDER STREET from a d o b e which stood in area shown in foreground. Other end was in saloon across street. On one occasion when "Most notorious bandit in California" was surprised by posse at door of Fandango Hall, he ducked into opening shown here and escaped from pursuers. State soon offered $5,000 for his capture, resulting in Murieta's ambush and killing at the mouth of Arroyo Cantova near Priest Valley by a posse of 20 State Rangers headed by Capt. Harry Love in July of 1853.
Murieta's head was severed and the problem arose as to how to preserve it as proof of the slaying. Capt. Love gathered all bottles of whiskey carried by the men which amounted to a total of three quarts. Paste of flour and whiskey was then smeared over grisly object and it was put in a keg, later being taken to a doctor who cleaned it off and more properly preserved it in alcohol. Head was then brought to Hornitos where Murieta had been so well known and lifted out by hair for identification by erstwhile drinking cronies. After this it was placed in glass jar and displayed all over California.

CHINESE "TREES OF HEAVEN" persist from oriental occupation, grow inside ruins of Ghirardelli store. In 1855 Ghirardelli, who previously had operated a trading post on the Stanislaus River, heard of the boom in Hornitos and felt it would be a good place to start a general supply house. Store was built by him and operated three years, when he moved to San Francisco and devoted himself to chocolate business. Upper floor was added to store and used as I.O.O.F. Hall, then as place to hold dances and meetings until demise of town.

BURIAL YARD of Catholic Church is heavily populated, casualties in early days many as result of "miner's consumption," frequent quarrels and violence in bordellos and opium dens. Cemetery has many plots with unique ways of arranging graves and stones. Here graves are covered by walk of stone and cement.

The gold rush changed all this. A gold camp called Quartzburg had sprung up not far away and was running in such wide-open fashion with murders rampant that the peaceful element forcibly ejected the prostitutes, gamblers and troublemakers. Hornitos being handy, these undesirables settled there, disrupting the idyllic course of the town's history. It was written: "Gamblers, girls and roughnecks . . . they were a tough lot, the worst in the southern mines. They reverenced nothing but money, cards and wine . . . blood was upon nearly every doorstep and the sand was caked in it." It was during this period the notorious bandit, Joaquin Murieta, moved in and made as permanent a residence as he did anywhere in

his unstable wanderings.

Almost every town in the Mother Lode was said to have been his "hide-out." Some historians have tried to destroy the Murieta legend but facts show there were several Mexican bandits during the period, three named Joaquin—two of these, Joaquin Valenzuelo and Joaquin Carrillo. Blame for the deeds of all was placed on Murieta even though two murders laid at his feet may have been perpetrated many miles apart. It is said Capt. Love and his Rangers were out for a reward and any Mexican would do as a means of collecting the money. It is also reported Murieta's sister made a trip to San Francisco to view the head of her famous brother. If she paid her dollar like other curious spectators she may have felt cheated, as she retorted: "This is not the head of my brother." No one ever claimed to have seen Joaquin Murieta alive after May, 1853.

Gold was plentiful around Hornitos although strictly speaking, the town was about fifteen miles from the Mother Lode proper. Caught with gold fever, the place grew even wilder and the usual entry of Chinese aggravated the situation. The Orientals were the very symbol of peace but they infuriated the whites by their willingness to work for so little on such a low standard of living.

One of these Cantonese was patiently gleaning the leavings of white miners in the gulch one day when a gang of white boys came along to torment him. After taking all this meekly for some time

Charley bristled at a particularly mean jibe and fired his gun into the air to scare the boys. The bullet hit a rock and angled into one of his annoyers, inflicting a skin wound. The boy ran home bawling and the resulting hue and cry was so loud Charley tried to run out of town. He was caught and clapped into the tiny jail.

In the middle of the hoosegow floor was (and still is) a short length of heavy chain attached to an iron ring. Ordinarily a rustler or horse thief made no more than a one night stay and to keep him safe, the ring was put over leg irons which were welded together, usually burning the culprit's leg. In the morning, after a quick "trial," he was taken out and hanged.

SLEEPY MAIN STREET shows gap in center where plaza is situated. Building at left was built of adobe and stone in 1852, was originally saloon, ten years later put to use as Masonic Hall, Lodge No. 98. It is said to be the only such hall where meetings are held on the ground floor.

MEXICAN-STYLE PLAZA is at extreme left, old Pacific Saloon at corner. Of simple adobe construction when erected in 1851, it was rendezvous of large cliques of French miners. Purchased in 1862 by Samuel McClatchy, saloon was "dolled up" by removal of old canopy, addition of brick trim around door. Result was so elegant, miners called it "The Bank." Next is thick walled adobe originally built by Mexicans as general store. Merchandise was piled on sidewalk during day where customers pawed over it. In 1860 Mrs. Marck arrived in town from France, bought building for bakery, sold such unlikely items as French pastry which had wide popularity in area.

For some reason, the Chinaman was allowed the freedom of the cell and late that night when he was craving his pipe, he heard voices outside and cringed against the opposite wall. The white men seemed friendly, chatting with him, telling him it was all a big joke and he would be released in the morning. In the meantime they would put his pipe and some tobacco on the ledge of the small window where he could reach it.

When the voices stopped Charley eagerly stepped up on the edge of the bunk to get at the high window. As he reached, his wrist was gripped and he was dragged closer, a noose slipped around his neck. Then several hands took hold of the rope, yanking him against the stone wall of the jail and letting him fall to the floor. This they kept up long after he was killed. None of the gang was ever punished. "It was good enough for the damn Chinks," was the popular opinion.

In spite of constant persecution, the Chinese for a time constituted a major element in the population of Hornitos. Their collection of hovels constructed of odds and ends was located just north of the original Mexican plaza. It was a fantastic labyrinth of basement opium dens with a ground level roof, stores made of packing cases, and some solid adobes. These latter gradually replaced the more flimsy structures and were built above the first "basement" establishments. Several of these remain today, being the first buildings to greet the visitor as he enters the village. The opium den was fitted up in approved fashion, bunks solidly lining the walls. A small opening near the ceiling allowed some of the stale fumes to escape. Here came not only the Orientals but many a white miner who had become addicted to the poppy.

Hornitos had passed through the original phase, the Mexican occupation with its fiestas, the Chinese influx with attendant racial clashes, and now came a new and more peaceful phase. The quartz gold deposits at Quartzburg so rich at first gave out. The white population moved over into Hornitos where the deposits were still productive. These people demanded a measure of law and order, and from then on, children played safely in the streets again.

CATHOLIC CHURCH in center of old burial ground is maintained in good condition, occasional Masses still observed in venerable structure. Note stone buttresses.

LITTLE STREAM WAS FILLED with miners panning the gravels in earliest days of gold rush. In '50s Chinese coolies were employed by hundreds to build stone walls to contain stock on hillsides at 25 cents a day. Remains of these fences extend for miles around Hornitos.

ALL'S NOT GOLD THAT GLITTERS

Knight's Ferry, Calif.

Well it was in the paper and they sent a reporter probably and he must have seen it . . . there—see the headline in the San Joaquin *Valley Republican?* "THE GREAT KNIGHT'S FERRY DIAMOND . . . here, I'll read it:

"The story goes that a party of miners were working a claim of sluice and hydraulic pipes at Buena Vista almost exactly opposite from Knight's Ferry. One night about dark a pipeman saw an object which he had washed out of the bank glittering on a pile of dirt and stones, about to be washed through the sluice. It's effulgent gleams lit up all the space in the vicinity, causing much astonishment to hardy workmen.

"The miner picked it up and moved along to show it to his comrades, but accidentally dropped it into the sluice where it was carried down by the current of the water into the mass of dirt and stones known as the tailings. A company of spiritualists from Knight's Ferry is now trying to locate the present locality of the jewel which is reported to be larger than the Koh-I-Noor."

All of which must have shown gold rushing settlers in California that newspapers were not just pulp and ink but human after all. With huge gold nuggets and gleaming yellow seams being uncovered every day since James W. Marshall discovered the first in the Sutter's Mill race January 19, 1848,

there was little headline value in ordinary gold finds. So, in the early 1850s the San Joaquin newspaper asked itself, why not jolt the public with a diamond discovery? Aw, it was all in fun, fellows.

In 1841 William Knight left Indiana with the Workman-Rowland party to become a farmer in California. He settled in the Sacramento Valley at a spot where the Sacramento River offered a natural landing place. Presumably he received a grant to the area, building a rude house on top of an ancient Indian mound termed by the natives "Yodoy." The shelter was of willow poles and reeds, tied with rawhide and plastered with mud. He established a crude ferry here and the location was called Knight's Landing.

On April 26, 1848, three months after Marshall's historic find, a San Francisco newspaper carried a story stating, "There are now about 4,000 white people, besides several hundred Indians, engaged in mining, and from the fact that no capital is required, they are working in companies on equal shares or alone as individuals . . . no other implement is required than an ordinary sheath knife to pick the gold from the rocks."

This decided William Knight to go to the Stanislaus River. It was one of the larger streams fed by Sierra snows and along its reach many early battles between Mexicans and Indians were fought, the war brought to a conclusion by a bloody clash in May of 1826. Leading the defeated natives was

EARLY SKETCH of Knight's Ferry shows suspension-type bridge apparently limited to foot traffic. Further upstream is another, possibly earliest covered bridge.

Chief Estanislao who was educated at Mission San Jose but turned renegade and incited his people to revolt. He lost his cause but his name is remembered in connection with one of the most romantic rivers in California's gold country.

The main road to Sonora, center of the Southern Mines, led from Stockton in the valley and crossed several streams of which the Stanislaus was the most formidable. Knight saw the difficulties the would-be miners were having and thought at once of the opportunity for a ferry. Instead of going on to the gold fields as intended he settled on the bank and put together a rude contraption that just did get the miners and baggage across.

He was able to be of service still further. Gen-

erally called "Dr. Knight" because of some education in Indiana, he built a small shelter for an infirmary and gave simple first aid to prospectors suffering from exposure and hardships. Fees for this may have been negligible but ferry fees mounted to $500 a day at height of traffic.

Yet Knight was not able to enjoy his prosperity very long, dying suddenly on Nov. 9, 1849. New owners improved the ferry and river property, enterprising brothers Lewis and John Dent. They also erected a grist mill on the bank and then joined with others to span the river with a bridge.

It was built in 1854 and a second, some historians saying a duplicate of the first, being still in service, completed in 1862. There is confusion here

VENERABLE COVERED BRIDGE still stands secure, author's heavy pickup camper making several crossings in August of 1967. Question: did U. S. Grant have a hand in designing it? This view is made from ruins of grist mill, water in foreground from Stanislaus River coming through penstocks during flood earlier in year.

GRIST MILL erected by Dave Tulloch in 1862 with Englishman T. Vinson as supervising stone mason, after original was wrecked with first bridge by flooding Stanislaus River. Material is locally cut pink sandstone. Well built, structure was still almost intact in 1940s, has since deteriorated with complete loss of roofs.

as old pictures of the town show a suspension-type bridge. And authorities differ about the engineering aid credited to U. S. Grant. One usually reliable source claims Grant "helped draw plans for the second bridge in 1862" yet there was a Civil War raging at that time which fully occupied the general's attention in East and South.

Grant was at Knight's Ferry in 1854. He left Fort Vancouver Sept. 24, 1853, by lumber vessel for San Francisco on his way to Fort Humboldt, site of the present Eureka. While stationed there Grant made several trips to San Francisco where he could indulge in his hobbies, jousting with bottles and handling horses.

His wife Julia, left behind in the East, while Grant served on the Coast, was a sister of the

Dent brothers. Sometime during that 1854 summer Grant made a visit to them at Knight's Ferry, a resident reporting in a diary that the captain was seen on one occasion driving down the street in "a peculiarly jovial mood." In front of his buggy were three horses in single file and behind it three empty buggies. Several other such lively incidents are related with no mention of the bridge or of Grant's reputed aid in planning it.

Whoever the designer, this early span was slung too low to allow for such a flood as occurred in 1862 when it was carried away. With the bridge went the grist mill, receding waters leaving a fringe of sacked flour along the lower banks. It was said the contents were quite usable after an outer crust was removed.

"Something wavering?
It could be your imagination!"

MARIPOSA, CALIFORNIA

The miners wanted to work and the Indians wanted revenge and loot. The latter raided the camps in trails of blood and the miners couldn't leave their families long enough to make pay dirt. So the story Charles Smithers heard until he died at 85 was part of the Mariposa pattern.

He was a baby when his father made a trip on horseback from Mariposa to one of the nearby mining camps. 25-year-old father Smithers completed his errand safely but on the way home his horse skittered and looking back, he saw several Indians following him. Spurring his horse he galloped straight into an ambush and as he tried to ride free, an arrow pierced his thigh, pinning his leg to the saddle. Nauseated by pain and loss of blood, he made it back to Mariposa where he fell from his horse, dragging the arrow through his leg.

Shortly after this bands of natives stationed themselves at strategic points around the town and other camps, levying tribute from all white travelers. James D. Savage, who owned three trading posts, one on the banks of the creek at Mariposa, had spearheaded a movement to rid the area of Indians and they retaliated by looting and burning his stores. Now thoroughly aroused, a large group of American miners and others organized a war party and took out after them. They came upon a large band camped on the North Fork of the San Joaquin, threw burning sticks of wood on their tents and as the Indians ran out, riddled

them with a fusillade of shots. Twenty-four, including the chief, were shot.

While this ended Indian forays temporarily, the governor sent Savage and the Mariposa Battalion into the high Sierra to track down any remaining Indians. One of the last of the scattered bands rounded up was hidden in the mountain valley later known as Yosemite and this ended the Indian episodes of Mariposa. The miners now settled down to work.

The jail at Mariposa, still standing, is built of dressed granite blocks from Mormon Bar, two miles south, mined from an intrusion which is the barrier terminating the Mother Lode on the south. Thus Mariposa becomes the end link in the "Golden Chain" stretching northward along Highway 49. Its history goes back some time before the discovery of gold at Coloma.

The first of several enormous land grants, one that was to effect the current of events for Mariposa, was handed out in 1844 by the Mexican Governor of California, Micheltorena. The recipient was Juan Batista Alvarado who, in August of 1849, sold out to John C. Fremont. This was eighteen months after James Marshall found those yellow flakes in the millrace of his sawmill. The original location of the grant was somewhere at the edge of the San Joaquin Valley but by a convenient and accepted process of the day the grant was "floated" to the Mother Lode country when the value of that area began to boom. This was accomplished merely by shifting the boundaries of the grant, which included 44,000 acres of land.

Mariposa Creek runs between "benches," more or less level, about the width of a city block and narrower. As a natural consequence of the panning and placering the town was laid out along the banks and composed entirely of tents, shacks and a few jerry-built frame buildings. When these got in the way of the creek workings a more substantial town was built on higher, drier ground nearby.

Hard rock mining followed close on the heels of the placering operations in Mariposa Creek, although at first this consisted of little more than scraping off the crumbly, gold-bearing quartz from the tops of the veins and running it through Mexican style arrastres. Kit Carson and two of his companions had found the Mariposa Mine as early as 1849, and by July of that year the production had already outgrown the capacities of

the primitive method of crushing. Palmer, Cook and Co. built one of the first stamp mills to handle the ore from the Mariposa Mine and were in full operation by '59.

All this time Fremont was fighting not only these "interlopers" but the owners of the Pine Tree, Josephine and Princeton and many smaller workings. He had no legal recourse under American law until he won his long battle in the courts and was given title to the Las Mariposa grant. He then unceremoniously ousted the erstwhile owners of these mines and reaped the harvest of their investments.

The golden years for the Mariposa Mine were from 1900 to 1915. Total production was estimated at $2,193,205. The shaft did not go straight down but inclined at about 60° and penetrated the lode a distance of 1550 feet. Signs of the mine workings may still be seen a mile south of Mariposa.

SCHLAGETER HOTEL built of brick and wood, has wide wooden balconies. Other old buildings in Mariposa are variously built of granite, soapstone from hills immediately east of town. Soapstone blocks are set in mud mortar on inside wall where weathering is negligible. Other interesting original buildings are Trabuco warehouse, present Bank of America, I.O.O.F. Lodge, Butterfly grocery and the jail.

MASONIC, CALIFORNIA

The bones of Masonic lie bleaching in the sun, huddled in a canyon close to the Nevada border. The elevation is enough to allow a sparse forest of small nut pine trees to clothe the hills above the town, supporting a colony of squirrels.

The animals are the only inhabitants now where once nearly a thousand people cast their lot for a few short years of prosperity.

The town is divided into lower, middle and upper sections, the central one being the oldest and largest. Most of the remaining ruins are here. There are some houses in fairly good repair, but most are ready to collapse and are filled with vines and debris. Here stood an enormous mill, now in ruins. It had received its raw material via an extensive tram system from the mines some distance away. The cars still dangle from the cables, and look ready to move at any time.

Gold was first discovered here in the 1860's and the Jump Up Joe mine soon was operating at the site. "Middle Masonic" grew up around the mill which was built at a more accessible location than the mine itself, accounting for the tram.

After the greatest values were exhausted, about 1901, Warren Loose of Bodie bought the claim. Extensive cyanide operations for more efficient extraction employed some fifty men by 1904.

Operations grew steadily less and less after those big days and at last ceased entirely.

Masonic is not well known to anyone now except sheepherders, who sometimes drive a band of "woolies" through the town, temporarily giving an atmosphere of life and sound.

"MAIN STREET," Masonic, California, was busy thoroughfare at turn of century. Pinon pines sparsely cover hill above town, nuts are bonanza to rodents, now the only residents of once roistering camp.

MASONIC'S TINY POST OFFICE was located in "Middletown" section. Window at right of door slid aside for dispersal of mail to eager, homesick miners. Flimsy little flagpole still stands, wired to building.

UNIQUE COMBINATION houses "convenience," left, chicken house, right. Former was lined with carpet and cardboard to help keep out wintry blasts, was "one holer." Hen house was complete with roosts for six birds, hopefully had nesting boxes for four. Tiny chicken run is at right.

MOKELUMNE HILL, CALIFORNIA

The Oregonians almost didn't make it. The fact that they did was due to the persuasive powers of two members of the party insisting they keep on digging after utter discouragement—and these two were forever blessed. The men were prospecting along the Mokelumne River in October, 1848, the pickings slim, provisions slimmer. Then the rich strike in the river sands and no one wanted to leave. Yet someone had to or they would all starve.

A man named Syrec finally made the break, promising himself to make up for all the wealth he would miss digging, by setting up a trading post. This he did with food, supplies and a tent he brought back from Stockton. He set up for business on a hill near the scene of operations.

The place was called Mokelumne Hill and other kinds of business ventures mushroomed around this first tent store, among them a boarding house, also in a tent. Later structures were more sturdy but in August 1854 fire levelled the camp. Subsequently building was largely of stone and several of these structures have survived.

Mokelumne Hill, during the hectic '50s, "enjoyed" a widespread reputation for wildness based on acts of violence of all sorts. Just south of town is Chili Gulch, scene of the Chilean War fought in December, 1849. This affair started over the prac-

MAYER BUILDING erected in 1854, showing beautifully tooled construction, Mokelumne Hill being blessed with local supply of light brown rhyolite tuff. Interior of one-time saloon is filled with "Trees of Heaven," evidences of Chinese population from several hundred to two thousand. At height of Oriental influx there were three joss houses and a "slave market" where young Chinese girls were put on the block.

tice of some mine owners, a Dr. Concha among them, of taking claims in the names of their peon help. Since claims were so rich they were limited to sixteen square feet, often yielding hundreds of dollars a day, American miners bitterly resented the Chilean method of acquiring extra claims. They passed stringent laws against the practice but Dr. Concha led a party of men into a gulch occupied by Americans who had dispossessed him and drove them out with several fatalities. The diplomatic dispute between the United States and Chile which followed was finally settled in favor of the Americans.

In the town itself, during a period of seventeen weeks, as many men were killed in arguments and fights. Then after a period of comparative calm, five more men met violent deaths one week end.

The French War was about as one-sided as any fracas could be. A group of French miners had made a fine strike on a small hill they called "French Hill" and in a burst of pride raised the Tricolor over their camp. Americans claimed this was an insult to their flag, stormed the hill, drove the Frenchies out and took over their claims.

Many other tales are told about life in Mokelumne Hill. There is a waggish one about a negro who entered the camp and innocently asked help in locating a claim. Jokers sent him to an area repeatedly prospected without success. The negro started to dig dutifully. Nothing was heard of him for several days until he came back to thank his benefactors. His bag was full of gold nuggets. Before he could return to the claim, the whites had swarmed in.

There is the Joaquin Murieta legend without which no Mother Lode town would be complete. A young miner named Jack, flushed with gold and whiskey, was playing poker with his cronies when the popular subject of the Mexican desperado came up. Jumping up on the table Jack loudly proclaimed: "I've got $500 here that says I'll kill the————the first time I come face to face with him!" This was the signal for a Mexican, unnoticed till now, to stand up and say: "I'll take that bet." In one swoop he grabbed the poke Jack was recklessly displaying and made for the door, vanishing in the dust of his horse's hoofs. Murieta, of course, in one of his more playful moments.

While American miners objected violently to the peon system of mining, claiming "slave la-

OLD CEMETERY in Mokelumne Hill is sombre with grove of Italian cypress, macabre effect heightened by flock of vultures wheeling overhead at dusk, seeking roosting places in trees.

bor" they condoned another and more vicious form of slave traffic. During the height of the gold rush and before women flocked to the camps, any female willing to share her bed with a lonely miner was worth hard cash, with few questions asked about color or race.

To fill this demand enterprising ship owners in San Francisco bought Chinese girls from poverty stricken parents in Canton and other Oriental ports, loaded them on ships under indescribably filthy conditions and brought them to San Francisco for distribution to the gold camps. Mokelumne Hill's big Chinatown was one outlet for the girls, sold outright to miners or housed in shacks and "rented out." Later the more aggressive white prostitutes crowded them out. The Oriental waifs returning to San Francisco to supply its burgeoning Chinese colony.

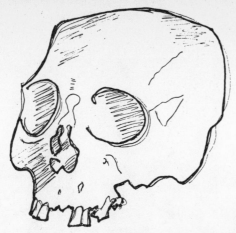

THE LADY FOUND A SKULL

Mormon Bar, Calif.

Mrs. Ellison wanted to plant a garden. "The spot where I wanted to plant my tomatoes," she reported, "was hard and dry. I diverted the spring water to spread over it and let it soak overnight. Next day it was so easy to dig I got carried away and made the planting holes deeper than necessary. At the bottom of one I uncovered a bone that looked human to me. A little more digging uncovered a skull that I was sure was human."

It was but it did not belong to one of the Mormons who in 1849 settled here on the west side of Mariposa Creek, two miles southeast of the old Mariposa gold camp. Mr. and Mrs. Ellison bought property here in recent years and found very little evidence of Mormon occupation. The Saints panned what gold there was in the creek and moved on to richer fields.

The Mormon Bar area is neglected by historians. Technically the spot is not on the quartz seam constituting the Mother Lode proper. The one-time village does not show on maps of the California Division of Mines' book *Geological Guide Book* on the Sierran Gold Belt, these showing the still active town of Mariposa as the southern terminus. Nevertheless the country around and along lower Mariposa Creek was the center of seething activity for a few years.

Just to the west was Buckeye where James Savage had one of his trading posts. A short distance south was Ben Hur and Bootjack lay slightly east. All these shared in the transient prosperity of Mormon Bar. Ranches established here later were fenced by miles of stone walls skilfully erected by Chinese coolies in 1862, each required to put up a rod and a half daily or lose his job. He was paid

"six bits" a day, the Chinese contractor receiving $1.75.

Until a few years ago there was a visible Chinese cemetery here. The ruins of several adobe buildings marked the site and still more recently a small frame store, all described in current guides as being viewable relics. They are no longer there. Cemetery occupants were exhumed for shipment to the Orient to be reburied. Grass and brush make the site uniform with the landscape, the adobe ruins gone, the store razed a few years ago.

Intrigued with the skull she found Mrs. Ellison called in Francis A. Riddell, State Park Archeologist from Sacramento. He reported that all evidences indicated a large village once existed here, at least several hundred years before the advent of the whites. Present Mariposa Indians have no knowledge of their predecessors. Exact dates of older occupancy are unknown, no radiocarbon tests having been made. Says Riddell, "I found eight or ten burials and numerous arrowheads during the course of my four days of excavation at the site. More scientific work should be done here."

And Mrs. Ellison has the answer to that. She says many more artifacts than stated were found in her garden, such as beautiful abalone bangles, pottery bowls in good condition. When she objected to giving up these relics for classifying purposes work was abandoned.

SITE of prehistoric Indian village lies at Mormon Bar. Granite outcropping offered conveniently situated **metate**, this multiple version rather unusual. In these holes aborigines ground abundant acorns into coarse flour for food.

MARIPOSA COUNTY COURT HOUSE is oldest one still in use in California. Front section, original part, was completed in 1854 at a cost of $12,000. Lumber was whipsawed from trees growing nearby, framework fastened with mortised joints and wooden pegs. Finished lumber was hand-planed, nailed with hand-forged square-cut nails. Fire-proof brick vault for safe keeping of records was added in '61, later enlarged. English-made clock with 267 pound bell was installed 1866, has chimed the hours ever since, musically struck five as picture was being made. Court room was scene of many legal battles, has remained exactly the same, with all original furnishings in place.

242

THE MOTHER LODE

No part of our country has a richer tradition or more fabulous history than a narrow stretch of Sierra Piedmont extending along the western slope from Mariposa to the Yuba River. That rainy day of January, 1848, when James Marshall burst in on John A. Sutter at Sutter's Fort stuttering almost incoherently a tale of his finding gold in the mill-race of Sutter's sawmill at Coloma, meant the end of "the happiest period any country ever knew."

Certainly it spelled the end of Sutter's vast domain, his agricultural empire, depleted of help when almost every man left for the gold fields. This particular incident was perhaps not vital to California as a whole but it signalled the end of a period, of the state's "Golden Age of Innocence." It meant the beginning of another kind of golden age, one which produced some $750 million in actual gold, part of it in chunks weighing as much as 195 pounds.

At first all the yellow metal was found loose in the stream beds, placer gold in the form of dust and small nuggets. When this easily garnered supply dwindled, the Argonauts had to start scratching and in many cases found the veins from which the loose stuff was weathering away. The Mexicans who were working the southern end of the strip called this vein, "La Veta Madre," and so the origin of the term, "Mother Lode," which came to apply more directly to that part of the gold bearing band between Mariposa and El Dorado. There is no geographical division between The Mother Lode, or Southern Mines, and the Northern Mines but an arbitrary line is usually drawn in the neighborhood of El Dorado or Placerville.

The author's treatment of this southern section by no means includes every Gold Rush town but is a generous and typical sampling both of well known ones and others off Highway 49, the main connecting link. The Northern Mines will be similarly covered in another volume and will include Coloma, Georgetown, Colfax, Dutch Flat and others.

NEVADA CITY, CALIFORNIA

John J. Kelly was a superstitious Irishman who worked in one of the steeply slanting shafts in the Nevada City mines. Kelly lost his partner in a mining accident and missed him sorely. This day he had been working alone and was now going to check the little wooden storeroom where dynamite and caps were kept. There was a hole in the door and it was Kelly's job to reach in and feel the latch on the inside to see that it was securely fastened.

It so happened one of Kelly's friends was in the powder room where a bucket of water was kept for emergencies, and the water was always cold down in the mine. When he saw the Irishman's hand come groping through the hole, he yielded to the impulse felt by a practical joker, stuck his hand in the cold water and then grasped Kelly's. The Irishman jumped with terror and ran up the shaft in a panic, screaming that the ghost of his dead partner had gripped his hand.

There are ghosts around Nevada City but the town itself is not dead. Its history concerns its place in the Northern Mines and it is full of gold rush color.

The first man to pan for the yellow metal in the area was the same one who first noticed flakes in the race of Sutter's Mill—James W. Marshall. His efforts at Deer Creek were disappointing and he moved on. He would later know that in the next two years there would be a rush of ten thousand miners to the area. Cabins began to go up in Gold Run just above the spot where Marshall dug in September, 1849, the first being that of Capt. John Pennington and his two partners.

A Dr. Caldwell erected a small building for a store on Deer Creek. Then as richer diggings developed seven miles above, he started a store there that became Caldwell's Upper Store, a name applying to the town also. In March, 1850, miners elected a Mr. Stamps to the position of alcalde of Caldwell's Upper Store. He was not one to put up with a name like that and taking his inspiration from the snowy mountains on the horizon, he named the town Nevada or "snowy" in Spanish.

In 1851 the county of Nevada was established with the rapidly growing city as its seat. Ten years later when the State of Nevada was formed, a hue and cry went up from the California city that it had the name first. Government officials said it was too late to do anything about the state's name but the city could add that word to its name. Citizens had to be satisfied with Nevada City.

During the first few months of the town's existence, strangers along the stream where placering was going on rubbed their eyes in disbelief—a woman was standing knee-deep in the cold water working a rocker right along with the men. The townspeople nodded and went on working. They knew Madame Penn. She worked hard and with some luck got enough gold together to start a boardinghouse, the first in Nevada City. The Union Hotel now stands on the site.

Swarms of hopeful prospectors and miners were pouring in at a record rate with all the excitement of the first placer gold, the loose stuff that could be scooped up from the creek bottoms. But this came to an end and as the old claims were exhausted and new ones impossible to find, the hard rock mining not yet started, some avid miners actually began to dig up the streets in search of gold—and found it.

One merchant, angered at the shambles in front of his store, protested to the man with the shovel: "See here—you can't dig up a public street like this!" The miner maintained he could, that there was no law that said he couldn't. The enraged storekeeper drew his gun to emphasize his words. "Very well, then—I'll make one. You git!" The miner moved operations to the next street.

A short distance from the town on Lost Hill a fantastically rich placering area was discovered. Several miners took out a quart of gold in a single day, worth $6,000. The dry gravels were covered by an overburden of soil and tunnels were necessary to get

DUMP WAGONS OF THIS TYPE were used throughout Sierra gold belt. Tree in background is also characteristic of country, though confined to medium altitudes. Called Digger Pine after native Indians, it does not penetrate loftier mining areas such as Sierra City, where it is replaced by Sequoia and other conifers. Digger Pine is distinctive, having lax, grayish needles and divided trunk. Picture taken in early March shows "candles," new growth starting at ends of branches.

at the gold-bearing material. The area became a maize of burrows and the resulting town was named Coyoteville. When it was swallowed up by the expanding Nevada City, the gravels were exhausted, but during the mad two-year rush a total of $8 million was removed.

One of the last good discoveries in the creek banks was made in the summer of 1859. John Burns, a resident of Nevada City, was walking along a ditch near Deer Creek and in crossing it, slipped on a wet plank and fell in the water. He floundered around and grabbed at the bank, dislodging a piece of decomposed quartz and exposing a yellow gleam. Burns clambered out and went home to change clothes, not because of discomfort but to attract no attention. He took a sack and shovel back to the ditch band and "cleaned out," the yield $2,000. The ditch company took over the new diggings the next day but Burns was happy to have enough nuggets for a string of wild days and nights.

Fourth of July celebrations were big days in mining camps. Two weeks before the holiday, about

NEVADA CITY IS UNIQUE in many ways, repays leisurely stroll on foot. Streets seem to have no set plan, original wandering burro trails may have influenced survey. Steep hills complicate pattern, narrow streets twist and turn unexpectedly; every angle offers architectural surprises like this "conservatory" linking hotel and annex. One house plant visible is Aspidistra, "Cast-Iron Plant" of Victorian times. Not popular or well-known these days, specimen could well have descended from lusty mining days when hotel was built.

1850, Nevada City was delighted to hear there would be a big fight between a jackass and a grizzly bear at nearby Grass Valley. The bear was billed as the most Ferocious Grizzly ever to be trapped in the Sierra, the donkey as The Champion Kicker of California, having killed a mountain lion in Hangtown and a bull in Sonora. On the morning of the festive day some two thousand miners went noisily by horse and foot to the "ring" of brush and stakes in Centerville, just north of Grass Valley.

Considerable dust was being stirred up along the way so a man carried a bottle of something to keep it wet and by the time the crowd arrived it was in a mood for anything. Every man paid his two dollars and pushed inside the stockade. There was the jackass, sure enough, nibbling at the grass at one side and there was the savage bear in a big wooden box. . . . "Don't get too close, gents!"

Then the play was ready to start and at a signal the gate was raised. The bear moved out slowly, a small brown one, timidly sniffing as if reluctant to leave the familiar shelter. A man forced him all the way out with a pole and when he saw the jackass, he ambled playfully toward it. When was the savage rush coming? The spectators waited anxiously.

Now the bear swung its head, obviously wanting to make friends. But the donkey was having none of that. He rolled his eyes, laid his ears back and when the bear got within range, two sharp hooves caught him in the ribs. Fully disenchanted, the bear slunk back and bounded over the barrier, disappearing into the chaparral. While the victor resumed his grazing nonchalantly, a thousand men set up a roar and if the promoters could have been found there might have been a lynching. A few had foreseen the outcome and were long gone for another bottle.

Something had to be done to relieve the tension so the miners who still wanted action took charge of the long-eared animal and led him at the head of a long, disgruntled procession toward, but not directly to, Nevada City. There were a lot of saloons along the way and the new hero would be welcome in all of them. None was passed up and in each he was toasted lavishly. By the time all got to Nevada City, there was only one of the crowd who could walk straight— the jackass.

The advent of quartz mining meant that Nevada City had come of age but with some placers still producing and only a few hard rock operations beginning, the transition was gradual and the camp did not suffer the setback experienced in other gold camps, notably Jackson, another Mother Lode town developing in a similar way.

In June of 1859 news came to the gold country which further depleted population and made an impact on Nevada City. The Nevada City *Transcript* of July 1 carried this item:

"J. T. Stone, formerly of Alpha but now living on Truckee Meadows, has just arrived here and reports the discovery of a vein of ore of extraordinary richness at the head of Six Mile Canyon near Washoe Valley. The vein is four feet wide and is traced a distance of three and a half miles. The ore is decomposed and works easily. It is like that from which silver is sometimes obtained. The discovery was made by a miner working in Six Mile Canyon, who found as his worked his claim, that it became richer as he approached the vein. The news has caused great excitement here."

Then the golden trumpet sounded again—far to the north. The clarion call spelled out "Cariboo" and away went the gold hungry drifters again, while the California camps were left to more decay. But Jackson and Nevada City stood out as examples of having something solid to fall back on when the bubble of loose placer gold broke.

Gold was still coming out of shafts penetrating far down into slide rock veins extending in quartz seams thousands of feet and producing if big companies were at hand to finance. Gone was the day when the individual prospector, equipped with only a pan and shovel, could stand in a stream and slosh riches in glittering gold out of the dripping gravel.

Nevada City, having successfully weathered the adjustment period, was displaying handsomely ornate mansions along Nevada and Prospect Streets, and by 1892 these homes gained further eminence with electric lights. The tiny power plant supplying this newfangled convenience was the nucleus of the giant Pacific Gas and Electric Company.

French nurseryman, Felix Gillet, started his business in the town, perhaps the first of its kind in the west. He was responsible for the beginning of California's huge English walnut production, introducing these and other nut trees.

Nevada City is a living monument to a fantastic era long gone. If it is not in itself a ghost, it is full of the wraiths of lusty, bearded miners and of sharpies who took their gold the easy way.

FIREHOUSE BUILT OF NATIVE granite and brick about 1851 was at first simple structure, Victorian-type balcony and gingerbread added later. It is likely most beautiful of many buildings remaining from heyday. Traditional iron doors and shutters are frequently encountered, one office building, "modernized" presents shock to history-minded observer; upper floor has several windows complete with ancient iron shutters, brilliantly painted chartreuse, alternated with purple.

NORTH SAN JUAN, CALIFORNIA

The long belt of gold rush towns stretching along the western foothills of the Sierra Nevada begins with Mariposa on the south and ends in a scattered cluster of high-perched camps in Sierra County to the north. The span includes many different geological formations, all having one important feature in common— the outcropping of gold. The belt is cut in two about the middle in the vicinity of El Dorado and Coloma, the southern section usually designated as "The Mother Lode," the northern, "Northern Mines."

Mother Lode towns were often settled by Mexicans, sometimes founded or named by them, as Hornitos and Sonora. Most of the camps farther north were settled or christened by Yankees and this includes North San Juan with its obvious Mexican name.

A German miner, Christian Kientz, did the naming. He had been with General Scott's army in Mexico and was deeply impressed with that country's geography, particularly by the hill on which sat the old Mexican prison of San Juan de Ulloa. When he saw the California gold area hill just north of a bunch of shacks beginning to be a town, he called it San Juan Hill and the town also took the name. By 1857 the place needed a post office, the authorities pointing out a much older town with the name San Juan already existing in San Benito County. They solved

OFFICE BUILDING, BUILT IN 1859 contained headquarters for numerous firms operating hydraulic mines, main source of income for North San Juan after placers were exhausted. When Sawyer Act became law and washing away of mountainsides ceased, prosperity of town ended, offices were emptied. Lower floor — originally large clothing store—was given over to succession of enterprises, in later years garage occupied quarters. At last, building was sold for valuable brick it contained and scaffolding was erected preparatory to wrecking historic structure. Mrs. Amelia Cunningham, long-time resident of North San Juan was outraged, bought structure, saving it from wreckers. However, Mrs. Cunningham died before starting renovation, estate is still in litigation, fate of building hangs in balance. Many hope State will take over, make Park of old town which contains so many relics of California's Gold Rush days.

the problem by simply attaching a "North" before the name.

The famous "Deadman's Claim" also had odd naming history. In January of 1853 two young men, West and Chadbourne, discovered a rich deposit in San Juan Hill. To get a sufficiently steep pitch to carry off tailings from the diggings, they were forced to make a deep cut. They were working at it when the whole bank caved in, burying both under tons of rock and dirt. Since there were no other claims near, and the boys were known for minding their own business and not fraternizing with other miners, they were not missed for several days.

When they were, it took several shifts of men to uncover the bodies. Both West and Chadbourne were found to have brothers, who were located and informed they owned a claim at North San Juan. Neither, it seems, was interested in mining, both selling out to Louis Buhring and Peter Lassen who paid $300 for the legal right to mine the spot.

The new owners had trouble with the water supply which either flooded out the equipment or disappeared and they barely made expenses, selling shares now and then to survive. Then a fluming company brought in a steady supply of water and fortunes changed drastically for the owners, now increased to seven. During the sixteen months ending in December of 1858, they took out a total of $156,000. The men continued to mine the claim by removing and washing the alluvial soil until in '60 nothing remained but bare bedrock.

What was probably the first "gold brick" swindle was perpetrated by a slicker posing as a lucky miner returned to the east from the North San Juan gold area. He announced to the New York assay office he had found a nugget of solid gold weighing 193 pounds Troy, and requested an assay. As he desired to display the chunk, he did not wish to mar its appearance and would samples please be removed at the places he indicated so they wouldn't show. Why, certainly. The assayed samples proved to be of the usual "fineness" of typical California gold.

Then the miner announced he was in a terrible predicament. He had a wonderful offer from a London firm for rights to display the nugget there. Yet he was tempted to cash in more directly by sending it to the Philadelphia mint but, in the meantime, he had to live. Could he have a loan, leaving the fabulous chunk of gold as security? Why, sure thing. The assay office advanced, the nuggeteer retreated. After what seemed a reasonable wait, the assayers dug more deeply into the glittering blob of treasure. Under a coating of gold there was a nice fat wad of lead.

MANY BEAUTIFUL EXAMPLES OF OLDTIME ART of marble sculpture exist in cemetery of North San Juan, most dating from about 1855. During period floral offerings now called "sprays" were made as flat bouquets in style shown on stone. Represented are lilies of the valley, callas, forget-me-nots, roses, morning-glories, lilies, tulips. Roses are "cabbage" type of that period, not high centered hybrid teas of today.

HUGE NOZZLE, CALLED MONITOR spewed streams of water at terrific pressures against hillsides, washing away tons of soil, resulting gold-laden mud to be diverted into sluices where heavier gold lodged against slates or "riffles" at bottom. Several millions in gold are said to remain in hills around North San Juan, hydraulicking being outlawed.

248

RANDSBURG, CALIFORNIA

Frederick Mooers was a newspaper man but he would never have been able to put the fire and excitement into a paragraph that he did in his eyes when he saw the particles of gold. "Boys!" he yelled to his two partners. "We've struck it! There's no need to look any farther."

This was the gold that started the Rand mine, that gave the name Rand to the mountains and town — "The fastest growing town in the west" — and there was much romance and human interest in the finding of it . . . unless you count the long days under the merciless sun, the desperate search for water with eyes almost glazed shut and the hunger for a kind word remembered from a boyhood in the shade back home.

The men responsible for Randsburg were three who had worked the scattered, played-out gulches around the fringes of the Mojave and had about given up ever making any big money. One was John Singleton, carpenter turned miner, who had gained much experience in the placers and hard rock mines but now was broke and discouraged. One was Frederick Mooers, clever newspaper writer but completely unfit to make a living, let alone a fortune. The third was Charles Austin Burcham, whose chief distinction was having a doctor for a wife. The total assets of the three were a team and wagon, bought with money Dr. Rose La Monte Burcham had earned delivering babies in San Bernardino.

JOSHUA TREES seem to form grotesque Conga line, posturing their way along sandy road in Red Rock Canyon. Several gold strikes brought series of rushes to gulches, leading into brilliant, eroded canyon. During one in 1893, prospector found $150 in four days, celebrated and returned with partner to take out $260 more. Tiny creek dried up and so did his hopes. Others, working on larger scale, did not depend on erratic stream flow, built "dry washers" operating on air blower principle. When all available gold was extracted prospectors left, to return when mountain storms formed Gully Washers in canyons. New beds of gold exposed, cycle started all over again.

Disgusted at finding no paying lode in Summit Gulch in 1895 — where Mooers and William Langdon had found some color earlier — the trio departed in the lumber wagon, heading for the hills where they spent a month until time and money ran short, as Burcham was nearing the end of a two-year limit imposed by his wife.

One night in April they made camp in a dry canyon not far from the Twenty Mule Team road between Death Valley and Mojave. The disheartened Mooers kicked his heels up the wash for fuel and gathered some greasewood stems when his eye caught a glint of yellow in a nearby ledge. Gasping, he dropped the brush and ran back for his pick. The first chunk of rock chipped off showed particles of gold all over it. "Boys!" he yelled, "we've struck it! There's no need to look any farther."

And for once the newspaper man made headlines with resounding effect. The three men secured eight claims and hired an expert quartz mining man to examine the ground, swearing him to secrecy. "You've got a good thing here," he reported. "Get a 100-stamp mill, shovel the whole mountain into it and your fortunes are made. The whole hill is good ore." Then he promptly broke the secret.

The news reached O. B. Stanton in Bakersfield who came running with cash. He liked what he saw and offered to spend $10,000 to get the mine started, erect a stamp mill etc., in return for one half interest. The agreement had the signatures of Mooers and Singleton but not Burcham. He was in Bakersfield giving his wife the good news and signing over to her half of his share, as agreed when she grubstaked him. "Now," Dr. Rose warned him, "don't you dare sign anything when you get back to the mine, at least until we know more about its value." Back at the mine Burcham was handed the document which he refused to sign. The deal fell through but the contract bearing the other two names would later be vital in endless and costly litigation.

Now here came the forthright doctor. In July she took charge of the mine situation while for the next several months the three men dug ore and crushed it by hand using a little water hauled from Cow Wells or Goler. Dr. Rose did the housekeeping and with blind faith of psychic assurance kept books while looking around for some way to finance and expand operations.

The partners got out enough ore to make two shipments to distant smelters in Montana. The rich ore was pulled down the mountain on sleds, transferred to wagons for hauling to Mojave and reloaded on flatcars. When the assay report came there was great rejoicing in camp and the four laid plans to begin mining on a larger scale.

SIDES OF RED ROCK CANYON are spectacularly eroded, giving effect of miniature Bryce. Harder rhyolite and sandstone of bright salmon-pink to red are moulded into fantastic forms, alternating with softer snowy-white clay in fluted columns. Canyon floor is composed of clean sand from walls, supports desert garden of cacti, "desert holly", greasewood, other shrubby growths, mostly prickly. One ampitheater-like area is filled with worshippers each Easter Sunday as first rays of sun enter gorge.

Meanwhile other mines were established — the Gold Coin, Napoleon, Bully Boy, Monkey Wrench, Wedge, Olympus, Trilby and King Solomon. One Swede miner called his claim The Big Norse. Si Drouillard found the rich St. Elmo, five miles from the original Rand, and this set off the big rush to Randsburg. Hopefuls from Los Angeles came as far as Mojave by train, boarding stages for Red Rock Canyon and Cow Wells where extra horses were hitched on for the steep stretch to Randsburg.

Every stage carried mail and a mixed assortment of humanity — miners, prospectors, legitimate business men who expected to open stores, as well as outcasts and riffraff from coast and eastern cities. Enough prostitutes, gamblers, pimps came along to populate a full-blown red light district, but gay and rowdy Randsburg never got a reputation for great violence. There were few killings as compared to those in other camps.

By 1897, Mooers, Singleton and Burcham had received something like $250,000 in payment for ore

RANDSBURG was built on whatever contour ground offered, one end of town much higher than the other. Main thoroughfare makes sharp hairpin curve into and out of town, following available levels. One comparatively level stretch, called Butte Street, intersected central business section. Building shown was famous Rinaldi's Market serving townspeople with meat and groceries over most of town's life.

DURING LUSTY DAYS, Randsburg's brothels were scattered among more reputable businesses, French Marguerite's exclusive bordello being immediately below Rinaldi's. Mothers, living still farther down gulch, forced to bring children past open doors often occupied by painted hussies, protested to civic authorities demanding that bawdy houses be segregated.

and their scraping days were over. Eventually revenues would amount to some $25 million from Randsburg mines. Legal disputes harassed the Rand mine, now called the Yellow Aster, some of them initiated by Mooers' former partner, William Langdon. He lost his case as did others who attacked the validity of the three partners' claims.

It was during this period that Daniel Kelsey struck it rich. A mule team driver, hauling borax for Coleman and Smith from the Harmony Works near Furnace Creek in Death Valley to Mojave, he quit the job because, as he said: "I just couldn't stand seeing those ornery critters go so long without water."

He made one trip with his own team, hauling lumber to the raw mining camp of Randsburg, stood enthralled in the midst of a thousand tents and a few board-and-canvas shacks, then bought some prospectors' tools and supplies. After a few weeks of fruitless picking and panning, he found some float in Yuma Canyon and tracked the ledge to its source. He chipped off a piece, showed it to a friend who invested $20,000 as a partner. The ledge started the famous Blue Daisy mine, which when sold for $170,000, sent the Dan Kelsey family on a grand tour of Europe.

Also during this period Pat Reddy finally gained what he had been refused in Randsburg's earlier days. Reddy was an attorney of sorts, self-educated and keen. He had never been admitted to the bar but made a reputation in the loosely conducted

courts of Nevada in the hectic '60s. In one scuffle at Aurora, he was wounded and eventually lost an arm. Reddy became state senator and then swung through the big mining camps where he fitted his talents into legal squabbles.

In Randsburg he approached the two-fisted Dr. Rose Burcham. "I tell you folks could do with a little cash to start things going," he said. "I'd be glad to advance say a few thousand dollars. Instead of repayment in cash, you can settle with me for a share of your mine." But Dr. B. was not about to see her project divided by even the smallest fraction no matter how much she needed money and no amount of pleading by Pat Reddy moved her. So smarting under the rebuff, he caught the next stage for Mojave.

When he later heard of the Yellow Aster's legal struggles, he hurried back and offered help. This time he found a desperate situation and his offer was accepted for a share of the mine. One phase of the case was won and Reddy's share eventually paid him enough to live on comfortably the rest of his life.

Over the years almost half the world's known minerals were found in the Rand and neighboring mountains. During the first years, if these were noticed at all, they were cast aside as worthless. Gold was all that mattered. But even the Rand's gold supply was not inexhaustible. When it thinned out and Randsburg's miners were scraping the bottom of the barrel, they found they had been overlooking

251

real money in tungsten. In 1895 rich deposits of this element of the chromium family were found five miles from Randsburg, close enough to infuse new life into the fading camp, although the town of Atolia grew up on the immediate site, the name derived from the two men involved in early development, Atkins and De Golia.

With the World War demand for tungsten, excitement ran riot in the gulches, the metal being found mostly in placer deposits. This frantic activity produced in all $65 million worth. Men working in mines were searched and their lunchboxes examined at the portals, and as contraband ore continued to flow, miners were forced to change clothes after work. A shopping bag quickly filled with the ore, scheelite, would bring $350.

Then came the end of the war and almost complete collapse of the tungsten market. With gold mining tapered off at the Randsburg mines, the area went into another slump. The Yellow Aster was in the doldrums and by this time all three of the original partners were dead. Dr. Burcham still held her shares and Mooers' son Edwin retained a part, but law suits, strikes and other labor troubles had brought the famous old mine to a virtual standstill. One strike lasted sixteen years, brought to an end in 1918. With only a skeleton crew of three still employed there, much of the population of the once

roistering, booming town had evaporated.

Then in 1919 came the discovery that a ridge of rock running down the slope of nearby Red Mountain was almost solid horn silver. Every former resident of Randsburg who could return to the dead town did so and again it served as in the tungsten boom. Two small centers sprang up close to the Big Silver, Osdick and Hampton, which were soon consolidated and ten years later given the formal post office name of Red Mountain. When the silver boom swelled to over $14 million in 1926, it showed signs of coming to an end. The mine was sold for $50,000 that year, the new owners doing nothing spectacular with it.

The Second World War made no stirring demand for tungsten and gold mining has made no comeback. Once again Randsburg has settled back on a comparative ghost town status. The inevitable tavern still operates, a desert museum is open on weekends displaying many of an almost endless variety of minerals and crystal specimens found in the surrounding hills. It is said of most dormant gold and silver mining towns that only a rise in prices of the metals would bring revival. In the case of Randsburg it would seem possible that one of the many minerals found hereabout and heretofore neglected, might suddenly become indispensable, causing history to repeat itself.

JOHANNESBURG, popularly Joburg, was less glamorous neighbor of Randsburg, contains few reminders of early days. It is busier today, being on highway, filled mostly with shanties and mobile homes. First houses were all frame, were destroyed by repeated fires. Later they were of adobe or as here, as scraps of tin or sheet iron — fireproof if not picturesque. Most prominent structure was 10-stamp mill, dominating town. One large hotel, boxy wooden structure, had about thirty-five rooms, was center of gay social events. Joburg also boasted several stores and saloons but no church, religious services sometimes held in school house.

ROUGH AND READY, CALIFORNIA

The "Great Republic of Rough and Ready" it was to be called. It was only a small mining camp and only a year old in 1850, but people in other towns had to admit the brash camp had ideas of its own and the courage of non-conformity. The scheme? To secede from the Territory of California and the United States, and to declare itself an independent country.

The hard-working miners had a point. They had laws, the mining laws they had worked out and which they figured were good enough to live by. Most of them had left Wisconsin to escape onerous restrictions and now with applications of U.S. laws about to be put into effect through territorial legislation, they were hot under the collar. They could expect all manner of irksome restraints now and, worst of all, they would be taxed the same as back home even though the basis

ROUGH AND READY IS FULL of romantic tales of heyday. Story of secession is well authenticated, less solid is story of Caroline, daughter of "slavegirl" who lived on this site. Caroline loved to ride, on one occasion came up to door-step on favorite pony, dismounted and with flourish stuck whip into ground. Whip, cut previously from cotton-wood tree took root, grew to be venerable giant, was blown down few years ago and part cut away. Caroline, growing up, went to San Francisco to go into "business" on her own. She caught sleeve on fire over lamp chimney while curling hair, rushed out to well for water, in her haste fell in, was drowned. Crumbling remains of W. H. Flippin blacksmith shop show in background.

would be different. They would even have to pay to operate their own claims, their very own by legal staking under miners' law.

Seething with the thoughts of these injustices, tempers suddenly exploded when a spark was unintentionally applied by a smart aleck from Boston. One of the original miners from Wisconsin was sweating at his claim and getting little gold, about ready to quit and "maybe chuck the whole shootin' match, maybe" when he looked up to see a dude watching him intently. On impulse the miner asked: "Say, Mister, how'd you like to buy this claim for three thousand dollars?"

The man in the city clothes shrugged his shoulders, took a step forward and made a counter offer. Nobody could be expected to buy a pig in a poke so he would work the claim all the next day to see how rich it was. Everything he dug over $200 the owner could have. Anything less would belong to him. Then at the end of the day they would decide. An agreement was reached.

The Boston man appeared the next morning still dressed fit to kill but with a helper who was ready to work for a promised $8. No sooner had he begun to fling the shovel at the rock when pay dirt showed up and before the day was over he had brought up $180 in gold. The helper was paid and left. The owner of the claim protested this thing wasn't fair, that he had never found more than a bare wage in a day and he should have a share in this find. The eastern man said no, the contract agreed upon was legal according to U.S. laws and there would be no reneging now. He intended to keep his clear profit—$172.

This reasoning pleased no one in Rough and Ready. Almost every miner sided with the claim owner and got hotter and hotter about it until an indignation meeting was held. Discussion dried men's throats and they repaired to the saloon, the Bostonian conspicuous by his absence. The original group expanded to include almost every adult male in the camp and not only was this most recent grievance hashed over but every other one as well.

When the issue of an impending tax on mines and

ROUGH AND READY SCHOOL, built around turn of century replaced original which was destroyed by fire. Now abandoned because of lack of pupils, it has been put to use as "Trading Post." Identification of little "tails" strung on line baffled curious photographer, even on close examination.

miners was brought up, the crowd exploded. One miner, E. F. Brundage, by way of being a leading citizen because of his ready and sonorous voice, loudly proclaimed—"We've had enough!" Everybody agreed, but what to do about it? Some were for appointing Brundage a committee of one to look into ways and means of combating the oppressive rulings and report a week later, same time, same place. But Brundage already had a solution which he proclaimed with a bullish roar—"Secede!"

After a brief, shocked silence followed by loud cheers, the resolution was passed unanimously and after a long pause for a few shots of Rough and Ready dust layer, a manifesto was drawn up. Climbing on a table, Brundage read the document which set forth a few complaints and ended with the resolution: "We, the people of Rough and Ready . . . deem it necessary and prudent to withdraw from the Territory of California and from the United States of America to form peacefully if we can, forcibly if we must, the Great Republic of Rough and Ready." With loud huzzas the resolution was passed unanimously, Brundage was elected president and all had another round of drinks. A constitution of twelve articles was drawn up and likewise approved.

The new government went into immediate action. Delegates were dispatched to the hotel room of the man from Boston. There was something about the pointed guns of the group that caused him to wilt and hand over the $172. Given five minutes to pack, he was prodded down the stairs, escorted to the edge of town and booted into the Territory of California.

The Republic waited expectantly for some reaction from Washington. Would it be disciplinary after suitable confabs? Would a regiment of soldiers make camp outside the boundaries of Rough and Ready, making plans to attack at dawn? The rebels organized a group of Vigilantes and felt prepared for any emergency—but nothing happened. It felt somewhat miffed at the complete silence, the insulting aloofness of the government—no recognition, no invasion. But gradually the miners settled down to their mundane labors, unhampered by United States law under Territorial jurisdiction.

Spring came and went. The month of June began to brown the green carpet of grass on the rolling hills. Thoughts began to form as to celebrating the Fourth of July in a proper way. Several miners, with others from Timbuctoo, discussed possibilities. Then while plans were sprouting, an appalling realization crashed down on the heads of all. The camp was no longer a part of the United States! Independence Day for it was no longer the Fourth of July. If there were to be a celebration, on what day would it be?

This was a quandary of cataclysmic proportions. No mining camp could hold up its head without a proper Independence Day blow-off. Something had to be done even if it meant restoring the new Republic to the United States. More meetings. More discussion. More whistle wetting. Then decision. Without asking if they might, the people of Rough and Ready voted it back into the Union. With this obstacle out of the way, plans were made for the dad-blamedest lid-lifting Fourth ever held in California.

Putting plans into effect was another thing. When they were going full tilt, on June 28, along came a disastrous fire, sweeping almost everything in town before it. Citizens did what they could with a Fourth of July parade down the little main street now bor-

dered by charred shells of once proud false-fronted businesses.

Rough and Ready was one of the first camps established in Nevada County. A party of men calling themselves the Rough and Ready Company arrived in the area September 9, 1949 under the leadership of a Captain Townsend. He had served under Colonel Zachary (Old Rough and Ready) Taylor, hero of the Mexican War. The men kept their gold discoveries secret for some time, getting out quite a bit of it before the tide of settlers and miners flooded in to make a town of a thousand by early spring, 1850.

A double row of buildings quickly formed, begin-

W. H. FLIPPIN BLACKSMITH SHOP is one of few remaining original buildings of Rough and Ready. At time of taking picture, venerable relic showed strong signs of imminent collapse. Peeks through cracks in walls revealed full complement of blacksmith's implements, forge and all.

ning at the foot of a transverse, oak-covered ridge. About twenty of them lined the camp's one street which had a crook in the middle to conform to the contour. At the end, and considerably elevated, stood an imposing church, complete with steeple and broad flight of steps. As was the custom, this elevation was dubbed "Piety Hill." If any of the founding party which had only "temporarily camped" on the spot ever thought of continuing on to Sacramento, he must long ago have forgotten it for the population remained stable for a number of years.

A Christian Association was organized during the first days holding meetings in one of the little clapboard shanties on the main street. Other religious organizations developed, generally of orthodox nature.

One "church" was headed by a "hell roaring" preacher, James Dinleavy, whose demands were greater than the satisfaction of soul saving and ran a popular and lucrative saloon on weekdays. As soon as he got together enough money, he sent for his wife who waited in San Francisco. Mrs. Dinleavy was the first woman to arrive in camp and excitement stirred the crowd into meeting her at the stage and deluging her with gifts including 21 ounces of gold dust.

The town continued to grow until about 1870. At its best period there were more than three hundred substantial houses, in spite of two crippling fires in '56 and '59. As placer deposits faded, so did Rough and Ready, and little is left of it today except the preposterous legend of secession.

PART OF OLD ROUGH AND READY HOTEL is incorporated in present conglomeration used as post office.

SAWMILL FLATS, CALIFORNIA

Three miles southeast of Columbia, a mile and a half south of Yankee Hill, is a clearing in a once dense forest. The nearly level area is on the banks of Wood's Creek, the same stream that figured so prominently in the histories of Sonora and a dozen other gold camps. Gold however did not bring the swarms of people there in the early 1850s. Here in the center of a bountiful supply of standing timber were established two large sawmills. Lumber was a scarce commodity in the early gold rush days and it brought a good price, creating a boom camp at Sawmill Flat.

At first not many Americans were willing to work in the mills, too many were eager to pan for gold or work for someone who had built a series of Long Toms or was sluicing the beds of the stream. There was always a possibility of pocketing good nuggets while guaranteed a daily wage of $2.50 a day. The first employees at the mills were almost all Peruvians and Mexicans. Being clannish, both races had established "segregated" saloons and stores, nearly every facility in town being duplicated. A population of over a thousand had grown up around the mills when an exciting event was noised around in spite of every effort to suppress it. Only a short distance north of the center of town a good strike of gold had been made.

Yet disappointment was due those who rushed up the creek to stake claims—disappointment and astonishment. The claims were already staked out —and by whom? By no one less than a strikingly beautiful Mexican woman! Her name was Dona Josepha Elisa Martinez and to discourage any too-ardent fortune hunters, she had brought from Mexico a motley crowd of peons, ready to defend their lady boss. The senora was already wealthy and the gravels of Wood's Creek and several shallow surface workings swelled her coffers earlier filled with gems and fancy clothes.

But being wealthy was not enough for the Dona Martinez. She was lonely. So it was opportune that a handsome young Mexican with curly black hair and luxuriant mustache called on her and introduced himself as Joaquin Murieta. He said he was a monte dealer who had fallen into some trouble and would she hide him for a while? Hide him she did and since that all happened before Murieta became notorious, his face familiar to many a victim of robbery and hold-up, he vanished completely from the posse on his trail.

Once he felt safe, he again took the bandit route and soon returned to hide with the lovely senora. This time she was able to conceal him only a short while. His hideout, the first of many to become known, was precarious. Murieta left hurriedly by the back door one night and Josepha Elisa, in her camp now called Martinez, as well as the populace of Sawmill Flats, knew him no more.

In 1857 a disastrous fire almost leveled nearby Columbia, the best customer of the mills. It was the worst but not the first of the fires that destroyed most of the flimsy buildings of the boom town. Columbia ruefully surveyed its ashes and decided that this time rebuilding would be done with brick. This was the death knell for Sawmill Flat and it gently folded. The rich deposits of gold at neighboring Martinez were soon scratched off and that collection of shanties also died, the senora returned to Mexico with her loot and without her swarthy bandit. The camp of Martinez vanished almost from sight and only a few shacks and cabins remained to mark the site of Sawmill Flats.

ONE OF FEW REMAINING CABINS at Sawmill Flats near collapse, with stone foundation and walls probably built of scraps from the sawmills. Ancient grapevine arches over south wall, leaves all but covering structure in summer. Buildings at site were all flimsy, show no sign of stone, adobe or brick walls. This wooden one has survived because high stone foundation kept rot from beams.

SHASTA, CALIFORNIA

Dick Barter might have lived out his life as an honest citizen but the cards were stacked against him. He arrived in California from Canada just too late to share in the first big bonanzas of the Sierra gold rush. His claim was on Rattlesnake Bar, near Auburn, and when he got there with a sister and cousin he found the gravels already depleted. Discouraged, his relatives went north to settle on a homestead at Sweet Home, Oregon.

But Dick stayed on, persistently working his claim. Never admitting its thin yield, he bragged about it so noisily in the Auburn saloons he was soon called "Rattlesnake Dick". If the nickname didn't force him into crime it at least made the rumors about his shady conduct easy to believe.

The first of these came about when a miner, who had taken a dislike to Dick's loud talk, reported he had seen the Canadian stealing from a little store near his claim. Dick was arrested, tried and acquitted, but the seed of suspicion was planted.

Next a Mormon named Crow missed his mule and brought charges of theft against Dick, even stating he had seen the accused taking the animal. This evidence was enough to convict the hapless man but before sentence was passed (which could have been death by hanging) the real culprit turned up, a man resembling Barter.

But now he was a marked man and it seemed to Dick that everyone looked at him with an accusing eye. Completely discouraged with his claim, he left the area for a mining town farther north — Shasta. It was enough removed, he thought, so he could start life again without the hated nickname and its sinister influence. Soon after arrival in the booming camp at the edge of the Trinity Alps he found work to his liking and settled down to what he hoped would be a peaceful existence.

He had two good years before some men from Auburn came to town and spotted him. In no time the information got around that "this man is Rattlesnake Dick, a fugitive from Auburn where he's been in all kinds of scrapes." And now he was looked at sidewise in Shasta. He was later quoted as saying: "I can stand it no longer. I have been driven to a hereafter. Now my hand is against everyone's as everyone's is against me."

Dick Barter lost no time in getting into his new way of life, holding up a man for enough to pay his way back to Auburn and more familiar territory. In best dime novel tradition, he "signed" his first dishonest deed, telling his victim: "If anyone asks who robbed you, tell them Rattlesnake Dick, the Pirate of the Placers".

For the first year or so his crimes were for chicken feed but he was laying plans to intercept a big shipment of gold that would come along the road through Shasta. The bullion would be sent south from Yreka by mules branded with the name of their owner, Wells Fargo. Therefore it would be necessary to transfer the gold to unmarked animals

OLD SKETCH SHOWS SHASTA before fire of June 14, 1853, which destroyed almost entire town in thirty minutes. Adams Express offices, Old Dominion and St. Charles Hotels, largest in town, shown here, were rebuilt within four years as solid brick, fireproof structures.

"TREES OF HEAVEN", grown from seeds brought home by nostalgic Chinese miners, are common sights in most milder climate mining camps. Photo shows bare limbs of early March outlined by low-angled sunlight.

immediately after the holdup. Dick knew where to steal the fresh mules and he would do this part of the job himself. George Skinner would be head of the gang performing the holdup, George's brother Cyrus helping gather up the new mules.

The robbery was committed without a hitch although the train was accompanied by twenty armed guards. George Skinner had only six men but the element of surprise helped him subdue the guards. They were tied to trees as Skinner's men made off with the loaded mules.

Arriving at the rendezvous site above Shasta, the high-spirited highwaymen waited for Rattlesnake Dick and his string of fresh mules. After several days of worry about Dick's absence and the possibility of a misunderstanding about the meeting place, Skinner and his boys were as jumpy as fleas. Expecting a posse from Shasta anytime, scouts combed the gulches and sentries kept constant

watch. In desperation a decision was made to make tracks with half the gold. The $80,000 in bullion represented far too much weight to carry without mules but, Skinner said, they could manage half of it and he would bury the other half alone. As he moved half the gold, a Mexican started to follow him and was shot on the spot. With part of the treasure buried, the gang headed for their hideout near Folsom, south of the American River.

They got there at night and buried the second half of the bullion, then started for Auburn to find out what had detained Dick. The fact was, the Auburn jail was detaining him now for he had been caught stealing the mules — but George Skinner would never know it. At Shasta, Wells Fargo detective Jack Barkley had deduced the job had been handled by Rattlesnake Dick's gang and knowing the location of the hideout, he took his posse in that direction. The two parties met in the moonlight on the Folsom-Auburn road and the first shot Barkley fired killed Skinner. Four men deserted the posse but the rest subdued the robber gang and brought them into Auburn. One of them, Bill Carter, received a pardon for revealing where the second half of the gold was concealed. With George Skinner dead, the first half was unrecoverable. The $40,000 in bullion remains hidden near Shasta to be added to the several other celebrated stories of hidden treasure in California.

Rattlesnake Dick broke out of the Auburn jail and made a brief return to his chosen career. One night, after a holdup, he was shot to death by a pursuing posse. On his body was found a pathetic letter from his sister, imploring her errant brother to give up his life of crime and join her on the farm.

While all this was going on, Shasta was not too much perturbed. The town was full of rough characters and accustomed to events of this sort. Stringing up her own horse thieves and holdup men from the gallows at the rear of the courthouse, she was not too much bothered by crimes outside of town.

STEEP BANK behind brick structures causes heavy runoff in rainy periods, while several semi-permanent springs flow most of year. Provision was made for drainage by bricked gutters between buildings. Here, in early March, rivulet is conducted to street as in 1850s.

LONG ROW OF FADING BRICK REMNANTS mark outlines of Shasta's once teeming business section. Most buildings retain fragments of iron doors and shutters commonly used, intended to keep burglars and fire out, or contain fires starting within.

Shasta was little more to start with than a camp at the gateway to the rich mines in the back country, a stage stop between the level valleys of the Sacramento and the snowy peaks of the Trinitys, the head of "Whoa Navigation" in the vernacular of the day.

Originally called "Reading's Springs" by the first settlers who arrived at the site shortly after Major Pierson Reading found fifty ounces of gold a day nearby, the name was changed to Shasta next year. The mountain for which it is named is not far to the north, is a magnificent old volcano of more than 14,000 feet in elevation, covered with spectacular glaciers on the north and east sides. At its foot is the present day town of Mount Shasta, not to be confused with the roistering old Shasta above Redding.

A hundred mule trains and teams were known to stop in Shasta on a single night. Its strategic position caused a fast growth of outfitters and suppliers. Mule trains heading for the mines in the

REAR OF OLD COURTHOUSE in Shasta shows jail on first floor, gallows on level with courtroom. First legal hanging here was that of a man named Higgins on November 10, 1855. Last of long succession was John Baker on August 24, 1874. Baker was one of pair guilty of holdup and murder. His companion, Charles Crouch, wanted execution over quickly but Baker stalled death for a few minutes by request that he be allowed to sing a song remembered from his childhood. It was granted and he sang "Faded Flowers", the last two stanzas being:

Oh! how dark looks this world and
   how dreary
When we part from the ones that
   we love;
But there's rest for the faint and
   the weary
And friends meet with loved ones
   above!

And in Heaven I can but remember
When from earth my proud soul
   shall be free
That no cold chilly winds of De-
   cember
Can take my companions from me.

layed obtaining full supplies until arrival in Shasta. One of the largest supply houses was that of Bull, Baker and Co. The firm erected a substantial brick building in 1853 replacing a wooden one destroyed by fire. The structure still stands today, a unit in the highly publicized, at that time, "longest row of brick buildings in California." The story is told of one of the Bull, Baker principals being stopped by a mule team owner on his way to breakfast. The latter was anxious to be on his way, joined the trader at breakfast and bought $3,000 worth of goods before the ham and eggs got to the table.

Shasta kept her position of shipping center until 1872 when the California and Oregon Railroad reached the six-mile distant city of Redding in the valley. This was a severe blow and when the neighboring placers became exhausted in 1888, the fading city lost county seat honors and quietly died.

MASONIC HALL shows through gaping doorway. Lodge building has been well cared for, is still in use. Treasured in vault is first charter of Western Star Lodge No. 2 which was brought from Missouri by Peter Lassen. He carried precious document in metal cylinder for protection against fire or water. Lassen made trip by ox train, became well known figure all over northern California, numerous prominent features including Lassen Peak being named for him.

SWANSEA, CALIFORNIA

Here was a good-sized livery stable, the forge almost intact. There was a boardinghouse with wide porches, once screened. A well-worn path led to a hole in the ground, a vanished "convenience." White talc rocks lined both sides of the trail, whether to satisfy the aesthetic senses or to facilitate stumbling feet in the darkness would be hard to tell. Adjoining the kitchen was a chicken pen of wire. A short trip from the coop to the table!

The town was named Swansea after the famous smelter town in Wales. Mary Austin has given the whole area a fitting name—"The land of little rain."

There is a dry lake a few miles back of the edge of the steep cliff. Its bottom is pure salt, and it's called Saline Lake. The salt was hauled to the edge of the cliff; then run down on a tram cable to the terminus, where it was shipped across the lake to Cartago, from there to San Pedro, thence to Swansea, Wales for refining.

BOARDINGHOUSE STANDS on east shore of vanished Owens Lake (background). Above, to west looms loftiest section of high Sierra, whose once-copious snows nourished lake. Mt. Whitney is above chicken-run at right.

TIMBUCTOO, CALIFORNIA

Jim Denton was a miner in Timbuctoo. His claim on the banks of the Yuba River paid him only the barest minimum in gold dust to keep body and soul together. His little cabin was furnished with only the simple essentials and he ate plain foods sparingly.

Nights along the Yuba even in June are cold and Denton was out of wood. He stopped working his rocker early one evening, June 20, 1860, and cut down the old oak near his cabin for firewood. He had planned to take it down because the aged tree had a badly decayed side and a strong wind might blow it over on his shack. He felled the tree and set about cutting it up. When he split the rotten section, he laid open a large hollow—and in it snugly reposed a buckskin sack.

As soon as Jim took hold of the soft leather, he

RAPIDLY FALLING INTO RUIN is pathetic shell of once busy Stewart Store. Patriotic groups mindful of value of historic relics have made effort to preserve old structure, placed sheltering metal roof over it. Struggle is futile against human vandals who pluck bricks and paint obscenities over old signs on building.

BEAUTIFUL EXAMPLE OF STONE-MASON'S work is crumbling rear wall of only building remaining in Timbuctoo. Native rocks, including river boulders, have been split so as to form facing. Doors and windows are lined with brick, furnished with iron shutters characteristic of period.

knew what he had and his hands trembled as he opened the drawstring and poured some of the contents into his hand. Nuggets they were, hundreds of them, with no quartz matrix sticking to them. He took the sack into the cabin and weighed the nuggets one at a time on his gold scales—total weight thirty-five pounds. He carefully counted the number of *chispas* and wrote down the figures.

An honest man, Jim took the bag to the store for safekeeping and then let out the story. He said all the rightful claimant had to do was give the weight and number of nuggets. No one in Timbuctoo or nearby Mooney Flat or Smartsville came forth and after waiting a reasonable period, Jim took the gold to Grass Valley where he sold it for $7,500. No claimant ever turned up and Jim Denton concluded the rightful owner had met with a fatal accident after pushing the bag into that hollow.

First miners to slosh gravels in their pans along that part of the Yuba camped there in 1850. In the party was a Negro, a refugee slave from the South. He had originally been captured by slavers in the French Sudan of West Africa, his native town being Timbuktu. He worked industriously in the little ravine above where the town was later built and found good colors in his pan. Happy over his discovery, he asked the others if he might call the place Timbuktu Gulch and they were agreeable. The colored man's first strike was followed by many more, news spread and a town grew up where the ground was more level. The name was preserved with American variations.

Getting started in 1855, the town grew steadily but not spectacularly. Then came the hydraulic mining era when the banks of the stream were literally washed away in a flood of thin mud and boulders. Results in gold production were so large that Timbuctoo boomed into the largest town in the eastern part of Yuba County. Churches, theaters, hotels, saloons and stores went up to serve a population of more than 1,200 people.

The flood of debris and mud soon raised another flood, that of protests from ranchers and the valley and the Sawyer Decision, 1884, put an end to this type of mining. The props that had kept up the economy of Timbuctoo were knocked out and the town quickly sank into oblivion.

266

"Stunted growths...
eached white... like skeletons!"

TUMCO, CALIFORNIA

Stark desert is the setting for the battered ruins of Tumco. Summers are witheringly hot for humans in the sandy wastes at the edge of the Cargo Muchacho Mountains. The small canyon, holding what is left of the camp, is twenty-five miles from Yuma, Arizona, where the thermometer often reaches 110 degrees or more. Winters offer luxurious temperatures of 60 to 80 with so much bright sunshine a Yuma resort offered "Free meals and lodging any day the sun doesn't shine."

Indians in prehistoric times carved petroglyphs on the canyon rocks near the twin cones of the Cargo Muchachos. The summit of these peaks is a bare 2,000 feet in elevation but they give the illusion of greater height because of the extremely low flat country, much of which in the nearby Imperial Valley is actually below sea level. Early Indians did considerable crude mining, as well as using the blackish "desert varnish" on the rocks. Their comings and goings to the mine sites and "picture galleries" were so constant their bare feet made conspicuous trails on the rocky ground, paths easily traced by the lighter color where the ancient patina has worn off. Along these primitive tracks are sometimes found potsherds and other artifacts.

From 1865 to 1870 Mexicans found gold in the gravels of Jackson Gulch but kept the discovery to themselves, working the area in a quiet and self-contained way. Production was low and not enough gold was brought into Yuma to cause a stir. A spark of excitement came in the early

'80s—news of a find made by a track walker named Hedges. He was apparently more interested in prospecting than sprung rails as his discovery was made in a canyon some distance from the railroad, a few gulches away from the Mexican claims—mica schist heavily laced with gold. Hedges promptly set a stake, quit his job with a small crew, set up mining operations on an enterprising scale.

Several methods of refining the gold were employed, first with crushing mills ranging up from one or two stamps to the hundred stamp mill considered to be one of the largest in the west, if not the world. Final recovery was generally accomplished in cyanide vats. The finished gold bars were hauled to the railroad at Ogilby, shipped to San Francisco mint.

The town growing up at the scene of the diggings was named after its founder and soon had over three thousand people. Water was piped in from Pilot Knob on the Colorado River. Hedges had all the trappings of the boom town except for the usual hotel, the men living in cabins of wood or stone, the natural building material as nothing was more abundant than rocks in this region so barren of soil, water and vegetation. Hedges had its Chinaman—Charley Sam who ran a grocery store.

During the town's period as Hedges it was free of the early day violence but it was responsible for one tragedy it would like to have forgotten. A handsome Mexican boy named Pedro

HOUSE IS QUAINT EXAMPLE of building with material at hand. Lumber for roof, lintels, etc., was imported, walls constructed of stones picked up within few feet, mud from desert floor holding them together, whole plastered with lime mortar.

worked at the twenty stamp mill at the entrance of a small side canyon. The adjacent cyanide plant had turned out three glistening gold bars in the morning but after lunch the men discovered there were only two in evidence. Pedro, being a "Mex" and handy, was promptly accused of the theft, but he vigorously denied any guilt. The men, determined to force an admission, tied his thumbs together and fastened them to the end of a rope thrown over a beam of the stamp mill. The rope was drawn taught. Still the boy protested his innocence. The men pulled some more until he was suspended, screaming with pain. Still no confession was forthcoming and he was lowered, only to have the rope made into a noose and placed around his neck. He was then forced to stand on a beam, the slack in the rope again taken up. Once again he was questioned, and promised that if he would tell where the bar was hidden he would be freed. The boy repeated

WRECK OF HUGE STAMP MILL comprising one hundred stamps, said to be one of the largest in the West. (Another of one hundred stamps stood at Melones in the Mother Lode country until it burned in 1942.) Mill was designed and built by '49ers who profited by mistakes in hard rock mines in Mother Lode where first crushers had square wooden stems and square iron shoes with no way of rotating them, a serious flaw as ore had to be broken by hand and shoveled into mill.

OGILBY, few miles from Tumco, was railroad shipping point for finished gold bars to San Francisco mint. In its heyday Ogilby was wild place, rowdiness not tolerated at Tumco mines. Men came here to spend money in honky tonks. With end of mining activity and close of Tumco, Ogilby languished and died. Buildings were hauled away or wrecked. When this photo was made in '61, only small shack remained near tiny cemetery. In '62 even this was gone and grave enclosures had been used for firewood.

he knew nothing about it. In a rage, several of the men gave the boy a shove and after a few convulsive jerks he was dead. Years later, when the mill was dismantled, a bar of gold was found in the foundations.

When Hedges was satisfied with his profits and tired of mining, he sold the whole operation to the Borden of condensed milk fame. Borden carried on under a corporation called The United Mining Company. He took the initials of the name and made Tumco of them, and so renamed the town. Ore became more and more free milling so that his profits increased as long as expenses were low. Then came the turn in events that caused so many camps to die, increasing costs while the price of gold remained fixed.

Borden closed down in 1909, and sold everything in the place. Machinery was hauled to Ogilby and shipped out, what little good lumber existed there was salvaged, and another ghost town came into being. Tumco today is a forlorn, completely deserted ruin. Particularly pathetic is the cemetery, well populated for a small town. Because of the acute water shortage, many mining operations were carried out dry when the drills and crushers should have been bathed in water. The dust penetrated lungs, resulting in what was called "miner's consumption" and was in time fatal. Excavations for graves were of the shallowest in this rocky terrain—a few inches had to suffice. Then rocks were piled up to form a cover about two feet high. These graves laid out appear in rows on a flat without a blade of grass or vegetation other than a few ocotillos and a little sparse grease-wood. Only one grave now has a splinter of wood which was once a cross. There is no identification on any of them, and a more lonely, barren and desolate resting place cannot be imagined.

269

VALLECITO, CALIFORNIA

The first discovery of gold at the site on Coyote Creek was actually made by John and Daniel Murphy. They were excited by their find and christened the infant camp Murphy's Diggings. But after a few months of panning the stream, the yield fell short of expectations and the brothers moved on to found the bigger camp of Murphy, after which the original location was called "Murphy's Old Diggings." Then the Mexicans drifted in to the Coyote Creek camp and satisfied with smaller amounts of gold dust, established a tiny village which they called Vallecito.

The word is the Spanish equivalent for "a little valley." Any Mexican settlement in such a situation was likely to be so called and there were a good many Vallecitos in California's early days. Only two have survived. One is an old Butterfield Stage station in San Diego county, the other a Gold Rush town in Calaveras county.

In 1850 the Mexicans arranged a little plaza

GILLEADO BUILDING, sole remnant of once boisterous gold town of Douglas Flat, two and a half miles northeast of Vallecito. Constructed in '51 of limestone blocks now stabilized with concrete, was used in several capacities, among them store and bank. At rear is small hole, reputed to be shotgun window for use of guard who watched safe full of gold. Other limestone buildings in Douglas Flat, relics of gold rush days, were torn down for material to build fences.

SHIP'S BELL used to call congregation to church, sound fire alarms, summon children to school, announce funerals and election results. Early in 1854 Vallecito sent delegation to San Francisco where ship had been abandoned when crew headed for gold fields. Ship's bell had been cast in Troy, N. Y. in '53, was purchased and brought to town. Since church had no steeple, bell was mounted nearby in large oak, served through life of Vallecito, then hung silent many years, finally falling to ground when tree blew down in hard wind of Feb. 16, 1939. In October of that year bell was mounted on monument at site by Native Sons of the Golden West. Stump of tree is shown at right. Other stories contradict legend on bronze plaque, insist bell is too large for ship type, not meant to be rung by lanyard connected to clapper.

after the fashion in their home land and put up temporary brush *ramadas* around it. In the next two years a few more substantial adobes were added and life moved along in sleepy siesta fashion.

Suddenly, in the fall of '52, all this was changed. A vein of gold far richer than the stream gravels was found to run more or less through the center of the camp. The Americans moved in and push-

ing the original miners out of the way, soon had the plaza plowed up and the buildings razed, establishing another center a block or so away. Saloons went up first, then a miner's hotel, fandango hall and several stores, followed by a bank, express office, school and finally a post office.

After the original burst, Vallecito settled down to a steady existence without much further expansion and had a good period of productivity.

VOLCANO, CALIFORNIA

Ill-fated from the start, Volcano went through several periods of travail in its life as a gold camp which may well be characterized by its name. But since the name came before many of its troubles it is explained by the bare rocks resembling lava flow or by the crater-like valley which the town occupied. During the first feverish expansion of the original strike at Coloma, many of Col. Stevenson's regiment of New York Volunteers ranged the hills and valleys of the Sierra Piedmont and found rich deposits in this gulch formed like a volcano.

These first comers averaged $100 a day per pan, the better spots giving up $500. When snow began to fly that fall most of the men prudently retired to the lowlands since no one had taken valuable time to erect shelter. Yet two young soldier friends decided to disregard the ordinarily mild winter climate and stick it out. They left no record of the troubles they endured through the bitter cold but a band of Mexican prospectors found their bodies in the spring. The creek diggings were called Soldiers' Gulch.

That same spring Capt. John A. Sutter, trying to recoup his fortunes, attempted to mine the area with Long Toms manned by a retinue of Indians and South Sea Islanders. He did well for a while with low labor costs and little outlay for equipment but his system had outlasted its day. American miners on the scene raised an outcry that the captain was using "slave labor," not too far from the truth, and Sutter was forced to decamp or face a noose.

Volcano's troubles had begun. With the first soldier-prospectors, Mexicans, Americans and a goodly number of aborigines were working the gravels and there was only just so much space to work in. The Indians held no regard for the white man's claims, dipping their pans where they saw fit. Tension grew until a quarrelsome white claimed an Indian had stolen some of his equipment. The chief of the Indian camp said he would go to the tribesman's tent and search for the missing tool. When he turned his back, a trigger-happy Texas Ranger, Rod Stowell by name, let fly with his rifle. The killing of the chief precipitated the pint-sized "Volcano Indian War" which ended with several fatalities on both sides.

The next several years were no more peaceful but the camp grew rapidly and soon had a respectable group of buildings, one of the most elegant a Masonic Hall, among the first in California. It had a sumptuous bronze chandelier adorned with no less than twelve "coal oil" lamps. The whole assembly could be lowered to trim wicks and clean chimneys.

The native blue limestone was quarried and blocks dressed to provide excellent building material and this was used for the brewery, Lavezzo and Wells Fargo buildings, two-storied I.O.O.F. building, Adams Express office and wine shop. The handsome brick St. George Hotel with three floors is still in good condition. Unfortunately when the rotting balconies were repaired a few years ago the beautifully turned spindles were replaced by common boards. The little jail is a departure from the prevailing construction, made of sheet iron sandwiched between layers of two-inch lumber.

Volcano's nearest neighbor of consequence is Jackson, still a thriving town. In the '50s the two camps were of similar size with a natural rivalry between them, their respective newspapers not above making derogatory statements about each

FAMOUS "TWO SALOONS" BUILDING was duplex affair, double-barreled threat to sobriety, connected inside. Patrons sometimes became confused, thinking to make exit into another bar instead, had to have one more. One of the two saloons, The Jug, was last to close its doors, later acted as store and meeting place.

272

other. A Jackson visitor in Volcano attracted some attention when he plunked down a $20 gold piece to pay for his lodgings. The local miners gathered around to eye the coin and the Jackson man reported to his home papers that the Volcano populace was so backwoodsy it had never seen such a large piece of money before. The Volcano editor was incensed at this kind of slur and retaliated to the effect that it wasn't so much the novelty of the gold coin that caused so much amazement but the fact that the Jackson man had so much money in his possession and had actually paid his hotel bill instead of skipping town.

During the fabulous fifties Volcano began to show signs of maturity after its roistering days. A Thespian Society was organized and put on performances of such classics of the day as "The Iron Chest" and "She Stoops To Conquer" and wherever it could, often in the hall of the Fraternal Building at the head of the main street. During these first years the miners were starved for any kind of theatrical entertainment and it wasn't long before the amateur efforts were replaced by more practiced ones of traveling theatrical troupes from San Francisco, the actors going where the money was.

Not from the metropolis across the Bay but from Grass Valley came that darling of the miners, the child star Lotta Crabtree, to perform her Highland Fling and other dances under the watchful supervision of her mother, Mary Ann. This one night stand was very profitable, the miners throwing nuggets and coins on the stage in their enthusiasm for the black-eyed charmer, who was to go on from these pick-and-shovel towns to world tours on a career to net her millions.

A group of earnest Volcano citizens felt the miners needed more culture and gave them a lending library, one of the first in California, which lasted until all the books were borrowed and none returned. During the middle '50s a volunteer fire department staged hose drills and parades in the streets but was not too efficient at putting out fires which plagued the town.

Most flashy of the civic groups was a militia company called the "Volcano Blues." Its showpiece was a salute cannon which was merely an emblem until the Civil War broke out. Then the fire department, Volcano Blues and two other organizations banded together to form the Union Volunteers. When a minority group with Confederate sympathies threatened to divert the camp's gold supply to Southern uses, the cannon christ-

LITTLE ASSAY OFFICE was operated by Madera Brothers through busy years of town—except for first few when mining was all by pan, Long Tom or rocker, and gold was self-evident. Later prospectors from hills with ore samples needed assayer's valuation. After Volcano died as mining camp, structure was taken over by Jack Giannini for barber shop. Another Giannini from Volcano founded Bank of America and Angelo Rossi, former mayor of San Francisco was born in Volcano.

ened "Old Abe," was wheeled out into the open. It might have been more of a threat if some Union man had thought to provide cannon balls. Instead some round cobblestones were fired with indifferent success but enough noise to discourage the Rebel cause in Volcano and the great Civil War engagement came to an end.

WEAVERVILLE, CALIFORNIA

Weaverville is a lively wraith now, ghostly only in that it is filled with relics and mementos of its boisterous past . . . of a time when board walks rattled with the clomp of miners' boots . . . when the streets were filled with Chinamen screaming in a tong war . . . of a period when newspapers could report on a Tuesday — "Sunday two persons were killed, yesterday buried and today almost forgotten."

In two blocks on both sides of the street the business section of Weaverville's Chinatown was crammed with 2,500 Chinese. Laundries, joss houses, gambling cribs and opium dens had oriental fronts and when the dives offered more for the customer than the white joints and cut into their profits, there was trouble. The Chinese lived anywhere — in warrens, back rooms of stores or in hovels on the fringes of town.

Most of them came from Canton or Hong Kong and the rival tongs under the two allegiances, were bitter enemies. Hatred built up until something had to give and a battle fought. In 1854 a day was set for it — July 4, popular in Weaverville for hangings, picnics, sporting events and now war.

Preparations went on for weeks, blacksmiths fashioning mining tools into cudgels and tridents, the latter favorite among feuding orientals since pitchforks were not available and guns strictly forbidden to Chinese.

On the appointed day rival forces of some six hundred Chinese gathered on a field above Five Cent Gulch, a mile east of town. Weapons flew and blood flowed until the up-to-now amused white spectators stepped in and stopped the mayhem.

Eight Chinese and one American were killed, many wounded and carried off the flat and a dozen or two with minor injuries limped home. Newspapers next day reprimanded the whites for allowing the bloody scrap but were tacitly reminded that they had encouraged it as a "coming attraction", and as one American defended himself: "We thought it was to be sort of a comic opera." Five Cent Gulch and the flat above it was shortly found to be rich in gold and was deeply mined.

It was in 1850 that John Weaver of Mississippi arrived in the locality, one of the wildest and most remote in California. Nothing disturbed the silence but an occasional scream of a mountain lion or the rushing sounds of the rivers. John (some say William) Weaver found gold to the extent of about $15 a day. The news got out and soon a village of log houses had sprung up. Steady growth was at first slow, so inaccessible was the gold field. Whichever

HANDSOME COURTHOUSE has been in constant use since construction in early days. Kept in good repair (note stucco over bricks), offices modernized but atmosphere of mid-nineteenth century is retained.

GRACEFUL SPIRAL STAIRCASES are unique feature of Weaverville's main street. Greatest building period was in 1850s when, as many wooden structures burned, solid brick ones replaced them. Many had offices and stores on second floors with balconies reached by outside, private stairways. Metal work was done in local blacksmith shops. Original iron doors are still in use upstairs in some buildings.

on dwindling reserves went sky-high. When the thaws finally did come and trains began arriving, morale had reached a miserable low. It was bad enough to have food stocks reduced to a little grain but the horrible catastrophe was — only a few gallons of whiskey left in the last keg.

Violence flared in Weaverville, with comic opera aspects along with grim results. There was the incident of the traveling man in the pig sty. He had arrived from Klamath in the morning, made calls on several prospects and had his pockets well lined by evening. This called for a celebration and he led the town on a round of the saloons. By midnight, thoroughly drunk, he groveled around for a place to sleep and settled for a cozy pig pen.

The drummer was still there in the morning but what had been in his pockets wasn't. He protested loudly that he'd been robbed and Weaverville's scapegoat, one Seymour, was brought to the sheriff for questioning. On previous occasions, when he had suddenly "come into money", he had headed for the closest bar. This time he had not. He was cold sober and had no money on him. Highly offended Seymour asked: "Why don't you look in the straw in that pig mud?" Sure enough, there was the missing cash. The weekly newspaper had some unsympathetic comments: "The money was found in the hog pen where the sot had found shelter and suitable companionship."

Not so funny was the fate of John Fehly, who also owed his troubles to the bottle. Stoned to the gills, he lunged from the Diana Saloon one day, shooting wildly in every direction. A random bullet caught well-liked Dennis Murray in the head and killed him. Fehly was seized by Dennis' friends and forced to jail. They all had lynch fever but Fehly had sobered up and was not about to let a noose be twisted around his neck without a struggle. He gave it but the hanging committee called for "The Infant", a gangling young giant, six feet six, and used to putting down insurgents. He threw a hammerlock around Fehly and jerked until the murderer gave

way the eager argonaut chose to get there he was up against hardships. Especially bad was the route from San Francisco by sailing vessel to Trinidad and the trip up the inner valleys by ox and wagon train, with Digger Indians always a menace. Yet Weaverville did grow and became the county seat of Trinity County very early — a dubious honor since she had no competition.

The Trinity Alps are often compared to the High Sierra but the differences are great. The latter range is strung out lengthwise, the Trinity mountains are bunched. Sierra altitudes reach far above 14,000 feet while most Trinity peaks are between 8,000 and 9,000 feet. The latter group is near the ocean and moisture laden storms pile up snow to depths unknown in the Sierra.

These snows made plenty of trouble for the first miners who were unprepared for them. The winter of 1852-53 was especially severe and flimsy-roofed cabins were crushed beneath the weight. Several homes back against the bases of steep slopes were smothered by avalanches, the slides most prevalent towards spring. To make matters worse, incoming mule trains carrying food and candles for lighting etc. were unable to get through the drifts and prices

276

up. "All right, you!" he panted. "At least put a coal in my pipe." Someone lit the pipe, the noose slipped over it and the trap sprung.

Weaverville got along without a jail for some years by the expedient of quick execution or release. "A man is either guilty or not guilty", the people said. But eventually the decision took longer and a wooden jail was built which was soon set on fire by a prisoner smoking in his bunk. A strong, fireproof one was built of brick and this set the trend for a change in the general aspect of the town, wood giving way to brick as fire forced the issue. Even before the town was changed, it had some 2,000 people and to serve them were fourteen saloons, four hotels, many stores, the inevitable gambling houses and girl joints.

There was wild jubilation in Weaverville in 1858 when the wagon road came through to Shasta which connected the town to the outside world. Commented the weekly TRINITY JOURNAL, started two years before: "Weaverville now assumes its proper place among the foremost cities of our fair state of California. The opening of the luxurious new wagon road ends our condition of isolation."

PLAINLY VISIBLE from State Highway 299 are evidences of huge devastation wrought by one of the largest hydraulic operations in world. Baron Le Grange mine, opened in 1851, directed powerful streams of water at slopes of Oregon Gulch Mountain, washing away tons of soil, running mud into sluice boxes where heavy gold settled to bottom, caught on slat ridges, was recovered in periodic "clean up". Mud flowed on downstream to spread over farm lands, ruining them. Destruction became widespread in valleys, finally resulted in federal Anti-Debris or Sawyer Act of 1883, putting end to all hydraulic operations. Later, restrictions were eased under certain conditions.

WHISKEYTOWN, CALIFORNIA

A miner could do without tears. He wanted no part of them unless they were tears of joy at finding a rich pocket of gold. But when a mule fell off a rocky cliff and with the mule went two kegs of whiskey, slam-banging down the rocky slope to end up at the bottom smashed to smithereens, the precious liquid dissipated into a stream . . well what could a poor miner do but cry?

This is what happened in the mountains between Redding and the Pacific Ocean, in general the Trinity River country of northern California. And when one miner sobbed: "This is sure one hell of a whiskey creek now", the stream was called Whiskey Creek and the miners revered the memory of the lost hooch by naming the camp Whiskeytown.

Jedediah Strong Smith opened up the country in 1828 on an expedition to Oregon. After pushing up the Buenaventure River (now Sacramento) he found the rocky hills coming so close to the river it was impossible to travel, so moved due west and then north up the Coast. He thus penetrated the Trinity Alps and found the going hard, rocks in the river bed "mangling the horses' feet." Smith's name served as the river's for years and when it was changed to Trinity, "Smith" became the name for another in Del Norte County.

Forced to leave the comparatively easy grade of the cascading stream, Smith's party veered almost straight up the mountainside, scrambling through thick undergrowth. Topping the ridge the party crossed into Humboldt County and eventually met the ocean. Jedediah Smith had opened up a trail that was roughly the foundation of today's roads between the Sacramento Valley and the Coast. In his footsteps followed trappers of Hudson's Bay Company on their travels to and from Oregon. Prospectors also used the route and in 1848 gold in large quantities were found in the Trinity and its tributaries. Although one report had "nuggets lying around in the gravel like walnuts" there was no such rush here as in the Mother Lode. Yet several wildly roaring gold camps sprang up in the Trinity Alps and Whiskeytown was one of the roughest.

At first a nameless clutter of shacks and tents on an anonymous stream, they bred more and got a proper name when the mule toppled off the high trail and the train headed for Shasta City, a camp farther up the creek and noted for its colossal thirst, was short one keg of whiskey.

As Whiskeytown grew large enough to petition for a postoffice, officials scoffed at such a crude name and suggested Blair, which in turn was ridiculed by the miners as was Schilling and Stella. Although called all these names sedately, it was Whiskeytown to the men with the picks and shovels.

OLD ROCK JAIL in Whiskeytown was stoutly built but couldn't resist modern bulldozers which cleared ground to be covered by waters of new lake. Still standing when author-artist Muriel Sibell Wolle took this photo, it was gone in 1963.

It was womanless for years until, said a valley newspaper of 1852: "Whiskeytown's first white woman has taken up her residence there", leaving the reader to guess her purpose. Later that year the paper reported one of the town's several bartenders was "insulted" by a fellow citizen and ventilated him with two bullet holes. The victim had many friends and with a rope over a tree branch they fixed the bartender so he could shoot no more of them.

Late in the '50s a man named Bon Mix erected "a commodious hotel" which embraced a fine saloon and dance hall. The girls employed there were described as "young ladies of probable virtue" but at the edge of town in a small row of cribs were several other ladies whose virtue was highly improbable.

Besides washing the gravel of Whiskey Creek, miners were working small hard rock mines, of a type known as "gopher holes." A man would start a horizontal tunnel, working in a prone position, enlarging the hole barely enough to crawl forward. He had just enough head room to hack at the rock and heap the chippings in a gunnysack ahead of him. When the bag was full he wriggled out hind-blind and dumped out the loose rock. There is no record of any of these burrowings paying off much, certain-

279

ly not enough for the hazard involved. Falling rock could have crushed a man or blocked off his exit.

Official records, always far below actual figures because of "bootlegging", showed $25 million was recovered from the gulches around Whiskeytown. Many other ghostly camps have a few stubborn inhabitants who stoutly maintain that the old place will boom again when the price of gold rises, there being plenty of the yellow stuff around. Not so in the case of Whiskeytown. Two hundred feet of cold mountain water covers the site.

The Bureau of Reclamation has diverted the waters of the Trinity River over twenty miles into the Sacramento by way of the newly created Whiskeytown Lake, formed by the dam of the same name, which was dedicated by President Kennedy in September, 1963, as one of his last official acts. High above, on dry land, a "new" postoffice, built of lumber salvaged from an old saloon in the original town, is plainly marked "Whiskeytown." No one argues about the name now.

RUSTY SKIP BUCKET was safely removed to level above rising waters, still lying in clutter of saloon lumber and other salvaged materials. Heavy container was used to remove ore from mine shaft, raised and lowered by ropes over windlass. When rope became frayed, miners stood clear of load.